New Historical Perspectives on Women and Economics

New Historical Perspectives on Women and Economics

Annual Supplement to Volume 54
History of Political Economy

Edited by Cléo Chassonnery-Zaïgouche, Evelyn L. Forget, and John D. Singleton

Duke University Press
Durham and London 2022

Printed and bound by CPI Group (UK) Ltd, Croydon, CR0 4YY
ISBN 978-1-4780-1740-0
This is the 2022 supplement to
History of Political Economy, ISSN 0018-2702.

New Historical Perspectives on Women and Economics

Annual Supplement to Volume 54
History of Political Economy

Edited by Cléo Chassonnery-Zaïgouche, Evelyn L. Forget, and John D. Singleton

Duke University Press
Durham and London 2022

Contents

Women and Economics: New Historical Perspectives

Cléo Chassonnery-Zaïgouche, Evelyn L. Forget, and John D. Singleton

Why Women and Economics?

Malthus. Ricardo. Mill. Marx. Menger, Jevons, and Walras. As Roy Weintraub (1999) observed a number of years ago, these names represent the figurative chapter titles to a "textbook" history of nineteenth-century economics focused on the development of economic doctrine. Indeed, as Joseph Schumpeter ([1954] 2006: 3) opened his influential account of the history of economic thought, "By history of economic analysis I mean the history of the intellectual efforts that *men* have made in order to understand economic phenomena or, which comes to the same thing, the history of the analytic or scientific aspects of economic thought" (emphasis added).

Certainly, the history of twentieth-century economics can be (and has been) written in a similar fashion: Marshall. Keynes. Hayek. Samuelson. Friedman. Arrow. Becker. Lucas. And so forth. Forward progress in economics forged through the intellectual accomplishments of leading

Correspondence may be addressed to Cléo Chassonnery-Zaïgouche, Fitzwilliam College, University of Cambridge, Cambridge CB3 0DG, UK (cc2006@cam.ac.uk); Evelyn L. Forget, Faculty of Medicine, University of Manitoba, 750 Bannatyne Ave., Winnipeg, MB R3E 0W3 (evelyn.forget@med.umanitoba.ca); and John D. Singleton, Department of Economics, University of Rochester, 280 Hutchinson Road, Box 270156, Rochester, NY 14627 (john.singleton@rochester.edu). We would like to thank Béatrice Cherrier, Erich Pinzón-Fuchs, and Steve Medema for multiple discussions along the way and during the conference.

History of Political Economy 54 (annual suppl.) DOI 10.1215/00182702-10085587

luminaries—almost exclusively men. Among its dozens of biographical profiles of economists, the most recent handbook in the history of economic thought, for example, contains only a single entry on a woman (Joan Robinson) (Faccarello and Kurz 2016). Likewise, Cléo Chassonnery-Zaïgouche, Catherine Herfeld, and Erich Pinzón-Fuchs's 2019 survey of major journals in the history of economic thought identifies just three female subjects (out of 145 authors mentioned in a sample of 205 published articles), of whom only one, Robinson, qualified as a professional economist.

But as many have argued, there are other ways to write histories of the sciences, including the history of economics (e.g., Coats 1993; Schabas 1992; Forget 2005). Weintraub (1999), for instance, points to perspectives that are informed by science studies, the Latourian framework of actors and networks, and through the lens of how economists are trained, socialized, and practice. To this list of alternative approaches can be added accounts that are informed by the fields of feminist philosophy, women's history, and gender studies. While Weintraub's plea for "thick" history—that is, "narratives with richness and complexity"—has been taken up by recent generations of historians of economics, accounts of economics in the twentieth century that "make women a focus of inquiry, an agent of the narrative" (Scott 1988: 7), and develop subjects and themes that emerge from that perspective, remain too few and far between.

The articles collected in this volume stem from a desire to produce and advance new knowledge about the history of women in the economics profession. This approach, which we view as helping to locate recent interest in the status and role of women within economics in historical contexts, has the potential to enrich understandings of economics in the twentieth century in several important ways. One is by "making visible" or—to use the historian of biology Evelyn Fox Keller's term—"recuperating" the contributions of women economists to the construction and stabilization of economic knowledge. While this purpose includes bringing to light the overlooked or neglected roles of female figures, it also stands to advance scholarship by orienting historical narratives toward describing the experiences of women themselves—and relating how those experiences differed from those of men in economics—as well as investigating the consequences for knowledge production. This focus thus goes beyond inquiries into how the social "process by which individuals become economists conditions and shapes the practice of those who identify as economists" (Weintraub 1999: 149) to center the socialization and practices of *women* economists. As such, this perspective can also foreground the gender-related barriers and constraints faced by women in the economics profession in various areas and at various points in time, a key theme that emerges from the articles in this volume. Margaret Rossiter's major contributions to the history of women scientists provide the main model for this approach (e.g., Rossiter 1982, 1998, 2002).

In addition, centering women economists as subjects of historical inquiry can be used to complement or challenge received interpretations of changes in economics and economic knowledge. The articles in this volume focus on the postwar period. An influential narrative of economics in the mid-twentieth century, told in Morgan and Rutherford 1998, emphasizes the rise of modeling, the passing from pluralism to modern "neoclassical" economics, and the mathematization of economics as crucial to understanding the development of economics after World War II. Moving forward, Roger Backhouse and Béatrice Cherrier (2017) identify and explore a later transformation in the status assigned to theoretical and "applied" work in economics since the 1970s. They emphasize a shift in "attitudes toward empirical work and how to do empirical work" (Backhouse and Cherrier 2017: 5) that accompanied changes in technology and emerging demands from clients and patrons of economic research, including policymakers. Historical objects contested in both transformations include notions, laden in the recent past in terminology like "credible" and "policy-relevant," of what it meant for economics to be "scientific" and "objective." Seen through the experiences of women economists (and their work), these transformations implicate previously overlooked social contexts and can take on added meaning as stories of marginalization, sometimes recognition, and perhaps appropriation. The contributions in this volume connect with and raise new questions for these metanarratives, for example, by tracing the origins and boundaries of feminist economics as a distinct field and by examining the production and transmission of economic knowledge about women, such as the gender pay gap.

A third and final way in which women-centered accounts can "thicken" recent histories of economics is through identifying, describing, and applying the construct of gender. As Joan Wallach Scott (1988: 25) has summarized, "If the group or category of 'women' is to be investigated, then gender—the multiple and contradictory meanings attributed to sexual difference—is an important analytic tool." The application of gender in this way stands to have two benefits for histories of economics. One is that it broadens the categories of analysis for describing and analyzing the experiences and practices of economists—women, but also men. Changes, such as the rising status assigned to particular kinds of empirical work or the growth of (and increasing value assigned to) collaborative work, thus take on gendered characters. Notions of objectivity and science at different points in time likewise can acquire and embody traditionally masculine (as opposed to feminine) beliefs and characteristics. This has informed recent work in the sociology of science, such as Etzkowitz et al. 2000 and Rosser 2004; the latter argues that gender-related barriers to success in scientific careers stem partly from a "tradition of male-centered approaches in labs, practices, and cultures" (Rosser 2004: xx). At the same time, using gender as a historiographical tool can help uncover "the metaphors with which scientists think" (Creager, Lunbeck, and Schiebinger 2001: 7) and describe how scientific practices in economics became gendered—for example, distinctions between "hard" and "soft" fields or the division of labor on research teams or the "identification police"—the figurative aggressive audience member who upholds rigor in empirical work by protesting the endogeneity of an explanatory variable on the first slide. Inspired by feminist philosophy, feminist scholars have been pioneers of this approach, producing important scholarship on gendered aspects of economics in historical perspective (Pujol 1992; Seiz 1993; Nelson 1992; Folbre 2010).

In developing and pushing forward a women-centered approach to history, this volume builds on important prior work relating to women in the history of economics. This foundational work includes biographies (Dimand, Dimand, and Forget 2000) and bibliographies (Madden, Pujol, and Seiz 2004) of women economists. Broad narratives on women in the profession include Madden 2002, which discusses female contributions to economic thought—and the barriers faced by women economists—in the first part of the twentieth century. Evelyn Forget (2011) presents an account of the phases of the status of women in the profession in the twentieth century: from a distinct minority in the early years to a relative retreat from academic economics into other spheres, before the "return" of women into academe in the 1950s (but in a lower proportion than before the 1940s). Informed by feminist perspectives, Maria Cristina Marcuzzo and Annalisa Rosselli (2008) survey and analyze work on the history of women, gender, and economics. Recent related scholarship contributes to bridging histories of the profession and histories of the knowledge produced (Madden and Dimand 2019). Conrad 2019 and Becchio 2020 are two recent accounts of the relationship between ideas on gender and the economics profession, while Chassonnery-Zaïgouche, Cherrier, and Singleton 2019 and Cohen 2019 both analyze historical links between strategies for advancing the status of women in economics and economic theorizing and evidence.

In our view as editors, there are important values at stake in the research agenda advanced by this volume. One value concerns what has been termed "epistemic justice." In their work, historians of science can reproduce and reaffirm social hierarchies concerning whose knowledge counts, for example, contributing (perhaps unwittingly) to the social processes that overlook, degrade, or otherwise deny credit to some groups or to some individuals. Writing women back into histories of economics is thus one step toward challenging and deconstructing such hierarchies. Also at stake, however, are the priorities moving forward of the community of those engaged in writing about economics' past. As Ann D. Gordon, Mari Jo Buhle, and Nancy Schrom Dye (1976: 89) observed several years ago reflecting on the "problem" of women's history, "We are learning that the writing of women into history necessarily involves redefining and enlarging traditional notions of historical significance, to encompass personal, subjective experience as well as public and political activities."

In the last section of this introductory essay, we reflect on the articles in this volume to consider "what's next" for this research agenda, arguing that it issues two important challenges to historians of economics. In the section below, we preview and describe the contributions included here to highlight and draw out several connected themes that emerge.

What's in the Book?

The articles gathered in this volume attempt to move the analysis of women, gender, and economics along in a variety of ways and from a variety of perspectives. There is an inherent ambiguity involved. "Women and economics" itself is an ambiguous way to designate women as economists (profession), women economists' ideas and practices (production of knowledge), and the subject of women in the economy (knowledge on women) as the objects of historical inquiry. One topic of interest is the evolution of women's roles as economists over the past century: how do particular women fit into a profession that has not always welcomed them, and how have the decisions that particular women made about their careers changed the profession itself? However, the knowledge produced by women economists is also of interest. Sometimes that knowledge involves a close look at the economic experiences of women, often but not always in the paid and unpaid labor markets. All the contributions here examine these topics to a greater or lesser extent.

"A Historical Portrait of Female Economists' Coauthorship Networks," by Erin Hengel and Sarah Louisa Phythian-Adams, presents an overview of women's representation within economics, particularly as authors in elite journals. This article raises as many questions as it answers. We might imagine we understand why women authors have become more prevalent over time, and have a sense that changing norms of coauthorship and institutional efforts to hire more women, to create more supportive work environments, and to ensure that women who are hired are well placed in productive research networks all complement one another to support women economists. However, the profession of economics is not alone in adopting these changes and has been demonstrably less successful than other fields of study (Lundberg and Stearns 2019; Liu, Song, and Yang 2020). And why were women authors so successful early in the twentieth century, only to become less so later? The trajectory is not monotonic.

In "Hidden Figures: A New History of the Permanent Income Hypothesis," Jennifer Burns investigates the roles played by a remarkable group of women at the University of Chicago during the middle years of the twentieth century. Dorothy Brady, Margaret Reid, and Rose Friedman were essential figures in the development of Milton Friedman's *Theory of the Consumption Function* (1957). Indeed, Brady, Reid, and Rose Friedman received praise and acknowledgment from Milton Friedman, Franco Modigliani, and others, but did one or more of them deserve greater acknowledgment, for example, in the form of coauthorship? This article documents an instance of what Margaret Rossiter (1993) has labeled the "Matilda effect"—the systematic discounting of the roles played by women scholars. As Burns (this volume) notes, "All this credit and recognition remained informal, confined to reputation and relationship, and did not translate into publications, research grants, or professional recognition."

Marianne Johnson examines the documentation of credit from another perspective in "Two 'Two Ostrom' Problems." This article documents the choices and decisions made by Elinor Ostrom, the first woman Nobel laureate in economics, as she attempted to build her career alongside that of her husband and research partner and to gain fair recognition for her own contributions to shared research programs. Johnson's narrative highlights the constraints facing Ostrom and the strategies she adopted, yielding new insights into the processes of marginalization and attribution in economics and the problem of scientific credit.

The issues of career trajectories and generational differences are explored outside the dominance of the United States by Andrés Guiot-Isaac and Camila Orozco Espinel in "Climbing the Obelisk: The Trajectories of Five Women Economists in Colombia, ca. 1950–70." The authors follow and document the career strategies of five successful women economists in Colombia who began their careers between the 1950s and 1970s. They show how the opportunities and challenges that women faced were distinct from those confronted by men and examine how their subjects leveraged the support of male colleagues, mentors, and family members to succeed in a setting not designed to facilitate their participation. This article also demonstrates how women economists relied on their ability to delegate to other, less well-situated women the care work they were still expected to provide to their families.

In "'Writing History as a Way of Life': The Life and Work of Margaret Marie Garritsen de Vries," Christina Laskaridis creates the opportunity to examine the life of a woman economist turned historian who built a career outside academe. As the official historian of the International Monetary Fund, de Vries faced the challenge of working in a context where women were absent because "money is considered just too important and too powerful to be entrusted to a woman." The discrimination that she and other faced, she believed, was less about explicit and intentional exclusion than about the "automatic" tendency to recommend only other men to fill vacant positions. Laskaridis writes, "To the frequent complaint of it being hard to find women to fill posts, [de Vries] would remind them of the quote by Juanita Kreps, who became secretary of commerce under President Jimmy Carter, that 'it depends on who's doing the looking.'" Throughout her life, de Vries struggled against sometimes unintentional behavior from colleagues who were and remained blissfully unaware of the devastating consequences their actions had on her own career.

Camila Orozco Espinel and Rebeca Gomez Betancourt, in "A History of the Institutionalization of Feminist Economics through Its Tensions and Founders," document the challenges associated with the creation and institutionalization of the discipline of "feminist economics." Noting that Barbara Bergmann used the term in 1983, a decade before the journal

Feminist Economics was founded, the authors use archival material and key informant interviews with leading figures in the movement to demonstrate how feminist economics grew to question the subject matter, methods, and theories throughout the discipline of economics. How, and to what extent, has feminist economics been able to maintain its integrity and identity distinct from other approaches to economics as it evolved?

Two of the articles in this volume explicitly address the difficulty that integrating women's experiences in the paid labor market posed for the economics discipline. Mainstream economics, with its focus on perfect competition, had little space for considerations of group power and conflict. Barbara Bergmann's occupational crowding hypothesis was at the core of this dispute. Sarah F. Small explores this contribution in "Tracing Barbara Bergmann's Occupational Crowding Hypothesis: A Recent History." She documents the relegation of Bergmann's hypothesis, which was explicitly framed to stand among mainstream theories, from its temporary and somewhat uneasy position in mainstream labor economics to feminist and stratification economics.

Daniel Hirschman builds on the same theme from a slightly different perspective in "Controlling for What? Movements, Measures, and Meanings in the US Gender Wage Gap Debate." He shows how the observed gender wage gap was used to demonstrate occupational segregation and the societal undervaluation of women's work through the 1980s, but by the end of the decade was increasingly attributed to women's choices and trade-offs between family and work in mainstream labor economics, thereby retreating from more radical "feminist" analyses and placing this "stylized fact" firmly within the mainstream economic paradigm.

Jennifer Cohen's contribution, "The Queen of the Social Sciences: The Reproduction of a [White] *'Man's Field,'*" offers the opportunity to reflect on what, exactly, has been meant by the term *professional* in a variety of contexts. In most ways, the challenges that women economists face building careers, dealing with colleagues, and negotiating credit are not especially different from the challenges faced by women working in any other field. However, there is one issue that economists alone confront. Only economists are theorizing about their own lives, decisions, experiences, and accomplishments as working women.

Several major themes emerge from the collected volume. Several of the articles, for example, examine the roles that women have played as professional economists. Phythian-Adams and Hengel investigate the changing roles that women economists have played as authors in key journals from a quantitative perspective, while the articles by Burns, Johnson, Guiot-Isaac and Orozco Espinel, and Laskaridis explore the tensions and compromises that particular women navigated as they built careers as professional economists and negotiated credit for their own work in particular times and places. Guiot-Isaac and Orozco Espinel, for example, examine the varied experiences of women in Colombia, while Laskaridis looks at the role of one professional economist outside academe. Burns investigates the challenges of working alongside high-profile male economists, while Johnson documents the career choices that allowed Ostrom to excel.

A second theme that emerges from these articles involves institution building. Orozco Espinel and Gomez Betancourt document the emergence of feminist economics as a separate subfield, while Small and Hirschman, from different perspectives, explore how the experiences of women in the paid labor market challenged the preconceptions of mainstream economics and supported the development of feminist economics. Small and Hirschman identify how the experiences of women as workers influenced the women economists theorizing about these issues and set the stage for the third theme in this volume.

The interplay of the personal and professional is an additional key theme that emerges. The interplay between women's experiences in the economy and women economists documenting, exploring, questioning, and theorizing about economics has not been systematically examined by historians of economics but has been the subject of feminist histories. Throughout many of the articles in the volume, the subjects were building their careers and simultaneously negotiating the meaning of professionalism and work: what does it mean to be a professional economist? The contribution by Cohen in particular shows how concepts of professionalism exclude diversity among practitioners and have protected the economics discipline from challenge, creating a hostile environment for women economists attempting to build careers, negotiate collaboration, and receive credit for their work.

What's Next?

The articles in this volume, and the research agenda of centering women in histories of economics to which they are connected, raise important questions moving forward for the community of those engaged with

economics' past. Here we reflect on two challenges and their consequences for future work in the history of economics.

This volume contains historical contributions related to women and
economics in the postwar period. At the same time, it represents a separate space within the field of the history of economics, broadly conceived,
that is devoted to a domain of knowledge that has too frequently been
ignored. Such separation is both common (the recent handbook on wom-
en's economic thought [Madden and Dimand 2019] providing another
example) and, in the context of recuperative history, often reflects a strategic choice to foster the development of a scholarly community. In this
way, the intellectual separation finds parallels with the history of the feminist movement, wherein a recurrent tension is between creating alternative venues and fighting for inclusion in male-dominated spaces. The
history of home economics provides a case in point: what was initially
recognized and promoted as a social advance for women (e.g., college
degrees and new academic jobs that explicitly recognize "feminine
expertise") was later perceived as a ghetto—the feminist avant-garde
of one time becoming the epitome of antifeminism for the next
generation.

Whatever the causes for separation of pursuits of knowledge, a potential consequence with which historians of economics must grapple is that
the institutionalization of separation can produce (or reproduce) social
hierarchies. In the case of historical research related to gender and women
in economics, separated spaces can reinforce a view that work on women
economists as subjects or on the history of economic thinking about
women and gender should not be priorities for the professional mainstream at-large. A fitting illustration of this is the "segregated pluralism"
of the annual Allied Social Science Associations meetings, wherein heterodox economics and American Economic Association–organized sessions both take place, but in separate rooms (or even separate hotels).[1]
Scott describes this "separate and unequal" state in history departments
in the 1980s:

> In the case of women's history, the response of most non-feminist histo-
> rians has been acknowledgment and then separation or dismissal
> ("women had a history separate from men's, therefore let feminists do

---

1. We thank Tiago Mata for the term, which he used to describe the status of heterodoxies at
ASSA meetings.

women's history, which need not concern us"; or "women's history is about sex and the family and should be done separately from political and economic history"). In the case of women's participation, the response has been minimal interest at best ("my understanding of the French Revolution is not changed by knowing that women participated in it"). (Scott 1986: 1055)

As editors, we worry that this volume, whatever its merits in advancing knowledge, enables this sort of separation (and dismissal) to persist in the history of economics. But the challenge issued to the community engaged with the past of economics is greater yet: Which histories should be told separately? Should, for example, the production of historical knowledge that centers racial and other minorities, including indigenous peoples, and economics likewise be separated—appearing mainly in dedicated handbooks, conference sessions, or special issues? When and how should the knowledge generated be integrated into the mainstream? In the case of women and economics, we have argued that mainstreaming gender as a tool of analysis, rather than its deployment in isolation, can facilitate integrating the history of economic thought by women with economics' history.

The second challenge that emerges from the articles in this volume concerns the "silences" of unwritten, undeveloped, and unpreserved work in the history of economics and how the community engaged with economics' past reflects on these. As historians, our "data" are naturally those historical artifacts that can be accessed in the present—for example, published articles in economics journals, book manuscripts, conference proceedings, autobiographical accounts, written correspondence stored in personal archives. But, as A. O. Scott (2021) asks in a recent *New York Times* review of Tillie Olsen's 1965 essay *Silences*, is there "a place in literature—in our canons and course listings, in our criticism and theory—for unwritten work?" The silences of work not completed—and completed work not preserved—stalk historical endeavors, especially those that focus or center on marginalized groups or bodies of knowledge.

In the case of women in economics, unequal access to academic careers and, for those who did enter academe, unequal access tools and networks important for professional success were historical barriers to advancement. The case of Sadie Alexander is representative of these missed opportunities for economics: the first black American to earn a PhD in economics, she nevertheless pursued a career outside it due to limited opportunities.[2] Moreover, what about those who "dropped out" altogether—the ones who are not even hidden but denied as scholars?[3] An example is Marion Crawford Samuelson, whose intellectual life is shrouded among the traces of her in her husband's archives (Backhouse and Cherrier 2019). Likewise, personal and collective archives of women economists are scarce, with even those of prominent figures still unprocessed (see Caroline Shaw Bell's archives at Wellesley and Phyllis Wallace's papers at MIT). This highlights gendered attitudes toward legacy and the role that historians may play in the social process of appraising and affirming worth: while some economists organize their archives early on with a clear view of their value to future generations, many women economists have been reluctant to even keep their papers.

Another form of silence concerns the impact of "nonscholarly" pursuits on scholars' academic output and professional trajectories. A case in point is Phyllis Wallace, who, like many African American scholars, waged urgent battles for racial and gender equality throughout her career. Issues of gender and racial inequalities requiring analyses or remedies (in society and in academe) have consumed the energy of scholars who have felt little choice due to circumstances of their life but to devote their energy to it—who else would have taken up the task? This energy, therefore, could not be devoted to becoming "brilliant scientists"—justifying their marginalization from historical accounts of scientific progress in economics. Wallace, for her part, produced original work on discrimination, but her main contributions were extra-academic: from influencing the principal litigation doctrine regarding discrimination (Chassonnery-Zaïgouche 2020) to urging the Boston Museum of Fine Arts to open a Nubian art gallery (Malveaux 1994). Her general theory of systemic discrimination was not written in the form of articles but scattered in different venues that did not fit the norm of scholarly excellence of the time. The challenge for the community of historians of economics is to recover the stories of the Phyllis Wallaces of the past in order to open spaces for the Phyllis Wallaces yet to come.

2. See the important work of Nina Banks (2021) in retrieving and publishing her economics writings.

3. This is a reference to the title of Aldon Morris's biography of W. E. B. Du Bois, *The Denied Scholar*, which describes the denial of Du Bois's general role in the history of scientific sociology and its "relegation" to activism.

References

Backhouse, Roger E., and Béatrice Cherrier. 2017. "The Age of the Applied Economist: The Transformation of Economics since the 1970s." In *The Age of the Applied Economist: The Transformation of Economics since the 1970s*, edited by Roger E. Backhouse and Béatrice Cherrier. *History of Political Economy* 49 (supplement): 1–33.

Backhouse, Roger, and Béatrice Cherrier. 2019. "Paul Samuelson, Gender Bias, and Discrimination." *European Journal of the History of Economic Thought* 26, no. 5: 1053–80.

Banks, Nina, ed. 2021. *Democracy, Race, and Justice: The Speeches and Writings of Sadie T. M. Alexander*. New Haven, Conn.: Yale University Press.

Becchio, Giandomenica. 2020. *A History of Feminist and Gender Economics*. London: Routledge.

Chassonnery-Zaïgouche, C. 2020. "Economists Entered the 'Number Games': The Early Reception of Wage Decomposition Methods in the U.S. Courtrooms (1971–1989)." *Journal of the History of Economic Thought* 42, no. 2: 229–59.

Chassonnery-Zaïgouche, Cléo, Béatrice Cherrier, and John Singleton. 2019. "'Economics Is Not a Man's Field': A History of the American Economic Association's CSWEP." Working paper.

Chassonnery-Zaïgouche, Cléo, Catherine Herfeld, and Erich Pinzón-Fuchs. 2019. "New Scope, New Sources, New Methods? A Survey of Contemporary Scholarship in History of Economic Thought Journals, 2016–2017." Working paper 2019-09, Center for the History of Political Economy at Duke University.

Coats, A. W. 1993. "What Can We Accomplish with Historical Approaches in an Advanced Discipline Such as Economics?" *History of Economic Ideas*, 227–65.

Cohen, Jennifer. 2019. "The Radical Roots of Feminism in Economics." *Research in the History of Economic Thought and Methodology* 37A:85–100.

Conrad, Cecilia. 2019. "Feminist Economics: Second Wave, Tidal Wave, or Barely a Ripple?" In *The Legacy of Second-Wave Feminism in American Politics*, edited by Angie Maxwell and Todd Shields, 99–136. Cham: Palgrave Macmillan.

Creager, Angela, Elizabeth Lunbeck, and Londa Schiebinger, eds. 2001. *Feminism in Twentieth-Century Science, Technology, and Medicine*. Chicago: University of Chicago Press.

Dimand, Mary Ann, Robert W. Dimand, and Evelyn L. Forget, eds. 1995. *Women of Value: Feminist Essays on the History of Women in Economics*. Aldershot: Edward Elgar.

Dimand, Robert W., Mary Ann Dimand, and Evelyn L. Forget, eds. 2000. *Biographical Dictionary of Women Economists*. Cheltenham: Edward Elgar.

Etzkowitz, Henry, Carol Kemelgor, and Brian Uzzi. 2000. *Athena Unbound: The Advancement of Women in Science and Technology*. Cambridge: Cambridge University Press.

Faccarello, Gilbert, and Heinz D. Kurz, eds. 2016. *Handbook on the History of Economic Analysis*. 3 vols. Cheltenham: Edward Elgar.

Folbre, Nancy. 2010. *Greed, Lust, and Gender: A History of Economic Ideas.* Oxford: Oxford University Press.

Forget, Evelyn. 2005. "Same View, Many Lenses." *History of Political Economy* 37, no. 2: 205–10.

Forget, Evelyn. 2011. "American Women and the Economics Profession in the Twentieth Century." *Œconomia* 1, no. 1: 19–31.

Gordon, Ann D., Mari Jo Buhle, and Nancy Schrom Dye. 1976. "The Problem of Women's History." In *Liberating Women's History: Theoretical and Critical Essays,* edited by Berenice A. Carroll, 75–92. Urbana: University of Illinois Press.

Liu, J., Y. Song, and S. Yang. 2020. "Gender Disparities in the Field of Economics." *Scientometrics* 125:1477–98.

Lundberg, Shelly, and Jenna Stearns. 2019. "Women in Economics: Stalled Progress." *Journal of Economic Perspectives* 33, no. 1: 3–22.

Madden, Kirsten. 2002. "Female Contributions to Economic Thought, 1900–1940." *History of Political Economy* 34, no. 1: 1–30.

Madden, Kirsten, and Robert W. Dimand, eds. 2019. *The Routledge Handbook of the History of Women's Economic Thought.* London: Routledge.

Madden, Kirsten, Michèle Pujol, and Janet Seiz. 2004. *A Bibliography of Female Economic Thought up to 1940.* London: Routledge.

Malveaux, J. 1994. "Tilting against the Wind: Reflections on the Life and Work of Phyllis Ann Wallace." *American Economic Review* 84, no. 2: 93–97.

Marcuzzo, Maria Cristina, and Annalisa Rosselli. 2008. "The History of Economic Thought through Gender Lenses." In *Frontiers of the Economics of Gender,* edited by Francesca Bettio and Alina Verashchagina, 2–18. London: Routledge.

Morgan, Mary S., and Malcolm Rutherford. 1988. "American Economics: The Character of the Transformation." In *From Interwar Pluralism to Postwar Neoclassicism,* edited by Mary S. Morgan and Malcolm Rutherford. *History of Political Economy* 30 (supplement): 1–26.

Nelson, Julie A. 1992. "Gender, Metaphor, and the Definition of Economics." *Economics and Philosophy* 8, no. 1: 103–25.

Pujol, Michèle A. 1992. *Feminism and Anti-feminism in Early Economic Thought.* Aldershot: Edward Elgar.

Rosser, Sue V. 2004. *The Science Glass Ceiling: Academic Women Scientists and the Struggle to Succeed.* New York: Routledge.

Rossiter, Margaret W. 1982. *Women Scientists in America: Struggles and Strategies to 1940.* Baltimore: Johns Hopkins University Press.

Rossiter, Margaret W. 1993. "The Matthew Matilda Effect in Science." *Social Studies of Science* 23, no. 2: 325–41.

Rossiter, Margaret. 1998. *Women Scientists in America: Before Affirmative Action, 1940–1972.* Baltimore: Johns Hopkins University Press.

Rossiter, Margaret. 2002. *Women Scientists in America: Forging a New World.* Baltimore: Johns Hopkins University Press.

Schabas, Margaret. 1992. "Breaking Away: History of Economics as History of Science." *History of Political Economy* 24, no. 1: 187–203.

Schumpeter, Joseph A. (1954) 2006. *History of Economic Analysis*. London: Routledge.

Scott, A. O. 2021. "Tillie Olsen Captured the Toll of Women's Labor—on Their Lives and Art." *New York Times*, March 25. https://www.nytimes.com/2021/03/25/books/review/Tillie-Olsen-tell-me-a-riddle.html?smid=tw-share.

Scott, Joan W. 1986. "Gender: A Useful Category of Historical Analysis." *American Historical Review* 91, no. 5: 1053–75.

Scott, Joan Wallach. 1988. *Gender and the Politics of History*. New York: Columbia University Press.

Seiz, Janet. 1993. "Feminism and the History of Economic Thought." *History of Political Economy* 21, no. 1: 185–201.

Weintraub, E. Roy. 1999. "How Should We Write the History of Twentieth-Century Economics?" *Oxford Review of Economic Policy* 15, no. 4: 139–52.

A Historical Portrait of Female Economists' Coauthorship Networks

Erin Hengel and Sarah Louisa Phythian-Adams

1. Introduction

In her 2002 *History of Political Economy* article, "Female Contributions to Economic Thought, 1900–1940," Kirsten Madden remarked, "Judging from the syllabi of most economics courses and the references contained in leading history-of-thought textbooks, students are likely to conclude that women, with the notable exception of Joan Robinson and, to a lesser extent, Rosa Luxemburg, have played a negligible role in the development of modern economics" (2).

Yet as Madden and others have documented, women have always been active in the field. Between 1900 and 1940, there were more than one thousand female-authored theses submitted for advanced degrees in economics and twice that many nonthesis scholarly outputs by women (Madden 2002). Edith Abbott and Sophonisba Breckinridge published numerous articles on women's employment and wages in the *Journal of*

Correspondence may be addressed to Erin Hengel, University College London, Social Research Institute, 27 Woburn Square, London WC1H 0AA, UK (erin.hengel@gmail.com); and Sarah Louisa Phythian-Adams, University of Liverpool Management School, Chatham Street, Liverpool L69 7ZH, UK (slpa@liverpool.ac.uk). We are grateful to Victoria Bateman, Cléo Chassonnery-Zaïgouche, Evelyn Forget, John Singleton, Sarah Smith, participants at the 2021 HOPE conference, and two anonymous referees for excellent and extensive comments and suggestions. We also owe a particular debt to Christopher Brunet for data collection, research assistance, and crucial input at an early stage of the project.

History of Political Economy 54 (annual suppl.) DOI 10.1215/00182702-10085601

Political Economy (Folbre 1998). Mabel Timlin made significant contributions to economic theory and Canadian immigration policy (Ainley 1999). Other influential women include Beatrice Webb, Edith Penrose, Margaret Reid—and of course, Rosa Luxemburg and Joan Robinson.

In this article, we document further evidence of women's contributions. Our focus, however, is on the authors and research published between 1940 and 2019 in the following general interest economics journals: the *American Economic Review (AER)*, *Econometrica (ECA)*, the *Economic Journal (EJ)*, the *Journal of Political Economy (JPE)*, the *Quarterly Journal of Economics (QJE)*, and the *Review of Economic Studies (REStud)*. We selected these journals for the influence they have had in setting the tone and agenda of economics research in the postwar period. The resulting analysis therefore catalogs and describes the women whose research has likely had the greatest impact on modern economics.

Our data confirm trends identified by Evelyn Forget (2011). The share of women publishing in influential economics journals follows a U-shaped curve that troughs in the late 1970s. Part of this decline appears to be related to a shift in the numbers and types of papers being published: immediately after the war, general interest journals published more papers and more coauthored papers, a change that coincided with a growing share of male authors. Nevertheless, we still find several women with substantial clout in the profession—for example, Ursula Webb, Eveline Burns, and Irma Adelman—as well as female-female mentoring relationships and coauthoring partnerships.

By the late 1970s and early 1980s, however, the share of women publishing in influential journals began to increase again, largely thanks to a rise in mixed-gendered papers—including between peers. For example, Janet Yellen published papers with William James Adams, her colleague at Harvard, and Nancy Schwartz coauthored extensively with Morton Kamien, her classmate from Purdue. We also see clear evidence of increased support for the next generation of female economists. David Gale, a professor at Berkeley, coauthored with several junior women, including Gabrielle Demange and Marilda Sotomayor. Schwartz and Kamien are noteworthy for creating an environment at Northwestern's Managerial Economics and Decision Sciences Department that facilitated the careers of many young women, including Esther Gal-Or, Jennifer Reinganum, and Nancy Stokey.

From the 1990s on, most prominent women in economics exclusively coauthored. This rise in women coauthoring with men coincides with a period of sharp growth in coauthorship—both in general (Seltzer and

Hamermesh 2018; Hamermesh 2013) and in our data. Between 1960 and 1979, 77 percent of exclusively male-authored papers were solo-authored; between 1980 and 1999, only 53 percent were. Yet coauthorship between women was almost nonexistent: conditional on publication in an influential journal, the percentage of exclusively female-authored papers that were solo-authored was the same in 1980–99 (94 percent) as it was in 1960–79 (93 percent). Indeed, over this entire forty-year period, general interest journals collectively published, on average, just one article per year that was coauthored by two or more women.

We see evidence, however, that this may be starting to change. Between 2000 and 2019, general interest journals published, on average, fourteen exclusively female-coauthored papers a year. There is also an initial emergence of identifiable clusters in women's coauthoring networks. A mapping of female-female and male-male coauthoring networks by decade suggests that female networks in 2010–19 roughly resemble male networks from 1940 to 1969. It also emphasizes the key role prominent individuals play in their formation.

Although papers by women coauthoring with other women still represent only a tiny fraction of all articles published in influential general interest journals (4 percent), their recent rapid growth may signal that research by female teams is receiving greater recognition and impact in the field of economics. Building on the "four-phases" construct of Forget 2011, we therefore tentatively suggest that we may be entering a new fifth phase in the representation of women in the profession—one that is characterized by more female-female collaborations.

This article contributes to several literatures. Our primary contribution is to document the coauthorship patterns and networks emerging from women's publications in influential general interest economics journals. In this sense, the papers closest to our own are Seltzer and Hamermesh 2018 and Hamermesh 2013, which find similar growth in coauthorship at a smaller set of journals and time periods. We add to this research by illustrating that past waves of increasing coauthorship have appeared to coincide with a relative decline in the share of female authors.

Second, we build on research highlighting women's contributions to economic thought and theorizing about the factors behind the historical evolution of their representation (see, e.g., Pujol 1992; Dimand, Dimand, and Forget 2000; Madden and Dimand 2019; Becchio 2020; Forget 2011). In particular, our study quantitatively investigates the hypotheses in Forget 2011 and extends her theory by suggesting that we may be entering a fifth phase of women in the economics profession, characterized by the increasing impact of research by women collaborating with other women. Our article also extends and complements the work of Madden (2002) by focusing on women's contributions in the postwar period.

Third, this article joins research documenting trends in economics research and how it is perceived by the most prestigious economics journals. For example, Hamermesh 2013 and Biddle and Hamermesh 2017 note a significant shift in the focus of papers published in general interest journals: prior to the 1990s, most of these journals published papers that used formal economic theory to identify questions and interpret results; by the early 2000s, however, research design was increasingly used as the guiding principle for identifying empirical questions. They argue that this shift suggests a change in the status and impact of applied fields relative to other areas of research. We contribute to this literature by documenting that the rise in the prestige of applied fields—as proxied for by top journal publications—coincides with (and is possibly connected to) an increase in the numbers of female authors published by these journals.

Finally, we contribute to the broader conversation on the underrepresentation of women in economics (see, e.g., Gamage, Sevilla, and Smith 2020; Bateman, Gamage, and Liu 2021; Auriol, Friebel, and Wilhelm 2022; Lundberg and Stearns 2019). Most relevant to our work, Erin Hengel (2022) highlights the dearth of female economists published in the *AER*, *ECA*, the *JPE*, and the *QJE* between 1950 and 2015; Hengel and Eunyoung Moon (2020) add data from *REStud* and describe further trends in men's and women's coauthorship patterns.

The article proceeds in the following order. In section 2, we discuss our data. In section 3 we show aggregate trends in the representation of women at general interest economics journals between 1940 and 2019 as well as trends in men's and women's coauthorship patterns. In section 4, we explore these trends in more detail in light of Forget's (2011) four phases by graphing and describing men's and women's coauthorship networks. Section 5 concludes.

2. Data

The purpose of this article is to document and analyze women's contributions to influential general interest economics journals between 1940 and 2019.[1] A complication, however, is that journal influence changes over

---

1. Madden (2002), in contrast, considers women's contributions from a broader range of research outputs, including monographs, books, and government reports.

Table 1. Article count, by journal and decade

Decade	AER	ECA	EJ	JPE	QJE	REStud	Total
1940–49	334	196	184	287	262	96	1,359
1950–59	233	291	315	332	331	215	1,717
1960–69	345	441	281	577	434	265	2,343
1970–79	710	744	331	779	377	466	3,407
1980–89	718	676	512	605	438	521	3,470
1990–99	707	495	844	513	435	393	3,387
2000–2009	928	601	780	411	426	436	3,582
2010–19	1,209	624	897	428	411	550	4,119
Total	5,184	4,068	4,144	3,932	3,114	2,942	23,384

Note: Papers published in the May issue of *AER Papers and Proceedings*, errata, corrigenda, and book reviews are excluded. Final row and column display total article counts by journal and decade, respectively.

time. In the early to mid-twentieth century, leading research was often published in the *AER*, *Economica*, and the *EJ*.[2] The *EJ* retained its outsized influence into the 1980s, but by 1995, the *AER*, *ECA*, the *JPE*, the *QJE*, and *REStud* had acquired a major lead (Ductor et al. 2020).[3]

Given the aims of our study and the effort involved in data collection, we decided to restrict our analysis to articles published in the following six journals: the *AER*, *ECA*, the *EJ*, the *JPE*, the *QJE*, and *REStud*.[4] The data were originally collected and analyzed in Hengel 2022 and Hengel and Moon 2020 and expanded in scope here to include the *EJ* and articles published between 1940 and 2019.[5] Unless otherwise mentioned, articles

2. For example, *Economica* (not to be confused with *Econometrica*) published A. William Phillips's famous paper, "The Relation between Unemployment and the Rate of Change of Money Wages in the United Kingdom, 1861–1957," in 1958 and Ronald H. Coase's "The Nature of the Firm" in 1937; see Gans and Shepherd 1994: 174 for qualitative evidence that the *EJ* was the "premier economics publication" for much of the first half of the twentieth century.

3. These latter "top-five" journals are particularly important to the economics profession today—e.g., publishing in them significantly increases one's probability of receiving tenure, decreases time-to-tenure, and positively influences career advancement (Ellison 2002; Heckman and Moktan 2020).

4. A more complete analysis would include *Economica*, given the influence it had in the earlier decades. Additionally, we emphasize that there are costs and benefits to restricting the data to these six journals. An important benefit is that by localizing data collection, we are sure to consistently identify research (and researchers) that have made an impact on the field of economics (as opposed to sociology or other related disciplines). However, the restricted sample may overstate the extent to which economics is elitist or male-dominated (Madden and Dimand 2019).

5. The original data set analyzed in Hengel 2017 included only articles published with an abstract between 1950 and 2015 in the *AER*, *ECA*, the *JPE*, and the *QJE*. Later, Hengel (2022) added articles published with a submit-accept date in *REStud*. A research assistant expanded

from the May (*Papers and Proceedings*) issues of the *AER*, book reviews, errata, and corrigenda are excluded. See table 1 for a breakdown of article counts by journal and decade.

Our final data set contains basic bibliographic information on 23,384 articles by 13,910 unique authors. For each author, we manually assigned a gender using the following hierarchy of information: (1) obviously gendered given names (e.g., "James" or "Brenda"); (2) photographs on personal or faculty websites; (3) personal pronouns used in text written about individuals; and (4) by contacting authors themselves or people and institutions connected to them.

3. Aggregate Trends in Female Authorship

Figure 1 plots the percentage of female authors published in the *AER*, *ECA*, the *EJ*, the *JPE*, the *QJE*, and *REStud* between 1940 and 2019. The U-shaped curve suggests women enjoyed a somewhat more prominent role in the profession during World War II, but their influence declined in the decades that followed (Forget 2011).

Part of this decline appears to be related to changes in the numbers and types of papers being published.[6] Immediately after the war, general interest journals published more papers and more coauthored papers. Article counts are almost three times higher in the 1970s than they were in the 1940s (table 1); between 1940 and 1949, 96 percent of papers were solo-authored; three decades later, only 72 percent were (see also fig. 2, top left-hand graph).

These changes led to an increase in male authors relative to female authors. In the 1970s, general interest journals published double the number of solo male-authored papers—but exactly the same number of solo female-authored papers—as they did in the 1940s. They also

these data sets to include articles published between 1940 and 2019 in the *AER*, *ECA*, the *EJ*, the *JPE*, the *QJE*, and *REStud* and gender coded the authors not already included in the earlier data sets.

6. It may also be related to the hypothesis that women were expected to cede the relative gains they had made in earlier eras in order to make way for men in the postwar period. Indeed, we find this sentiment reflected in the words of Mary Anderson (then head of US Department of Labor Women's Bureau) in a 1942 letter to Mary Barnett Gilson: "We would do well not to quibble over who is going to have the jobs after the war is over." Eleanor Lansing Dulles remarked in 1958 that "[the Federal Public Service] is a real man's world if ever there was one. It's riddled with prejudices. If you are a woman in Government service you just have to work ten times as hard" ("Eleanor L. Dulles" 1996).

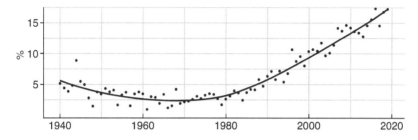

Figure 1. Percentage of women publishing in influential general interest journals. Figure plots female authors as a percentage of all authors published in the *AER*, *ECA*, the *EJ*, the *JPE*, the *QJE*, and *REStud* by year. Lines of fit estimated using a quadratic LOESS model (smoothing span $\alpha = 0.75$).

published nineteen times more papers coauthored exclusively by men; however, mixed-gendered papers increased only by a factor of four, and papers coauthored exclusively by women were almost nonexistent. As a result, the share of women publishing in general interest journals declined in the postwar period.

Starting in the 1980s, however, it began to increase again, largely thanks to a rise in mixed-gendered papers. The first two graphs in the second row of figure 2 plot the numbers of solo female-authored papers and coauthored papers with a single female author, respectively. Between 1980 and 1999, there was a sharp increase in mixed-gendered papers, alongside a more modest rise in solo female-authored papers. Around 2000, general interest journals also began publishing a nonnegligible number of articles by female teams (fig. 2, bottom right-hand graph).

4. The Evolution of Female Coauthoring Networks

In this section, we investigate how female coauthoring networks have evolved. To structure our analysis, we interpret empirical patterns through the lens of Forget 2011. Forget 2011 divides the history of women in the economics profession into four phases. The first phase (before 1918) predates our data, but created the conditions that enabled many influential female economists to study economics and thrive in the profession several decades later.[7] During the second phase—which coincides with the first

7. A defining feature of phase 1 was the expansion of women's colleges in the United States, many of which supplied the women who went on to earn graduate degrees in economics

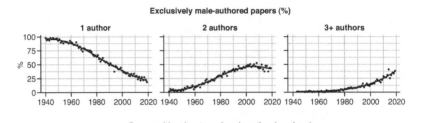

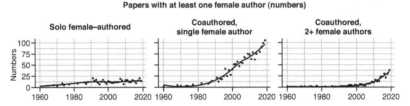

Figure 2. The rise in coauthorship. Top row of graphs show the percentage of exclusively male-authored papers published each year that are solo-authored, coauthored by two authors, and coauthored by three or more authors. In the second row of graphs, the first graph plots the absolute number of solo-authored papers by women published each year, the second graph plots the numbers of papers coauthored by a single woman and at least one man, and the third graph plots the number of papers coauthored by at least two women. Lines of fit estimated using a quadratic LOESS model (smoothing span $\alpha = 0.75$).

decade of our data (1940–49)—women were often routed from "core" economics subjects toward adjacent disciplines (e.g., social work and home economics). They returned to the "core" in phase 3 (1950–69), thanks in part to increased demand for the statistical skills many women had learned while working as government researchers. The final phase (post-1970) is characterized by more rapid growth in women's representation as barriers fell and women began to enter the profession in substantially higher numbers.

To make patterns in the data more obvious, we graphically map collaborations over time. Results are shown in figure 3. Its top two rows display graphs of male-male and female-female coauthorship networks by decade. The table below the graphs displays the number of unique authors (N), average degree (Deg.), average weighted degree (Wt. deg.), and the average clustering coefficient (Clust.) for men and women publishing in the

elsewhere and then hired them back to teach economics to the next generation of students. Consistent with this hypothesis, we noted while hand-coding author gender that many women publishing in the forties and fifties had an earlier connection to the women's liberal arts college Bryn Mawr.

	1940–49		1950–59		1960–69		1970–79		1980–89		1990–99		2000–09		2010–19	
	M	F	M	F	M	F	M	F	M	F	M	F	M	F	M	F
N	755	45	970	43	1,.422	45	2,300	91	2,454	146	2,722	308	3,280	568	4,623	1,110
Deg.	0.15	0.00	0.32	0.00	0.57	0.09	0.88	0.15	1.30	0.07	1.57	0.16	1.85	0.30	2.41	0.66
Wt. deg.	0.16	0.00	0.39	0.00	0.64	0.18	1.01	0.15	1.56	0.07	1.88	0.17	2.13	0.31	2.84	0.72
Clust.	0.71	0.00	0.66	0.00	0.41	0.00	0.47	0.00	0.51	0.00	0.55	0.00	0.59	0.81	0.67	0.70

Figure 3. Network decomposition by decade. Graphs in the top rows plot the network evolution for male-male and female-female connections over decades. Each diagram is restricted to individuals who have authored a paper in the *AER* (including available *P&P* issues), *ECA*, the *EJ*, the *JPE*, the *QJE*, or *REStud* during the relevant decade. Nodes represent individual authors; the size of a node reflects the number of coauthoring relationships (regardless of coauthor gender) an author has in the data. Authors of the same gender who coauthor with each other are connected by a line, where the weight of that line is determined by the number of papers the pair have coauthored together. The table below the network graphs displays the number of unique authors (*N*), average degree (Deg.), average weighted degree (Wt. deg.), and the average clustering coefficient (Clust.) for men and women publishing in the relevant decade. Average degree is the average number of edges per node on a graph and is calculated by dividing the number of coauthoring pairs in the data (number of edges) by the number of authors (number of nodes). The average weighted degree is the degree weighted by the number of papers a pair of authors have coauthored together. The average clustering coefficient measures the extent to which nodes in a graph cluster together (i.e., how often an author's coauthors also coauthor with each other). Network visualizations were created in Gephi using the Fruchterman and Reingold (1991) algorithm.

relevant decade. (See the notes for figure 3 for each statistic's definition.) By diagramming these relationships, we aim to better understand how women's research connections to one another have evolved since 1940 (conditional on publication in a general interest economics journal), analyze the extent to which they differ from men's, and observe whether the two are converging.

4.1. Phase 2 (1940–49)

Forget's (2011) second phase overlaps with the first ten years of our data (1940–49). During this decade, 80 percent of women published in general interest economics journals solo-authored; the rest coauthored with men—there were no female-female coauthoring relationships during this period. Among men, 92 percent of research contributions were solo-authored, and another 7 percent were coauthored with other men; the remaining 1 percent were coauthored with women.

These patterns are also apparent in figure 3. The network graph for female authors consists only of disconnected nodes and its average degree is zero,[8] confirming that there were no female-female coauthoring relationships in the 1940s. Men's network graph suggests they were more connected to one another; however, its average degree is still only 0.15—like women, men in the 1940s predominantly solo-authored.

The two most prominent female authors during the 1940s were Joan Robinson, a theorist, and Ursula Hicks (née Webb), a public finance economist. Both women largely published solo-authored papers in the *EJ* and *REStud*. Hicks and Robinson were founding members of *REStud*'s Board of Editors (*Review of Economic Studies* 2021), and Hicks served as its managing editor from 1933 to 1961 (*Review of Economic Studies* 2013).

Other prominent female authors during this period include Grace Gunn and Eveline Burns. Each published several articles in American journals (the *AER*, the *JPE*, and the *QJE*). Burns's research was in the area of social insurance systems and entirely solo-authored;[9] Gunn worked on marginal productivity and production functions with Paul Douglas, with whom she helped develop the Cobb-Douglas production function (Douglas 1976; Biddle 2020).[10]

Several women during this period coauthored with their husbands. Examples include Gladys and Roy Blakey, who coauthored two papers in the *AER* on the Revenue Acts of 1940 and 1941; Gertrude and Alfred Oxenfeldt conducted a survey of businessmen and jointly published the results in the *JPE*; Winifred and Charles Hyson coauthored a paper in the *QJE* in the area of regional economics. During the 1940s, Nancy and Richard Ruggles both published solo-authored papers in general interest

8. Average degree is the average number of edges per node on a graph. It is calculated by dividing the total number of edges (i.e., the number of coauthoring pairs in the data) divided by the total number of nodes (i.e., the number of authors).

9. Burns was a member of President Franklin D. Roosevelt's Committee on Economic Security, where she helped design the 1935 Social Security Act (Kasper 2012).

10. In the acknowledgments of his paper "The Cobb-Douglas Production Function Once Again: Its History, Its Testing, and Some New Empirical Values," Paul Douglas (1976: 903) writes, "Work on the production function was carried on by a large number of persons who deserve to be credited as coauthors. Foremost among these is Grace Gunn who participated, over a period of 40 years, in no less than three separate phases of the work."

journals—Nancy published two papers on marginal cost pricing in *REStud*; Richard published a paper on wage rates in the *QJE*. The Ruggleses would go on to coauthor frequently together in later decades (Qian 2020).

Despite the important work that female economists were conducting at the time, many still had to fight for recognition. For example, after thirteen years working as a lecturer at Columbia University, Eveline Burns was told "that there is no possibility of advancement to professorial rank or to permanent status" (Burns and Haig 1940). Some women may have also published under pseudonyms—for example, Raya Dunayevskaya used the pseudonym Freddie Forest[11]—while others like Edith Hirsch may have adopted their husbands' names ("Edith Hirsch" 2003).[12] Finally, many women left the profession entirely. For example, Carrie Glasser earned a PhD in economics from Columbia University and later published "Some Problems in the Development of the Communications Industry" in the September 1945 issue of the *AER*. After her husband (and fellow economist) took a position at Stanford, however, she left the profession to become an artist (David, McKinnon, and Wright 2003).

4.2. Phase 3 (1950–69)

The next two decades (1950–69) correspond to Forget's (2011) third phase. Solo-authoring continued to dominate, although to a slightly lesser extent: 66 percent of women's contributions during this period—and 75 percent of men's—were solo-authored. When women coauthored, they usually did so with men: of the forty coauthored papers by women, 90 percent were coauthored with men.

Nevertheless, the 1960s produced two female-female coauthoring relationships in our data. The first pair was Irma Adelman and Cynthia Taft Morris, who published three development economics papers together—two in the *QJE* and one in the *AER*. Adelman and Morris formed a long-lasting research partnership that emphasized the importance of political and social forces for economic performance (Headlee 2013); toward the

11. Raya Dunayevskaya was a prominent Russian economist and philosopher who specialized in the study of Marxian economics. She published an article on Marxian economics in the *AER* in 1944 under her actual name.

12. Hirsch's husband, Julius, published an article in 1944 in the *AER* titled "Facts and Fantasies concerning Full Employment." It is not clear whether Julius wrote the article or Edith did under his name.

end of phase 3, they even published two books together: *Society, Politics, and Economic Development* (1967) and *Economic Growth and Social Equality in Developing Countries* (1973).

The second female-female coauthoring connection was between the Australian mathematician and statistician Alison Harcourt (née Doig) and the British economist Ailsa Land. Land and Doig worked together on a project for British Petroleum at the London School of Economics (Informs 2021), and in 1960, they published their landmark paper "An Automatic Method for Solving Discrete Programming Problems" in *Econometrica*. It developed an optimization algorithm now known as "branch and bound."

Ailsa Land is also the first woman in our data who was clearly mentored by another woman: Helen Makower (Land 2018). Makower studied at Newnham College, an all-women's constituent college of the University of Cambridge; she earned a PhD from the London School of Economics, where she later joined as faculty. Makower was a mathematical economist with very strong links to the Cowles Foundation (*History of Economic Thought* 2021). She also solo-authored theory papers in *REStud* (1945) and the *EJ* (1953).

Most other contributions by female economists during this period were by a small number of prominent women in particular subdisciplines, including Joan Robinson in economic theory, Edith Penrose in managerial economics, Anne Krueger in macroeconomics and trade, and Margaret Reid in household production and consumption. Most prolific by far was Robinson, who published sixteen solo-authored papers between 1950 and 1969, most of which revolved around the Cambridge Capital Controversy.[13] Irma Adelman published the second-highest number: in addition to her three papers with Morris, she solo-authored two papers in the *AER* and one in the *EJ*, and published another in *ECA* that she coauthored with her husband, the physicist Frank Adelman.

Finally, employment opportunities for women were undoubtedly better between 1950 and 1969 than they had been in the 1940s; nevertheless, female academics still had to fight for recognition and equal access to university jobs. For example, despite significant publishing success, Irma Adelman had difficulty securing a tenure-track position; instead, she accepted various nontenure appointments at the University of California

13. The Cambridge Capital Controversy was a dispute Robinson and several other faculty members at the University of Cambridge had with Paul Samuelson and Robert Solow at MIT.

at Berkeley, Mills College, and Stanford (Adelman, Zilberman, and Kim 2014).

These authoring patterns are apparent in the network topology of figure 3. The 1950s and 1960s graphs for women largely consist of disconnected nodes. In the 1950s, women's average degree was zero; a decade later it rises to 0.09 thanks to the Adelman-Morris and Doig-Land partnerships. In contrast, men were forming stronger connections to one another. Compared with the 1940s, men's 1950s and 1960s network graphs include noticeably more connections. Their average degree is also two to four times higher.

4.3. Phase 4 (Post-1970)

In the 1970s and 1980s, general interest journals continued to publish a number of solo-authored papers by prominent women. For example, in 1974 Krueger published her famous "rent seeking" paper in the *AER*, and Barbara Bergmann solo-authored several papers in the *AER*, *ECA*, and the *JPE*.

However, women during this period were also increasingly collaborating with men—and especially with their male peers. For example, Katharine Abraham coauthored papers with Henry Farber (1987, *AER*), James Medoff (1980, *QJE*), and Lawrence Katz (1986, *JPE*). In 1985, Yellen coauthored three papers with her husband, George Akerlof: two were published in the *QJE* and one in the *AER*; while an assistant professor at Harvard, she also coauthored papers with William James Adams, another junior faculty member at the time (1976, *QJE*; 1977, *EJ*) (McCulloch 2017).

The most prolific female author during this period, Nancy Schwartz, also coauthored. Schwartz was an industrial organization theorist, an associate editor of *ECA*, on the board of editors at the *AER*, and the first woman appointed to an endowed chair at Northwestern's Kellogg School of Management (Kamien 1998). Schwartz coauthored extensively with Kamien, her classmate from Purdue (Kamien 1981) and (later) colleague at Northwestern.[14] During the 1970s, Kamien and Schwartz published three papers in *ECA*, another three in *REStud*, two in *AER*, and one in *QJE*.

---

14. Both Schwartz and Kamien were hired by Stanley Reiter, who had been a faculty member at Purdue during their doctoral studies and supervised Schwartz's PhD (Kamien 1998).

Schwartz and Kamien were well known for nurturing young talent at Northwestern's Managerial Economics and Decision Sciences Department. According to their colleague Donald Jacobs, "Mort and Nancy had an unwavering belief in caring for the basic work and for the people who would make real contributions. The culture and department were set up to give people what they needed to advance their work— guidance, colleagues to help them discuss ideas, relief from teaching" (quoted in Lindell 2011). Schwartz and Kamien jointly supervised PhD students Jennifer Reinganum and Esther Gal-Or. During the 1980s, Gal-Or published three solo-authored papers in general interest journals; Reinganum published six—including a paper from her dissertation that built on Schwartz and Kamien's earlier work on patent races.

While at Northwestern, Reinganum also worked closely with Stokey, an assistant professor hired by Schwartz and Kamien. Reinganum thanks Stokey in several of her papers, and in 1985 they published "The Importance of the Period of Commitment in Dynamic Games" in the *International Economic Review*. Stokey, in turn, is a well-known mathematical economist and served as *ECA*'s first (and until 2020, only) female editor. Between 1970 and 1989, she solo-authored four theory papers in the *JPE*, the *QJE*, and *REStud*; she also coauthored with Jerry Green (1983, *JPE*) and her partner Robert Lucas Jr. (1987, *ECA*).

During the 1970s and 1980s, the University of California at Berkeley was another incubator for young female theorists. Beth Allen and Graciela Chichilnisky studied at Berkeley under Gérard Debreu. In the 1980s, Chichilnisky and Allen each published three solo-authored papers in general interest journals. Around the same time, Gabrielle Demange and Marilda Sotomayor studied with David Gale, another prominent mathematical economist at Berkeley. Demange solo-authored two papers in *ECA* and coauthored a paper with Gale in the *JPE*. In 1986, Sotomayor, Demange, and Gale published "Multi-item Auctions" in the *JPE*;[15] three years later, Sotomayor also published a paper in *ECA* with Alvin Roth.

Despite growth in coauthorship more generally, papers by women coauthoring with other women were still relatively rare. During the 1970s, women's average network degree was 0.15 (fig. 3) thanks to several collaborations between women, including Irma Adelman and

---

15. Sotomayor, Demange, and Gale also worked closely with Myrna Wooders at the Institute des Hautes Études Scientifique (Sotomayor 2009). Wooders published three papers in *ECA* during the 1980s and 1990s: two solo-authored and one coauthored with William Zame.

Cynthia Taft Morris, Adelman and Barbara Bergmann, Rachel McCulloch and Janet Yellen, and Barbara Wolfe and Anita Summers (née Arrow). In the following decade, however, general interest journals published only one coauthored paper exclusively by women—"Women's Labour Supply and Marital Choice," by Shoshana Grossbard and Shoshana Neuman (1988, *JPE*). As a result, their average degree returned to the single digits (0.07).[16]

From the 1990s on, most prominent women in economics exclusively coauthored. For example, between 1990 and 1999, Janet Currie and Raquel Fernández each published seven coauthored articles in general interest journals and Anne Case published five; the following decade, Esther Duflo, Marianne Bertrand, and Susan Athey collectively published twenty-seven articles, only three of which were solo-authored. Figure 3 suggests that coauthorship between women was also becoming more common. Between 1990 and 2009, women's average network degree doubled each decade: in the 1990s, general interest journals published twelve papers coauthored exclusively by women; the following decade, they published thirty-one—including three papers coauthored by three women.

This steep increase in women coauthoring—with men and other women—coincides with the rising prominence of applied empirical microeconomics (Biddle and Hamermesh 2017). Although Anne Case and Raquel Fernández continued to rely heavily (or exclusively) on theory in their earlier papers—for example, Fernández's "Strategic Models of Sovereign-Debt Renegotiations" (1990, *REStud*) and Case's "Vote-Seeking, Tax-Setting, and Yardstick Competition" (1995, *AER*)—Janet Currie's approach put less of an emphasis on formal theory.[17] The following decade, Duflo pioneered the use of randomized controlled trials in economics, and Bertrand has focused on field experiments and inference using observational data. Athey, however, is an applied theorist—in fact, her PhD was supervised by Paul Milgrom and John Roberts, two of Nancy Schwartz's protégés (Bryan 2016).

---

16. However, in the 1980s, general interest journals published four mixed-gendered papers coauthored by at least two women—e.g., the paper by Sotomayor, Demange, and Gale already mentioned.

17. Nevertheless, even Currie did not entirely avoid theory, particularly in her earliest papers. Indeed, one of her first papers in the data, "An Experimental Comparison of Dispute Rates in Alternative Arbitration System" (1992, *ECA*), interpreted its results through the lens of a formal model of arbitrator behavior.

4.4. Phase 5?

Since 2010, female-female collaborations have continued to rise. Between 2010 and 2019 general interest journals published 73 exclusively female coauthored papers—including four by four women—and 148 mixed-gendered papers by at least two women. As a result, women's average degree doubled again, a trajectory that mirrors the growth rate in men's average degree between 1940 and 1969. Figure 3 also suggests that women's average clustering coefficient—a measure of how frequently one's coauthors collaborate with each other—has resembled men's since 2000.

Women's 2010 network graph in figure 3 further suggests an initial emergence of identifiable clusters. Figure 4 explores in more detail the largest of these, which is centered on several prominent women working in or adjacent to the field of development economics: Nava Ashraf, Marianne Bertrand, and Esther Duflo. Ashraf, Bertrand, and Duflo are professors at the London School of Economics, Chicago Booth School of Business, and MIT, respectively. Bertrand was coeditor at the *AER* from 2011 to 2017 and the *EJ* from 2004 to 2005. Duflo is the current editor of the *AER* and a winner of the 2019 Nobel Prize in Economics.

Conditional on publication in a general interest journal, Ashraf has coauthored with Oriana Bandiera—her colleague at the London School of Economics—Alessandra Voena, and Erica Field. Duflo has coauthored with Rohini Pande, Petia Topalova, Rema Hanna, and Marianne Bertrand. Bertrand has also coauthored with Hanna, as well as Adriana Lleras-Muney and Sandra Black, her classmate from Harvard. Pande and Lleras-Muney are further connected to Seema Jayachandran, and Jayachandran, in turn, is connected to Ilyana Kuziemko, who studied with her at Harvard. Finally, Petia Topalova has coauthored with Pinelopi Goldberg, the editor of the *AER* from 2011 to 2016.

Authors' connections to one another are actually much thicker than figure 4 suggests. For example, Topalova (2005) and Hanna were close friends and roommates while studying at MIT. Several authors have also coauthored with each other on papers published in journals outside the six we cover—for example, Jayachandran and Field have published together in the *American Economic Journal: Economic Policy* and the *AER P&P*; Field has also coauthored a paper with Voena (2017, *AER P&P*).

Many of the authors in figure 4 are also indirectly connected to one another via a third author. Pande, Bandiera, and Bertrand have all

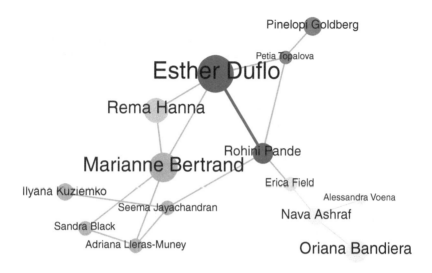

Figure 4. Ashraf-Bertrand-Duflo cluster of female-female collaborations. Graph represents the largest component network from the female-female coauthorship network structure shown in figure A1. Nodes represent individual authors who are highly connected (having four or more coauthoring relationships in the data); their size is increasing in the number of coauthoring relationships they have (and the smallest nodes indicate authors who usually solo-author). Authors who coauthored with one another are connected by a line, and the weight of that line is determined by the number of papers the pair have coauthored together. Network visualizations were created in Gephi using the Fruchterman and Reingold (1991) algorithm.

coauthored with Robin Burgess; Topalova (2005) and Pande (1999) thank him in their PhD theses. Both Topalova (2005) and Hanna (2005) thank Sendhil Mullainathan in their theses; Mullainathan in turn was Ashraf's PhD adviser and has frequently coauthored with Bertrand. Benjamin Olken has coauthored with Duflo, Pande, Jayachandran, and Hanna. Olken—who is married to Amy Finkelstein—also links the Ashraf-Bertrand-Duflo network to the Finkelstein network shown in figure A1. Other "connecting coauthors" include Jesse Rothstein (coauthor with Bertrand and Black), Ray Fisman (coauthor with Bertrand and Kuziemko), Edward Glaeser (coauthor with Ashraf and Bertrand), Claudia Goldin (coauthor with Kuziemko, Lleras-Muney, and Bertrand), Emir Kamenica (coauthor with Bertrand and Ashraf), and Nina Pavcnik (coauthor with Topalova and Goldberg).

Several of the individuals in figure 4 are also connected to each other via their PhD supervisors. Together with Michael Greenstone, Duflo supervised Hanna's PhD; she also cosupervised Topalova's with Abhijit Banerjee, her own PhD supervisor, later husband, and cowinner of the 2019 Nobel Prize. Greenstone and Banerjee have coauthored with Pande; Banerjee has also worked together with Bertrand. Michael Kramer—who shared the 2019 Nobel Prize with Duflo and Banerjee—supervised Ashraf's and Jayachandran's PhD dissertations. Ashraf was also advised by Lawrence Katz, as were Black, Kuziemko, and Bertrand. Voena was supervised by (and has coauthored with) Michèle Tertilt, who has also coauthored with Field.

Finally, many of the women in figure 4 are further connected to one another through their PhD students. Pande supervised Lori Beaman and Jessica Leight. Beaman coauthored several papers with Duflo, Pande, and Topalova; Leight has worked with Field and Ashraf. Goldberg supervised Nina Pavcnik, who has gone on to work with Topalova. Ashraf supervised B. Kelsey Jack, and they also coauthored a paper together with Bandiera. Jack has also coauthored with Jayachandran and Michael Greenstone.

5. Conclusion

Immediately after the war, general interest journals published more papers and more coauthored papers. These changes appear to have coincided with—and possibly led to—a decline in their shares of female authors. Nevertheless, we still find pockets of women during this period who continued to publish, including Joan Robinson, Ursula Webb, Eveline Burns, Edith Penrose, Anne Krueger, Irma Adelman, and Margaret Reid. There are also instances of women collaborating with each other—Ailsa Land with Alison Doig and Irma Adelman with Cynthia Taft Morris—and at least one case of a senior female economist (Helen Makower) mentoring a junior woman (Ailsa Land).

Thanks to a rise in mixed-gendered papers, the share of women publishing in influential journals began increasing again in the late 1970s and early 1980s. For example, Janet Yellen coauthored with George Akerlof and William James Adams; Nancy Schwartz collaborated extensively with Morton Kamien.

The 1970s and 1980s are also noteworthy for the level of support provided to the next generation of female economists. Schwartz and

Kamien were well known for nurturing young talent at Northwestern's Managerial Economics and Decision Sciences Department—including Jennifer Reinganum, Esther Gal-Or, and Nancy Stokey. At the University of California at Berkeley, Gérard Debreu and David Gale mentored several other influential women, including Beth Allen, Graciela Chichilnisky, Gabrielle Demange, Myrna Wooders, and Marilda Sotomayor.

From the 1990s on, most prominent women in economics exclusively coauthored—and since 2000 (and especially post-2010) increasingly with other women. As a result, we observe an initial emergence of identifiable clusters in women's coauthoring networks. These networks center on several prominent female economists, all of whom have mentored (and often coauthored with) junior women. Building on Forget 2011, we hypothesize that this rise in women collaborating with other women suggests that we may be entering a new phase in the representation of female economists in the discipline.

There are undoubtedly a multitude of factors driving the recent rise in female-authored papers published in general interest journals. We do not, however, believe that increasing coauthorship alone has been a fundamental cause of it. Indeed, the initial increase in coauthorship that occurred during the 1960s and 1970s did not coincide with rising shares of female authors. Moreover, given gender homophily in coauthorship networks (Ductor, Goyal, and Prummer 2021) and the fact that journals have historically published so few female coauthored papers, we suspect that any trend toward greater coauthoring that occurs in isolation may actually reduce women's influence in the profession.

Instead, we believe other factors—either on their own or in combination with increasing coauthorship—have probably contributed to the rising share of women that we see in the data. These include cultural changes within economics departments and efforts to increase the share of women in influential research networks like the National Bureau of Economic Research. We hope that future work will explore these and other hypotheses in more detail.

Our sample of coauthoring relationships is, by design, highly selected. For that reason, we have so far refrained from drawing general conclusions about women's collaboration patterns. Yet if we do, there are several plausible hypotheses that might explain the patterns we see. First, women may have always collaborated with one another but published their research in other outlets—either due to personal choice or, as argued in

Hengel 2022, Card et al. 2020, and Hengel and Moon 2020, because general interest journals hold female-authored papers to higher standards. A second hypothesis is that women are now flocking to the profession thanks to shifting norms about the value of empirical research (Biddle and Hamermesh 2017). A related hypothesis is that the rise in prestige of applied work has been driven by prominent female economists who value this type of work and serve as strong advocates, role models, and mentors for future generations of women—for example, Barbara Bergmann was an influential supporter of the (then controversial) applied empirical work championed by David Card and Alan Krueger (Bergmann 2005) as well as a vociferous advocate for women in the profession (see, e.g., Bergmann 1998).

We conclude by asking whether it matters if general interest journals publish research by female teams. Why can they not simply publish papers by women coauthoring with men? Although our data cannot directly answer this question, we stress that the majority of published papers are predominantly male-authored: even in 2019, most were either entirely authored by men (67 percent) or have at least one male coauthor (94 percent). Thus the research that sets the tone and agenda for the economics profession is still predominantly written from the viewpoint of men. It is difficult to appreciate the consequences such a one-sided perspective has had, but one obvious repercussion may be a body of evidence that disproportionately relies on male-only samples (Manchester and Wasserman 2022).[18]

Moreover, Irma Adelman attributes the productivity of her coauthoring relationship with Cynthia Taft Morris to a mutual bond fostered by their close friendship: "[Morris] and I really hit it off, not only in terms of our social commitment but also in terms of our personal attributes. We really liked each other" (Adelman, Zilberman, and Kim 2014: 15). While men and women can and do form collaborative partnerships from strong friendships, such relationships are probably more likely to be found within genders than between them, all else being equal. Thus, as they publish more research by female teams, journals may also be incentivizing a more efficient allocation of available resources and improving the overall quality of economic research.

18. This is actually an issue that medical practitioners and public health officials have been grappling with for years. For example, until recently, many health trials excluded women. As a result, some health issues specific to women have been historically understudied and more poorly understood and may have led to worse health outcomes for women (see Holdcroft 2007).

References

Adelman, Irma, David Zilberman, and Eunice Kim. 2014. "A Conversation with Irma Adelman." *Annual Review of Resource Economics* 6, no. 1: 1–16.

Ainley, Marianne Gosztony. 1999. "Mabel F. Timlin, 1891–1976: A Woman Economist in the World of Men." *Atlantis* 23, no. 2: 28–38.

Anderson, Mary. 1942. "Letter to Mary Gilson." Economics in the Rear-View Mirror. https://www.irwincollier.com/chicago-mary-barnett-gilson-upon-retirement-1941/.

Auriol, Emmanuelle, Guido Friebel, and Sascha Wilhelm. 2022. "Underrepresentation of Women in the Economics Profession More Pronounced in the United States Compared to Heterogeneous Europe." *PNAS* 119, no. 16.

Bateman, Victoria, Danula K. Gamage, Erin Hengel, and Xianyue Liu. 2021. *Royal Economic Society, Silver Anniversary Women's Committee Report: The Gender Imbalance in UK Economics.* Report to the Royal Economic Society Women's Committee. https://www.res.org.uk/uploads/assets/575c241a-fbff-4ef4-97e7066fcb7597e0/women-in-academic-economics-report-FINAL.pdf.

Becchio, Giandomenica. 2020. *A History of Feminist and Gender Economics.* London: Routledge.

Bergmann, Barbara R. 1998. "Two Cheers for CSWEP?" *Journal of Economic Perspectives* 12, no. 4: 185–89.

Bergmann, Barbara R. 2005. "The Current State of Economics: Needs Lots of Work." *Annals of the American Academy of Political and Social Science* 600:52–67.

Biddle, Jeff E. 2020. *Progress through Regression: The Life Story of the Empirical Cobb-Douglas Production Function.* Cambridge: Cambridge University Press.

Biddle, Jeff E., and Daniel S. Hamermesh. 2017. "Theory and Measurement: Emergence, Consolidation and Erosion of a Consensus." In *The Age of the Applied Economist: The Transformation of Economics since the 1970s,* edited by Roger E. Backhouse and Béatrice Cherrier. *History of Political Economy* 49 (supplement): 251–70.

Bryan, Kevin. 2016. "Bengt Holmström and the Black Box of the Firm." VoxEU. https://voxeu.org/article/bengt-holmstr-m-and-black-box-firm.

Burns, Eveline M., and Robert M. Haig. 1940. "Correspondence between Dr Burns and Professor Haig." Economics in the Rear-View Mirror. https://www.irwincollier.com/columbia-eveline-m-burns-parts-ways-with-the-economics-department-1941-1942/.

Card, David, Stefano DellaVigna, Patricia Funk, and Nagore Iriberri. 2020. "Are Referees and Editors in Economics Gender Neutral?" *Quarterly Journal of Economics* 135:269–327.

David, Paul A., Ronald McKinnon, and Gavin Wright. 2003. "Memorial Resolution: Moses Abramovitz." *Stanford Report,* July 9. https://news.stanford.edu/news/2003/july9/abramovitzmeml-79.html.

Dimand, Robert, Mary Ann Dimand, and Evelyn L. Forget. 2000. *A Biographical Dictionary of Women Economists.* Cheltenham: Edward Elgar.

Douglas, Paul H. 1976. "The Cobb-Douglas Production Function Once Again: Its History, Its Testing, and Some New Empirical Values." *Journal of Political Economy* 84, no. 5: 903–15.

Ductor, Lorenzo, Sanjeev Goyal, Marco van der Leij, and Gustavo Nicolas Paez. 2020. "On the Influence of Top Journals." Mimeo.

Ductor, Lorenzo, Sanjeev Goyal, and Anja Prummer. 2021. "Gender and Collaboration." *Review of Economics and Statistics*, forthcoming. https://doi.org /10.1162/rest_a_01113.

"Edith Hirsch, 103, Commodities Economist." 2003. *New York Times*, February 3. https://www.nytimes.com/2003/02/03/business/edith-hirsch-103-commodities -economist.html.

"Eleanor L. Dulles of State Dept. Dies at 101." 1996. *New York Times*, November 4. https://www.nytimes.com/1996/11/04/world/eleanor-l-dulles-of-state-dept-dies-at -101.html.

Ellison, Glenn. 2002. "The Slowdown of the Economics Publishing Process." *Journal of Political Economy* 110, no. 5: 947–93.

Folbre, Nancy. 1998. "The 'Sphere of Women' in Early-Twentieth-Century Economics." In *Gender and American Social Science: The Formative Years*, edited by Helene Silverberg, 35–60. Princeton, N.J.: Princeton University Press.

Forget, Evelyn L. 2011. "American Women and the Economics Profession in the Twentieth Century." *Œconomia* 1:19–31.

Fruchterman, Thomas M., and Edward M. Reingold. 1991. "Graph Drawing by Force-Directed Placement." *Journal of Software: Practice and Experience* 21, no. 11: 1129–64.

Gamage, Danula K., Almudena Sevilla, and Sarah Smith. 2020. "Women in Economics: A UK Perspective." *Oxford Review of Economic Policy* 36: 962–82.

Gans, Joshua S., and George B. Shepherd. 1994. "How Are the Mighty Fallen: Rejected Classic Articles by Leading Economists." *Journal of Economic Perspectives* 8, no. 1: 165–79.

Hamermesh, Daniel S. 2013. "Six Decades of Top Publishing: Who and How?" *Journal of Economic Literature* 51, no. 1: 162–72.

Hanna, Rema. 2005. "Essays in Development and Environmental Economics." PhD diss., MIT.

Headlee, Sue. 2013. "Remembrance of Cynthia Taft Morris." 2013. https://eh.net/wp -content/uploads/2013/10/Remembrance-of-Cynthia-Taft-Morris.pdf.

Heckman, James J., and Sidharth Moktan. 2020. "Publishing and Promotion in Economics: The Tyranny of the Top Five." *Journal of Economic Literature* 58, no. 2: 419–70.

Hengel, Erin. 2017. "Publishing While Female: Are Women Held to Higher Standards? Evidence from Peer Review." Working paper 1753, Faculty of Economics, University of Cambridge.

Hengel, Erin. 2022. "Are Women Held to Higher Standards? Evidence from Peer Review." *Economic Journal*, forthcoming. https://academic.oup.com/ej/advance -article/doi/10.1093/ej/ueac032/6586337.

Hengel, Erin, and Eunyoung Moon. 2020. "Gender and Quality at Top Economics Journals." Mimeo.

History of Economic Thought. 2021. "Helen Makower, 1910–1998." http://www
.hetwebsite.net/het/profiles/makower.htm.

Holdcroft, Anita. 2007. "Gender Bias in Research: How Does It Affect Evidence
Based Medicine?" *Journal of the Royal Society of Medicine* 100:2–3.

Informs. 2021. "Ailsa H. Land." 2021. https://www.informs.org/Explore/History-of
-O.R.-Excellence/Biographical-Profiles/Land-Ailsa-H.

Kamien, Morton I. 1981. "It's Just Like New York!" In *Essays in Contemporary
Fields of Economics: In Honor of Emanuel T. Weiler.* West Lafayette, Ind.: Purdue
University Press.

Kamien, Morton I. 1998. "Nancy L. Schwartz." In *Frontiers of Research in Economic
Theory: The Nancy L. Schwartz Memorial Lectures, 1983–1997.* Cambridge:
Cambridge University Press.

Kasper, Sherry D. 2012. "Eveline Mabel Burns: The Neglected Contributions of a
Social Security Pioneer." *History of Economic Thought* 34, no. 3: 321–37.

Land, Ailsa. 2018. "Professor Ailsa Land." 2018. https://www.lse.ac.uk/Mathematics
/assets/documents/Prizes/PROFESSORAILSALAND.pdf.

Lindell, Rebecca. 2011. "In Memoriam: Professor Emeritus Morton I. Kamien,
1938–2011." 2011. https://www.kellogg.northwestern.edu/news_articles/2011
/morton_kamien_memoriam.aspx.

Lundberg, Shelly J., and Jenna Stearns. 2019. "Women in Economics: Stalled
Progress." *Journal of Economic Perspectives* 33, no. 1: 3–22.

Madden, Kirsten K. 2002. "Female Contributions to Economic Thought, 1900–
1940." *History of Political Economy* 34, no. 1: 1–30.

Madden, Kirsten K., and Robert W. Dimand. 2019. *Routledge Handbook of the
History of Women's Economic Thought.* London: Routledge.

Manchester, Colleen Flaherty, and Melanie Wasserman. 2022. "Gender Diversity in
Scholarship." Presentation, ASSA Annual Meeting.

McCulloch, Rachel. 2017. "Why Collaborate in International Finance?" In
Collaborative Research in Economics, edited by Michael Szenberg and Lall B.
Ramrattan, 257–73. Cham: Palgrave Macmillan.

Pande, Rohini. 1999. "The Economics of Public Policy: Interventions in Electoral
Representation, Information Transmission and Investment Choices." PhD diss.,
London School of Economics.

Pujol, Michèle A. 1992. *Feminism and Anti-feminism in Early Economic Thought.*
Aldershot: Edward Elgar.

Qian, Lisa. 2020. "Giving Economist Nancy Ruggles Her Due." *YaleNews*, March 10.
https://news.yale.edu/2020/03/10/giving-economist-nancy-ruggles-her-due.

Review of Economic Studies. 2013. "Directory of Current and Past Board
Members." http://www.restud.com/wp-content/uploads/2013/02/HISTORY_13
_dec_2013. doc.

Review of Economic Studies. 2021. "History of the *Review of Economics Studies*."
http://www.restud.com/history/.

Seltzer, Andrew J., and Daniel S. Hamermesh. 2018. "Co-authorship in Economic
History and Economics: Are We Any Different?" *Explorations in Economic
History* 69:102–9.

Sotomayor, Marilda. 2009. "My Encounters with David Gale." *Games and Economic Behavior* 66, no. 2: 643–46.

Topalova, Petia. 2005. "Three Empirical Essays on Trade and Development in India." PhD diss., MIT.

Appendix A

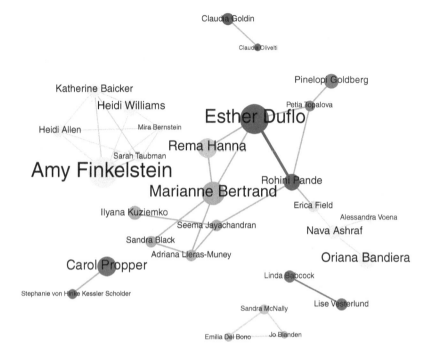

Figure A1. Largest subnetworks among identifiable female-female clusters. Graphs are the largest subnetworks among identifiable female-female clusters publishing in general interest journals between 2010 and 2019 and include available publications in the *Papers and Proceedings* issue of the *AER*. Nodes represent individual authors who have four or more coauthoring relationships in the data; their size is increasing in the number of coauthoring relationships they have. Authors who coauthored with each other are connected by a line, whose weight is determined by the number of papers the pair have coauthored together. Network visualizations were created in Gephi using the Fruchterman and Reingold (1991) algorithm.

Hidden Figures: A New History of the Permanent Income Hypothesis

Jennifer Burns

To the graduate students she was not a hidden figure but a distant one, "always carrying a pile of books with statistical data." In winter, she walked with particular care through the snow with a box of meticulously arranged punch cards, headed toward the computer center. To her colleagues she "carried her own weight," even if she did not head her own workshop. Instead, she was a regular at others' workshops in the University of Chicago's vaunted economics department. "Milton gave her a certain amount of credit in his 'permanent income hypothesis,'" reflected longtime department chair Arnold Harberger (Harberger and Edwards, forthcoming; Goldin 2021: 46). Indeed, her name surfaces in the introduction to Milton Friedman's *A Theory of the Consumption Function*, which presented the idea. But few economists of her day knew much about Margaret Reid, despite her nearly half-century tenure as a full professor at one of the nation's leading economics departments. One exception was the Italian American scholar Franco Modigliani, who lauded the "highly imaginative

Correspondence may be addressed to Jennifer Burns at jenniferburns@stanford.edu. I am grateful to John Singleton and Cléo Chassonnery-Zaïgouche for the invitation and encouragement to write on this topic. I received helpful comments on earlier versions of this article from attendees at the 2021 History of Political Economy Conference, a 2018 Economic History Seminar at the Stanford University Department of Economics, a 2018 Gender History Workshop at the Stanford History Department, and the 2015 Women in Intellectual History Workshop at the Stanford Humanities Center. This research was supported by Stanford University, the National Endowment for the Humanities, and the Hoover Institution Library and Archives.

History of Political Economy 54 (annual suppl.) DOI 10.1215/00182702-10085615

analysis of Margaret Reid (unpublished)" as a "fundamental contribution" to consumption economics. Reflecting on his career after receiving the Nobel Prize, Modigliani (1986) also highlighted the "path-breaking contribution" of two other women: Dorothy Brady and Rose Friedman.

Building on Modigliani's and Harberger's casual reminiscences, this article uses archival sources to reconstruct an alternate history of Milton Friedman's *A Theory of the Consumption Function*, spotlighting the contributions of Margaret Reid, Dorothy Brady, and Rose Friedman to the work that ultimately helped Milton Friedman win a Nobel Prize. Although Milton Friedman offered public credit to his wife and their two close friends, none received formal recognition or reward for their contributions. Despite Friedman's efforts, disciplinary norms along with the broader culture obfuscated the collaborative and gendered nature of this economic breakthrough. Understood as his accomplishment alone, Friedman's challenge to the Keynesian consumption function was immediately lauded by professional economists and contributed to his growing reputation in the field. Yet it was a joint discovery with origins in conversations, research, and debates among a group of female scholars working in uneasy relationship to academic economics. For detailed discussion of the hypothesis and its reception by economists, see Nelson 2020, 1:192–213.

Restoring this history underscores the centrality of women's contributions to economics, a recovery project still necessary decades after the dawn of women's history. Scholars have documented the Matilda effect—the systemic discounting of women's intellectual contributions—in the natural and social sciences, including economics (Rossiter 1993). The specific history of the permanent income hypothesis adds to this scholarship while also introducing an important distinction between formal and informal credit and recognition. By the middle decades of the twentieth century, female economists had made inroads into professional economics, particularly in government agencies and affiliated research groups. Their male colleagues were willing to rely on their research skills and accord them limited access to graduate degrees and teaching positions. As the case of Modigliani demonstrates, some were even willing to be fulsome in their praise. But all this credit and recognition remained informal, confined to reputation and relationship, and did not translate into publications, research grants, or professional recognition. Attending to this distinction in other cases of the Matilda effect will help scholars determine whether this informal credit should be seen as an intermediary stage along the path to further inclusion or a mechanism for forestalling meaningful reallocation of disciplinary power.

Emphasizing Friedman's engagement with the women's world of consumption economics also offers new insight into the origins and meaning of his ideas. At the very least, it provides a new answer to the question, "Why is there no Milton Friedman today?" (Klein et al. 2013). Considered more broadly, however, rooting the permanent income hypothesis in the work of women economists and the female-dominated world of consumption economics provides a new genealogy for the school of thought known as "Chicago economics." Scholars have recognized the importance of Friedman's student Gary Becker's exploration of household economics. To some, Becker's interest in pricing the priceless bonds of household labor and familial connection is the paradigmatic example of neoliberalism, an economic and social philosophy said to define the late twentieth century or post-Fordist era (Foucault 2008: 269–70). There has been only minimal investigation, however, of the continuities between Becker's work and that of his female predecessors at Chicago. The case of Friedman's consumption function suggests another place to seek the feminine face of neoliberalism.

The story begins with a tragedy: the stillbirth of Milton and Rose's first child in 1941. The couple had recently moved to Washington, D.C., where Milton took a job at the Treasury Department. They planned to raise their child in the rambling Maryland farmhouse of Aaron Director, Rose's brother. But without a baby, this imagined bucolic playground transformed to a stark landscape of loss. Hastily changing plans, the Friedmans rented an apartment in bustling Dupont Circle. Longtime friend Dorothy Brady offered Rose the ultimate distraction—a part-time job at the Bureau of Home Economics.[1]

In 1940s Washington, D.C., this was quintessential woman's work, but neither Brady nor Rose Friedman had a typical profile for a government employee. At once steely and sensitive, Brady held a PhD in mathematics and raised her son as a single mother after her marriage to a UC Berkeley economics professor foundered. Rose described her as "closer to perfection than anyone I have ever known," emphasizing her empathy and

---

1. Little has been written about Brady, whose papers do not survive. Her career is briefly described in Forget 2004: 80–81; Reid 1987; and Iowa State University Economics Department 1986.

emotional intuition (Friedman and Friedman 1998). The two had met a few years earlier, when Brady worked with Milton Friedman on the Study of Consumer Purchases, a massive government survey of consumer behavior (Stapleford 2007).

Rose was midway through her PhD at the University of Chicago, where she had studied with the department's titan of price theory, Frank Knight. Rose was a rarity not only for being a female graduate student in economics but for avoiding consumption economics, that unusual domain where being female was considered an asset. Most other women who studied economics at Chicago came to work with Hazel Kyrk, the department's lone female professor and an expert in household consumption. Rose instead fell in with a cluster of students who idolized Knight, among them her brother and her future husband. Having completed all her coursework, she arrived in D.C. with vague plans for a dissertation in capital theory, Knight's current research interest. In truth, Rose was beginning to lean out when the stillbirth bounced her back into the working world she was ready to leave behind. As a result, she brought an unusual training in neo-classical price theory to the Bureau of Home Economics, whose staff members were typically steeped in the other major economic approach of the era, institutional economics.

Despite her narrow job title—she was officially a "home economics specialist" in the USDA's Bureau of Human Nutrition and Home Economics—Brady's research was anything but a backwater. Prewar Washington was still grappling with a changed economic and political landscape carved by the Great Depression and the New Deal. The administration of Franklin Roosevelt (1932) had started eclectic and experimental, unified by little other than the president's conviction that in an era of mass unemployment, there was a new "duty and responsibility of Government toward economic life." By the late 1930s, however, leading economists and policymakers had begun to converge on the diagnosis of John Maynard Keynes's *General Theory of Employment, Interest, and Money*. The problem of the Great Depression, as Keynes saw it, was a fall in aggregate demand, and the solution was government spending to bolster national income.

But what was national income, and how much of it did the United States have? Although economists had long measured output and prices in specific sectors or commodities, only recently had they tried to combine numerous indexes into one aggregate figure of "national income." In 1934 a comprehensive statistical study, Simon Kuznets's *National*

Income, 1929–1932, became a minor sensation in D.C. Funded by the Commerce Department, it would eventually shape policy at the highest levels. With national income a defining concept for policymakers, the flip sides of income—consumption and savings—were hot topics.

Consumption was also critical because of another Keynesian concept, the multiplier. Drawing on ideas of his student, Richard Kahn, Keynes argued that a dollar spent was not simply a dollar spent but would ramify throughout the economy according to a "multiplier," as each individual passed a portion of this new income to another through consumption. But how much of this new dollar would be spent, and how much saved? This question was critical to calculating the multiplier and hence the appropriate amount of government stimulus. Keynes (1964: 96) argued that there was a sort of "psychological law" that people would "increase their consumption as their income increases, but not by as much as the increase in their income." This relationship between income and consumption, quickly dubbed "the consumption function" in the new language economists began to use for parsing Keynes, was assumed to be a stable and predictable relationship.

Yet as researchers threw themselves headlong into testing, refining, and elaborating the Keynesian consumption function, puzzle after puzzle emerged. In 1942 Kuznets published another groundbreaking work analyzing nearly a century's worth of American income and consumption data. He found savings and consumption ratios to be remarkably consistent, even as incomes rose. But fresh data from the Study of Consumer Purchases and other nationwide budget studies pointed in the opposite direction. It turned out that farm families had different savings patterns than urban families; so did residents of cities and villages. Both results could not be true, nor could the problem be resolved in light of Keynes's formulation. All of this had immediate policy relevance. If the consumption function was unstable or unknowable, the basic logic and efficacy of New Deal spending could also be questioned. It was the first shadow of doubt falling across the emergent paradigm.

Rose's new project plunged her into the thick of the so-called Kuznets paradox (Bunting 1989).[2] Broadly speaking, Dorothy and Rose were trying to make sense of the mounds of data generated by the Study of

2. By contrast, J. J. Thomas (1989) argues that the impact of both Kuznets's statistics and Keynes's consumption function have been overstated, emphasizing that earlier budget studies had already made economists aware of the complexities of consumption relationships.

Consumer Purchases. The specific challenge they took up was teasing out the relationship between spending and saving in different communities. Their data could be broken down into at least twenty-four different groups, including those identified as farm families, white families, Negro families; west-central middle-size cities, New England villages, southeast villages, Atlanta, Portland, Omaha, Columbus, Providence, Chicago, and New York. Were there any commonalities across these diverse groups? What discernable patterns linked income, consumption, and savings? Their research unfolded within the auspices of the National Bureau of Economic Research, a hybrid academic-private research institution with close links to Columbia University. A few years earlier, Milton Friedman had helped establish NBER's Conference on Research in Income and Wealth, an ongoing project that coordinated the activities of worker bees like Brady with luminaries like Arthur Burns, Wesley Mitchell, and Kuznets.

Rose and Dorothy's research culminated in "Savings and the Income Distribution," a nineteen-page paper that marked a significant shift away from the social and cultural explanations characteristic of earlier consumption research. The authors began with a nod to the traditional way income differences had been interpreted, "in terms of the income of the individual family, its size, occupational group, race and national origin, region and size of community," noting that corresponding variations in consumption patterns had been treated "as not yet susceptible of expression in a numerical relation of any form." By contrast, Brady and Friedman (1947: 247) noted these relationships could also "be expressed in quantitative terms." Keeping with Brady's statistical bent and the training Rose had received at Chicago, the paper would analyze numerical income distributions rather than digging into the qualitative differences between rural and urban families. Still, their mathematics remained simple, with their major conclusions explained textually and displayed in basic scatter-plot diagrams.

Across all twenty-six community categories, Rose and Dorothy reported they had found one key pattern: "Variations in the pattern of consumption and savings among groups of families at given income levels may be explained to a considerable degree by differences in the level and distribution of income" (247). What mattered to savings and spending, the authors explained, was not the *absolute* income a family received but its *relative* income, for example, whether the family was in the twentieth or fiftieth percentile vis-à-vis its neighbors. And in turn, this varied from community to community, again with some discernable patterns. In communities with fewer high-income families, savings rates for all families were higher. The denser the population, the lower the savings, across all groups.

Dorothy and Rose's conclusions did retain some intriguing qualitative conclusions. Coming clearly through the data was "the apparent tendency for families, whatever their income, to relate their consumption to the community income situation," suggesting a residue of cultural analysis remained. Was it norms, traditions, or some other force that accounted for these regularities? In the end, this was not a speculation the authors indulged, other than a brief closing note arguing that black family spending was "doubtless influenced by consumption patterns of the white community as well as by their own social world" (250, 265).[3] Yet nothing more could be done with the present information; the paper closed with an unobjectionable call for more data and analysis.

However modest the paper's overt claims, Brady and Rose Friedman were in fact making a bold play for relevance in the emerging debate over Keynesianism. As the Yale economist James Tobin understood, their paper threatened the entire edifice of policy and politics coming to rest on Keynesian concepts of savings and consumption. Tobin recognized that Brady and Rose Friedman's paper, along with the work of the Harvard economist James Duesenberry, established a new "'relative income' hypothesis" that challenged the Keynesian "'absolute income' hypothesis." This new hypothesis was appealing, Tobin (1951: 135–36, 152) wrote, in light of Kuznets's findings: "It explains the relative constancy over the last 70 years of the percentage of national income saved. This invariance cannot be explained on the simple Keynesian theory that the saving ratio is a unique function of absolute real income" (Duesenberry 1940).[4] In turn, the relative income hypothesis suggested that a quick and easy prediction of national income from family income was impossible. A leading defender of Keynes, Tobin presented his own data in defense of the

3. Brady may also have been influenced by the Berkeley economics professor Jessica Peixotto, a colleague of her former husband, who developed what one historian describes retrospectively as a "relative-income theory of consumption" in her 1927 study of college professor budgets (Peixotto 1927; Cookingham 1987: 47–65).

4. Despite Tobin's critique, Brady and Friedman's paper is often omitted even from detailed discussions of the topic. For example, Thomas 1989 closely examines early progenitors of the relative income hypothesis but cites only Duesenberry. Duesenberry did not cite Brady and Friedman (he did cite two of Brady's statistical papers).

absolute income hypothesis, at the same time arguing that a fully developed theory must account for wealth and historic growth in asset holdings.

On the surface, Dorothy and Rose had published a basic research report. Considered in the bigger picture, their conclusions spoke to the politically charged question of consumption. Was the paper deliberately framed as an attack on Keynes?[5] Both women were dedicated empiricists, and the problem in the data was compelling. At the same time, the solution they came up with dovetailed nicely with each woman's intellectual inclinations. The paper's emphasis on relative income reflected the traditional approach of consumption research that Brady knew well, which often pointed to cultural factors as determining parts of family economic life. Brady's long tenure in reformist D.C. agencies suggests that like most consumption economists, she was probably sympathetic to New Deal social spending. By contrast, although Rose has left little trace of her thinking in this period, she was among the most loyal of Frank Knight's students, and his teachings would have primed her to be skeptical of both the New Deal and Keynesian concepts newly popular among economists.

While it is difficult to parse Rose's distinct contribution, and harder still to detect if Milton played any role in the project, the combination of Rose and Dorothy was uniquely generative. At this stage in her career, Brady was an able technician but not a groundbreaking scholar. Her other publications during this time were applications of the ideas laid out in her paper with Rose or discussions of the inadequacy of various data sets (Brady 1938, 1951, 1952). By contrast, Rose's Chicago training emphasized finding a general principle or relationship within the specific data and moving quickly to the wider implications for policy or economic theory. Working together, they created an empirically rich and theoretically ambitious paper. As one historian of the era notes, their paper was a "first attempt to provide a unifying hypothesis" to explain a widely noted anomaly (Hynes 1998: 29). In this respect, the paper captures both Rose's intellectual potential and the loss to economics that came with her move away from active research.

---

5. Duesenberry (1940: 1, 116), for one, admitted his book "began as a critique of the Keynesian consumption function," while hastening to underscore, "It is not, of course, intended to argue that nothing needs to be done about depressions."

By the time Dorothy first presented their findings at the Conference on Research in Income and Wealth—nearly three years after their collaboration—Rose had long since moved on.[6] However fruitful, working with Dorothy had been at best only a distraction from her dominant goal of starting a family. After about six months, she stopped working in order to focus on her health. The formal collaboration was over, but the conversations and intellectual bonds remained.

Nearly a decade later, Rose had the two children she desired and Milton had secured a coveted tenured professorship at Chicago. Dorothy was still burrowing through consumption data. In 1948, Milton intercepted a paper on food expenditures she had sent to Rose. Building on their earlier publication, the paper attempted to correlate the consumption function to the income distribution. Friedman found the paper "enormously intriguing" but doubted Brady's results could support the hypothesis. He referenced a few points they had discussed in a recent visit and went on to make a number of suggestions about ways to analyze her data.[7]

Brady responded with a letter accepting some of his criticisms and pushing back against others. Pointedly, she referenced his work on smoothing at the Study of Consumer Purchases, noting many of the same issues he had faced remained unresolved. She agreed, however, that her paper was incomplete, offering a sentiment that almost exactly anticipated Friedman's famous 1953 essay on methodology: "Fundamentally, the only real test of a theory is in reasonably accurate prediction and this experiment did not lead to a 'formula' that could be used for prediction."[8] Friedman's next letter to Brady, coming after another conversation, pointed her toward a chapter in his dissertation coauthored with Simon Kuznets, published as *Income from Independent Professional Practice*. "It's in this chapter that we present the material and breaking down an income of an individual into various components," he explained.[9]

6. Brady first presented the paper in November 1945 at the Conference on Research in Income and Wealth.

7. Milton Friedman to Dorothy Brady, May 4, 1948, Milton Friedman Papers, Hoover Institution Library and Archives, Stanford University, box 21, folder 18.

8. Brady to Friedman, May 13, 1948, Friedman Papers, box 21, folder 18. This comment, along with discussion of the desired features of a scientific theory in the introduction to *A Theory of the Consumption Function*, suggests the 1953 essay was cross-fertilized by the group's work.

9. Friedman to Brady, November 8, 1948, Friedman Papers, box 21, folder 18; Friedman and Kuznets 1945.

Friedman closed with hopes that Brady was settling in to her new position at the University of Illinois, Urbana.

Brady carried Friedman's reference to her new colleague, Margaret Reid. A former student of Hazel Kyrk, Reid's lifework was measuring the economic contribution of household work, previously considered nonproductive activity. After receiving her PhD in economics from Chicago, Reid accepted a professorship at Iowa State College. During the war years, Reid took two leaves of absence from Iowa and accepted federal appointments in D.C., during which time she helped establish nutritional and food-expenditure standards to inform appropriate levels of government support for poor families. Reid was drawn to Washington by a combination of factors, including a reformist desire to shape policy, political controversy at her home department in Iowa, and a rich network of economists interested in similar questions.[10] Among these economists was Brady, whom Reid described in glowing terms as "unusually intelligent, clear thinker, high standard of workmanship, marked social conscience, able, systematic, thorough, sensitive to people, sense of humor."[11] Perhaps the most powerful lure of all, however, was the trove of data on consumption that could be found in D.C. and nowhere else.

Here her goals and Brady's goals were particularly symbiotic. Brady had the data, but Reid had the time. Eventually, Reid was able to secure Brady a temporary position at her next employer, the University of Illinois. As Reid wrote in a later grant proposal,

> I think you are aware that Dr. Dorothy Brady and I hoped, by coming to the University of Illinois, to have an opportunity to do research in consumption of a type not possible in the day-to-day rush in Washington. We have both felt for a long time that there are data in many Washington, and other files that should be but are not being analyzed. Analysis tends to be neglected because the effort of staffs to such a large extent must go to getting current data which have immediate value, and because of lack of staff to meet both current needs and do long run research.[12]

10. Reid's ideas and career trajectory are described in Yi 1996 and Forget 1996.

11. Margaret Reid, typed diary entry, July 19, [1943], Margaret Reid Papers, University of Chicago Regenstein Library, box 53, folder 1.

12. Margaret Reid to Kathryn V. Burns, Acting Head, Home Economics Department, January 19, 1949, Reid Papers, box 1, folder 15.

Given her base in the Midwest, Reid was keenly interested in patterns of income, savings, and consumption among farm families. Brady was not just a valued collaborator but brought access to data that could help her situate farmers in a broader national context.

One of Reid's specific goals was to analyze consumption across multiple years.[13] Here the Friedman and Kuznets reference was apposite. The chapter Friedman cited to Brady discussed the concepts of permanent and transitory income. To better compare the incomes of dentists and doctors, Friedman and Kuznets had drawn a distinction between onetime "windfall" or transitory income, and more regular permanent income. Reid was focused on an entirely different group—farmers—and she was interested in consumption. But consumption was, after all, the obverse of income. And farmers were beset by an extreme version of the dynamic that Friedman and Kuznets had detected. Vagaries of weather, prices, and the need for new equipment could make farm consumption swing wildly from year to year. Permanent income suggested a way to smooth out these cycles and gain a more robust estimate of income over the long term. Thus Brady brought more than data to Reid: she introduced her to an important theoretical framework.

Brady also drew Reid firmly into the Friedmans' social orbit. Reid became a regular visitor to Rose and Milton's New Hampshire summer home, "the Hideaway." Located near the Connecticut River in Orford, the Friedmans' getaway was a modest cabin surrounded by a thick grove of pine trees. Arthur Burns had first introduced them to the area, which was popular with New York economists due to the proximity of the Dartmouth College library. After buying the Hideaway in 1949, the family spent every summer there. When Friedman was not battling mice, porcupines, or raccoons, Orford became the site of his deepest thinking. Near the house—but not too near—was an artists' studio, with a large glass window looking out to the woods and perfect light (Friedman and Friedman 1998: 164).

Splendid isolation worked for Friedman, but what got Rose thinking was her friends. When Dorothy and Margaret visited, the evenings became an impromptu seminar on consumption research. They were sometimes joined by Ruth Mack, an economist neighbor who had worked with Friedman at the Treasury Department (Shoup, Friedman, and Mack

13. Reid to Burns.

1943).[14] As the children drifted off to sleep in a balcony above the firelit living room, they heard below the steady hum of adult voices.

At the crux of their conversation was the Keynesian consumption function. According to Keynes, there was a fairly straightforward relationship between income, savings, and consumption. As income rose, people would increase their spending. Their savings would also increase. This relationship, which economists termed "the consumption function," was critical to the multiplier, which in turn determined the amount of additional investment needed to stimulate a moribund economy or maintain growth. Yet the empirical puzzle continued, as detailed surveys of income and spending revealed a variety of contradictory patterns. Almost a decade earlier, Rose and Dorothy had been among the first economists to suggest a rival theory, now called the relative income hypothesis. Other economists, notably James Tobin, had suggested an alternate explanation that seemed to redeem the original Keynesian idea: the wealth-income hypothesis. Yet as Dorothy and Margaret explained what they were finding, neither explanation really seemed to fit.

Slowly, over the summers of 1949 and 1950, yet another hypothesis began to evolve through the group's conversations. The scholars added Friedman and Kuznets's concept of permanent income to the consumption data Brady and Reid were analyzing and began to think through the implications. What if spending was not the result of income, per se, but of "permanent" income? What if consumers—like Reid's farmers—based their spending and savings on a forecasted average of income over several years, or even their lifetimes? If transitory or windfall income was factored out in favor of permanent income, would the data make more sense?

Taking such a perspective did not mean setting aside entirely Rose and Dorothy's first insight on relative income. Comparative spending could still be a factor, even if it was less important than the crucial elements of time and anticipation. It was even possible to integrate Tobin's argument that wealth played an important role in savings. Some consumption—for example, of durable goods—could be understood as a form of savings. But as their conversations progressed, the scholars became convinced that their permanent income hypothesis, as Milton Friedman (1957: 6) claimed in the finished work, was an idea that was "potentially more fruitful and is in some measure more general" than the alternatives.

---

14. A Columbia PhD and longtime staffer at NBER, Mack appears to have joined the group occasionally and offered comments on a late-stage draft.

An important spur to discovery was the sudden possibility Reid and Brady might secure faculty positions at the University of Chicago. Hazel Kyrk was on the cusp of retirement, and while there was no rule her replacement need be a woman, both department tradition and the nature of the appointment—joint with Home Economics—opened a rare opportunity. Simultaneously, Friedman was coming into his own as a force within the department, fighting a guerrilla war against a rival group of economists at Chicago, the Cowles Commission. In Friedman's view, the Cowles Commission econometricians were not really economists but glorified mathematicians. Rather than building predictive mathematical models, economists should develop and test theories by closely examining data from the real world—just the sort of work Brady and Reid were doing. Friedman saw the chance to supplant his intellectual enemies with two women he admired as scholars and knew as personal friends.

In March 1951, Reid and Brady sent department head T. W. Schultz a long memo outlining a program for consumption research. Landing amid Friedman's maneuvering against the Cowles Commission, and no doubt written at his urging, the memo suggested an alternate focus for the Chicago department. Along the way, it boldly defended and celebrated the unsung work of consumption researchers. Consumption had moved to "the forefront of economic discussion" due to the Keynesian revolution, the memo noted. Yet economists had ignored a century-old tradition of empirical work. "The early efforts to discover the consumption function through the use of family data were carried on almost as if nothing had previously been done in this field," Brady and Reid declared tartly, leaving unspoken the truism that women had done most of the prior research. Because it ignored the field's pioneering scholarship, the new work "has been spotty and much of it shoddy," the two women declared. They went on to propose a program in consumption research, centered at a university.[15]

The department took up the hiring question in May. With Friedman operating behind the scenes, the department's chair, Shultz, led discussion. The retirement of Kyrk, Schultz noted, opened up the possibility of "undertaking to put resources into the field of consumption research." The

15. Margaret G. Reid and Dorothy S. Brady to T. W. Schultz, "Memorandum: Proposed Research Project on the Consumption and Savings of Families," March 12, 1951, p. 4, Friedman Papers, folder 18, box 21. Friedman later rewrote this memo, so we know this version was written without his substantive input.

department should even consider "a full scale workshop directed by a team consisting of Miss Reid and Mrs. Brady."[16] For now, though, they had funding for one appointment, joint with the Home Economics Department. Reid soon emerged as the lead candidate. Unlike Brady, who held a PhD in mathematics, Reid had already established an academic career in economics. She was also known to Schultz from their time as colleagues at Iowa State College, and perhaps most important, she had the invaluable credential of a Chicago PhD.

In a second meeting, Schultz pressed for a detailed resolution stating that the department would hire Reid "as the first move in the establishment of the research enterprise, with the hope that Miss Reid soon could be joined by Mrs. Dorothy Brady." The motion to hire Reid passed unanimously, but the department supported only a tepid "continuing interest in consumption economics as a field of research," declining to record a more detailed resolution.[17] Any future moves would depend on outside funding and the department's willingness to offer Reid a workshop akin to those run by her colleagues.

As these deliberations unfolded, Friedman decided to write up the ideas he called "our tentative hypothesis."[18] He sent a copy to Brady, Schultz, and Reid. He also rewrote the proposal Brady and Reid had already submitted and forwarded a copy to Schultz. This document was generous with credit. "Dorothy Brady and Margaret Reid have concluded from their recent work that no one of these is acceptable. Together with Milton Friedman, they have developed an alternate hypothesis," he wrote.[19] In another letter to Brady, Friedman referenced "the consumption hypothesis we have so far arrived at."[20] Brady wrote back encouraging Friedman to develop it into something publishable. "I believe that you included all of the logic as I remember your oral summary late one night a month ago," she noted.[21] With Reid now heading to Chicago and leaving Illinois, Brady returned to her government job. Friedman continued to

16. "Minutes, Meeting of the Department, May 23, 1951," University of Chicago Department of Economics Records, Regenstein Library, University of Chicago, box 41, folder 2.

17. "Minutes, Meeting of the Department, May 28, 1951," Department of Economics Records, box 41, folder 2.

18. Milton Friedman to Brady, June 14, 1951, Friedman Papers, box 21, folder 18.

19. Milton Friedman, "A Program for Consumption Research," June 11, 1951, Friedman Papers, box 232, folder 12.

20. Milton Friedman to Brady, July 15, 1951, Friedman Papers, box 21, folder 18.

21. Brady to Milton Friedman, July 17, 1951, Friedman Papers, box 21, folder 18.

lobby for Brady's hiring at Chicago, even suggesting her as a potential director of the Cowles Commission.[22] He would eventually succeed in securing her a temporary position.

When the permanent income hypothesis appeared six years later in *A Theory of the Consumption Function*, Friedman gave credit to both Reid and Brady. It was Reid, he claimed, who had first tested the theory "with characteristic enthusiasm, persistence, and ingenuity." She had then pressed him "to write up the underlying theory so that she could refer to it in a paper presenting her conclusions" (Friedman 1957: ix). Reid was working on a paper, "The Relation of the Within Group Transitory Component of Incomes to the Income Elasticity of Family Expenditures," that did reference Friedman's theory.[23] This paper was never published, but portions of it were presented at the 1953 Annual Meeting of the American Economic Association (Reid 1953). But from his correspondence at the time, it appears Friedman spontaneously wrote up the hypothesis as part of broader efforts to secure Reid and Brady faculty positions at Chicago. Moreover, it appears that Brady was the first to press Friedman to write something for publication. Separately, Reid may have done the same, and she may have urged him in person rather than through a letter.

But why would Reid have wanted Friedman to take this next step, rather than write it up herself? She may well have believed herself to lack the technical training and knowledge to do the hypothesis justice. This had not, however, been an obstacle in their conversations.

Perhaps she understood that her work would go farther, faster if it rested on a theory developed by a well-known male economist.[24] Indeed, at the very same moment Friedman's other major collaborator, Anna Schwartz, was struggling to secure a doctorate despite her prodigious research output.[25] Reid's memo to Schultz indicates she knew well how economic research by women, no matter how relevant, could be systematically overlooked.

22. Milton Friedman to T. W. Schultz, March 29, 1954, Department of Economics Records, box 42, folder 10. Friedman's energetic advocacy can be contrasted to Paul Samuelson's tepid support of his student Margaret Garritsen de Vries (see Laskaridis, this volume).

23. Margaret Reid, "The Relation of the Within Group Transitory Component of Incomes to the Income Elasticity of Family Expenditures," unpublished paper, Reid Papers, box 10, folders 8–9.

24. The sociologist Robert Merton even suggested this as a strategy that lesser-known scientists might deliberately employ to spread their ideas (Rossiter 1993: 326).

25. This episode is covered in Jennifer Burns's forthcoming biography of Milton Friedman.

Regardless, it was Friedman who ultimately took ownership, turning it from "our tentative hypothesis" into "my hypothesis."[26] After Reid's hiring, the ideas languished until the summer of 1953, when Friedman went on a tear. "I have been meaning to write to you all summer, for you have been much in my thoughts," he told Reid. "I finally got around to writing up the theory of consumption, and naturally drew much on your paper." The result was "a beast" and "a mammoth" of a manuscript, running to 140 handwritten pages. It had turned out better than he dared even hope, Friedman wrote, for much of the evidence conformed to the hypothesis. "I am beginning to believe we really have something," he reported excitedly.[27] His second letter, sent ten days later, slipped between "my paper" and "our approach," as he referred to the completed paper, which Brady was having typed up and would send to her.[28]

In the fall, Friedman headed to Oxford for a year abroad, leaving the hypothesis to be tended by Reid and Brady. In his absence, a thunderstorm descended on Brady. She was suspended from her government job in early 1954 due to a loyalty investigation. Brady had been caught up in the McCarthyite dragnet most likely due to her ex-husband, a known political radical. Although they were long divorced, decades-old associations with suspected Communists could still end careers.[29] Or possibly she was a victim of the lavender scare; Dorothy had a female partner, and this relationship could have been deemed a security risk. Unable to work until her case was resolved, Dorothy was stressed and haggard. "She looked dreadful," Anna Schwartz reported to Friedman, passing on Dorothy's thanks for a letter he had written on her behalf.[30] A month later, Brady's case was closed and she was able to resume work. But she remained "whipped" by the experience, as Schwartz saw it.[31] She returned reluctantly to her former job at the Bureau of Labor Studies.

At this stage, with Friedman overseas, Reid's link to the emerging hypothesis was common knowledge in Chicago. Director of Graduate

26. Cf. Milton Friedman to Brady, June 14, 1951, Friedman Papers, box 21, folder 18, and Milton Friedman to Ruth Mack, August 31, 1954, Friedman Papers, box 109, folder 8.

27. Milton Friedman to Margaret Reid, August 7, 1953, Reid Papers, box 6, folder 1.

28. Milton Friedman to Margaret Reid, August 17, 1953, Reid Papers, box 6, folder 1.

29. Brady's name appeared as belonging to a "Red Front" in a report of the Dies Committee, likely the original source of the investigation. See "Government Employees Listed by Dies as in Red Front," *New York Herald Tribune*, October 26, 1939, 8.

30. Anna Schwartz to Milton Friedman, January 19, 1954, Friedman Papers, box 90, folder 7. David Friedman, interview with author, Stanford, Calif., October 16, 2014.

31. Milton Friedman to Schwartz, February 1, 1954, Friedman Papers, box 90, folder 7.

Studies Gregg Lewis sought out Reid to discuss a possible appointment of James Tobin as director of the Cowles Commission. After Tobin and Reid had a lengthy discussion, she reported back to Friedman that he was not inclined to support a major grant for research in consumption. "However Dorothy feels and I do that he can be educated," Reid wrote. The dream of a consumption workshop was still alive. She also noted that Tobin's visit, along with her AEA presentation, had raised the interest of a visiting scholar, Sigbert Prais. A Cowles affiliate, Prais wanted to "translate my hypothesis into algebra."[32] Prais wrote an eight-page paper analyzing Reid's longer paper alongside Friedman and Kuznets's book.[33] Reid also shared her extended take with Franco Modigliani, her AEA copanelist. Twenty years later he cited the never-published paper, along with the article by Rose and Dorothy, in his Nobel Prize address.[34]

If field specialists and the Chicago department knew of Reid's involvement in Friedman's latest project, he declined to share this information when corresponding with Tobin. This was a curious omission, given that Tobin had publicly commented on the very first iteration of the hypothesis, Dorothy and Rose's now obscure 1947 paper. Arriving back in the United States the following summer, Friedman felt confident enough to alert Tobin, whom he identified with the absolute income hypothesis, to his criticism and seek a response.[35] By August 1954, Friedman was preparing the manuscript for submission to the National Bureau of Economic Research. It had now definitively become, in the words of NBER director Solomon Fabricant, "your manuscript."[36] And when Friedman debuted the completed manuscript to the field at a Princeton conference, Brady, Reid, and Rose had faded away entirely. In a sad irony, NBER hired Rose to check the footnotes on the finished work. The experts at the conference may have known about Dorothy and Rose's original paper. But their remarks addressed Friedman and offered him credit and blame for a

32. S. J. Prais, "An Exegetical Note on Some Recent Work on Income Variations," eight-page typescript, Friedman Papers, box 232, folder 13.

33. Margaret Reid to Milton Friedman, February 7, 1954, Friedman Papers, box 232, folder 13.

34. Margaret Reid to Milton Friedman, February 7, 1954, box 232, folder 13; Modigliani 1986.

35. Milton Friedman to James Tobin, July 24, 1955, Friedman Papers, box 109, folder 10.

36. Solomon Fabricant to Milton Friedman, October 26, 1954, Friedman Papers, box 232, folder 12. The book was published by Princeton University Press as part of an NBER series.

hypothesis they found at once "splendid and stimulating" yet not entirely convincing.[37]

Ultimately, the book would do much to revive Friedman's flagging reputation in the field. Unlike his work in monetary theory, which was not then a high-prestige research area, *A Theory of the Consumption Function* addressed critical issues in the mainstream of the field. And while there was a political tint to the work, economists need not share Friedman's policy preferences to recognize the contribution. The Yale economist James Tobin, a frequent Friedman sparring partner, laid down a favorable verdict: "Research on the consumer behavior will be different in the future than it has been in the past as a result of this work. The kinds of phenomena that will have to be investigated in any future study have been changed as a result of this work."[38] It was the ultimate academic compliment. Even if they did not know it, Friedman had forced the field to contend with the woman's world of consumption economics.

Did Friedman unfairly claim singular credit for *A Theory of the Consumption Function*? In the book's introduction, he went so far as to call it "a joint product of the group," humbly claiming "my hand held the pen" (Friedman 1957: ix). But there is no evidence he seriously attempted to publish the book as a coauthored work, even though much of his early work was jointly authored.[39] In the informal world of intellectual give and take—where the actual thinking and discovery happened—Friedman was generous with his praise and credit. In the formal world of publication and peer review, Friedman defended his own interests.

This was less an indictment of Friedman and more testimony to the power of norms. In fact, Friedman's willingness to champion the work of Brady and Reid set him apart from the field. Not only did Friedman want to hire his friends, he wanted them to have real institutional power, a position his peers did not share. In his work with Anna Schwartz, Friedman not only published as coauthor but successfully pushed Columbia faculty to grant her the PhD. In both cases, however, women economists found their options constrained by formal structures of power and recognition.

37. Friedman was not able to attend the conference in person, but two attendees, Eugene Lerner and Warren Nutter, sent a transcript of remarks. Lerner to Milton Friedman, October 28, 1955, Friedman Papers, box 232, folder 13.

38. James Tobin, transcript of "Conference on Consumption and Economic Development," Princeton University, October 21–22, 1955, 6, Friedman Papers, box 232, folder 12.

39. Friedman (1945) wrote most of *Income from Independent Professional Practice*, which listed Simon Kuznets as coauthor. The book served as Friedman's Columbia University doctoral dissertation.

Reid could become a valuable member of the Chicago department, recognized within that sphere for her tangible contributions. But never would she get her own workshop, the place where the real work of the department occurred. Schwartz could be given operational control over the NBER study on monetary cycles that culminated in *A Monetary History of the United States*, but the credential of a PhD came only grudgingly.

What if *A Theory of the Consumption Function* really was a solo work, with Friedman doing all the heavy analytic lifting and the women acting as passive sounding boards, cheerleaders, or simply suppliers of unprocessed research data? In other words, was Friedman justified in excluding Reid, Brady, and his wife from formal authorship or recognition? Given the difficulty of pinning down the process of intellectual discovery, this question is tricky to answer. Since Friedman took it upon himself to write up the hypothesis in extended form, and since the general concept had first appeared in his dissertation, no doubt he appeared in his own mind to deserve full credit. (Perhaps Kuznets got stiffed too.) Before accepting this interpretation of his female collaborators' reduced role, however, we should reflect on how commonly these framings have been used to sideline women whose substantive contributions can be thoroughly documented. We should also listen to Friedman himself, who in private correspondence conceptualized the project as joint until the final stages when it assumed formal shape.

Another approach is to ask, Would Friedman have hit on the permanent income thesis by himself? Certainly one tributary came out of his dissertation research with Kuznets. Yet the more fundamental context was the group of woman economists he had known for decades who brought him a steady stream of ideas and provocations—not to mention painstakingly gathered data. Rose's role was critical; as their son reflected, "she was part of a cluster of people and ideas out of which the consumption function came."[40] Without her, there would have been no long summer evenings, no letters from Dorothy Brady, no plots and plans to create a consumption workshop at Chicago, and no reason for Milton to divert his thinking away from money. One element of Friedman's profile that particularly impressed the Nobel committee decades later was his versatility. He was not simply a monetary theorist, but a consumption researcher and a historian. Without the women in his life, he would simply have been the first.

Beyond Rose, another influence was the Chicago tradition in household economics. Since the 1920s, the department had distinguished itself by

---

40. David Friedman, interview with author, Stanford, Calif., October 16, 2014.

keeping at least one woman on the faculty. The title of Friedman's book was a hat tip to Hazel Kyrk, whose first book was *A Theory of Consumption*. Friedman may have been the first to realize the possibilities of this fact, but he was not the last. A decade later, Gary Becker would make waves with audacious claims to measure in dollars and cents the value of children and the price of housework—the very sorts of calculations household economists had been doing for years.[41] Friedman had started a new twist on an old tradition, laundering women's economics for consumption by a male-dominated profession.

What is at stake in understanding the true history of *A Theory of the Consumption Function*? First, it clarifies that women were important contributors to the fundamental disciplinary debates surrounding Keynesianism in the twentieth century. Friedman, for one, saw *A Theory of the Consumption Function* as a direct blow against the Keynesian consensus, claiming that "acceptance of the permanent income hypothesis removes completely one of the pillars of the 'secular stagnation' thesis." A key part of New Deal thinking, the idea of secular stagnation held that higher incomes would lead to higher savings, less investment, and continued economic sluggishness. One solution was taxing and redistributing high incomes. Yet the permanent income theory suggested higher income did not necessarily lead to higher savings; the relevant concept was permanent income. Friedman spelled out the implications: "It destroys the case for one proposed remedy," he argued. Reducing inequality would not automatically increase the propensity to consume and stimulate the economy. This was not merely Friedmanism grafted onto the text; surviving letters show he and Dorothy regularly discussed income inequality, how to measure it, and its social and political implications—even referencing the ideas of Alvin Hansen, a leading American Keynesian.[42]

Friedman (1957: 237) went on to argue that the theory downgraded the importance of the multiplier, thereby revealing "an inherently cyclically more stable system." This went to the crux of the matter: did capitalism need government intervention to function? *A Theory of the Consumption*

41. Kyrk's career is covered in Kiss and Beller 1999. Reid's relationship to Friedman and Becker is discussed in Yi 1996. For Becker's role in the development of New Household Economics, including an analysis of how the field became less hospitable to women, see Grossbard-Shechtman 2001. A revised and shortened version of the article presents Becker in a more positive light. See Grossbard 2006.

42. See, e.g., Brady's undated Friday letter to Friedman, which references past conversations on the topic and hopes for continued discussion (two-page handwritten letter, Friedman Papers, box 21, folder 18).

Function reminds us that monetarism was not Friedman's only challenge to Keynesianism. Indeed, while the Keynesian-monetarism debates petered out by the end of the 1980s, permanent income remains a fundamental economic and sociological concept; only its roots in the female networks of consumption economics remain obscure.

Second, *A Theory of the Consumption Function* touches on the boundary-crossing drive of neoclassical economics—so-called economics imperialism. Attending to consumption and household economics shows that this male-driven colonization project drew in fundamental ways on a protofeminist impulse to understand, value, and price the unpaid household labor of women.

Finally, while most critics of twentieth-century economics do not share Friedman's politics, they do share his judgments that economics became too theoretical, too arid, too wedded to a formalist interpretation of human behavior. In short, economics became a science of the artificial.[43] The recent emergence of behavioral economics as a corrective shows the wide resonance of this critique. But what drove this turn to formalism, and how can its mistakes be avoided in the future? One overlooked factor is how an earlier generation of academic economists stigmatized and sidelined the corner of their field engaged in extended study of how households and individuals actually made economic decisions in real life, not in simulations. It was women who gathered and analyzed critical information on economic behavior, from income to consumption to savings. In an age of economics driven by big data, it is worth remembering that the original computers were women (Grier 2005).

And what of our opening question—was informal credit a stepping-stone or a dead end? Vexingly, it was both at once. It would take broad shifts in social norms to open traditional markers of professional success to women in economics. And there was no making up for lost time. Yet when these shifts finally began under the pressure of feminism and the rights revolutions, informal credit could sometimes transform into something more.[44]

43. For a historically rigorous version of this thesis, see Mirowski 2002.

44. Outside the scope of this article is the example of Schwartz. Friedman's intervention secured her a doctorate, and she was recognized as coauthor of *A Monetary History of the United States*. Nonetheless, Friedman's Nobel citation identified *A Monetary History* as his work alone. By the 1980s, Schwartz had become more widely known to economists for her work on the Shadow Open Market Committee, and to a wider public for her service on the US Gold Commission in 1981.

After her children departed for college, Rose Friedman turned once again to her husband's work. "With the assistance of Rose D. Friedman" proclaimed the cover of Milton Friedman's 1962 popular work, *Capitalism and Freedom*. Once again, there were hints her role had been essential. By Milton's account, she "pieced together the scraps of the various lectures, coalesced different versions, translated lectures into something more closely approaching with written English" (Friedman 1962: xvi). In fact, just as *A Theory of the Consumption Function* would never have appeared without Rose, so did *Capitalism and Freedom* owe its existence to her presence. Rose consistently pushed Milton toward political engagement, sharpening his political identity and encouraging him to take up public-facing opportunities like his *Newsweek* column. By 1982 she appeared as a coauthor of *Free to Choose*, a best-selling book based on Milton's PBS documentary, of which she was a coproducer (Friedman and Friedman 1980). In the documentary itself, she remained always offstage.

Rose's ideas, be they economic or political, remained subsumed by her husband. "My husband never wrote anything without my reading it over and talking about it," she bragged to an interviewer in Singapore. "Now you can't tell who wrote what, the style is the same throughout the books. I always tell people we work as one; we are one." Rose was not bothered that all the attention went to Milton, she maintained. "I'm not a competitive person, or I would have ordered my life differently."[45] Still, at times there was a burn. Whenever she was introduced as Dr. Friedman, Rose confessed to another interviewer, "I feel upset inside when that happens. It's hard to come out and say at the time, 'I'm sorry, but I'm not a doctor,' but I don't want to fly under false colors." In 1986, that problem was solved when Pepperdine University awarded her an honorary doctorate. A picture of glowing Rose, surrounded by family at the commencement ceremony, was the last photograph included in the couples' joint memoir (Ullrich 1976; Friedman and Friedman 1998).

In the end, Dorothy Brady found her place in academe, but not as a consumption expert. Nonetheless, it is entirely possible her work with Friedman made a difference. After a brief stint as a visiting professor at Chicago, in 1958 she was hired as a professor of economics at the Wharton School, University of Pennsylvania. Had Friedman pushed for her hiring there, as he had at Chicago? Brady's papers do not survive, making it hard

45. "And Friedman Chose a Rose . . . ," *Straits Times*, Saturday, October 18, 1980.

to know for sure. But doubtless a year at Chicago burnished her résumé as an economist. At Wharton, Brady's interests began to shift toward economic history, where she drew on her statistical studies to depict economic life and relative prices in the nineteenth century. By the time of her death in 1977, she was a beloved figure to former colleagues and students (Easterlin 1978).

During most of her decades at Chicago, Margaret Reid was actually an emeritus professor, assuming that rank as required by mandatory retirement in 1961. Still, she remained a fixture on campus, regularly attending economics workshops and seminars. Undergraduates knew her as the lady in the library "taking up two whole tables with her stuff." Graduate students were slightly more informed, telling one another, "There goes one of the ancients. She was important and, amazingly, she is still doing research!" Decades later, the Harvard professor Claudia Goldin reflected that Reid was "the only female economist I knew as a graduate student." Reid maintained an active research program into her eighties, passing away in 1990 (Hershfield 1985; Goldin 2021: 49, 266n46).

Had she lived five years longer, Reid would have witnessed an upwelling of interest in her work, symbolized by the special issue of *Feminist Economics* devoted to her life and career. In 2021, Goldin hearkened back to Reid as a pioneer. "I wish I had possessed enough foresight to have struck up a conversation with Margaret when I was a graduate student," she lamented. "How naive I was for not recognizing her importance to the field of economics!" Goldin summarized major themes in Reid's work beyond the permanent income hypothesis, including her work designing the consumer price index. She highlighted as particularly relevant Reid's unsuccessful push to include women's unpaid labor in measures of national income (Goldin 2021: 47).

Before Reid passed away at the age of ninety-four, she was able to enjoy a formal marker of disciplinary prestige beyond her Chicago job. In 1979 she was elected a Distinguished Fellow of the American Economic Association, the field's major professional organization. It was small beans compared with the Nobels and Clark Prizes of her colleagues, but nonetheless a triumph to be savored. As the first woman so honored, Reid was determined to get credit at last. At her request, the traditional wording of the citation was changed, with an updated pronoun that recognized "her contribution" to the field of economics (Hershfield 1985).

References

Brady, Dorothy. 1938. "A Realistic Approach to Teaching Clothing Expenditures." *Journal of Home Economics* 30, no. 9: 612–16.

Brady, Dorothy S. 1951. "Research on the Size Distribution of Income." In *Studies in Income and Wealth*, 14:2–60. New York: National Bureau of Economic Research.

Brady, Dorothy S. 1952. "Family Savings in Relation to Changes in the Level and Distribution of Income." In *Studies in Income and Wealth*, 15:103–30. New York: National Bureau of Economic Research.

Brady, Dorothy S., and Rose D. Friedman. 1947. "Savings and the Income Distribution." In *Studies in Income and Wealth*, 10:247–65. New York: National Bureau of Economic Research.

Bunting, David. 1989. "The Consumption Function 'Paradox.'" *Journal of Post-Keynesian Economics* 11, no. 3: 347–59.

Cookingham, Mary. 1987. "Social Economists and Reform: Berkeley, 1906–1961." *History of Political Economy* 19, no. 1: 47–65.

Duesenberry, James S. 1940. *Income, Savings, and the Theory of Consumer Behavior.* Cambridge, Mass.: Harvard University Press.

Easterlin, Richard. 1978. "In Memoriam: Dorothy Stahl Brady, 1903–1977." *Journal of Economic History* 38, no. 1: 301–3.

Forget, Evelyn. 1996. "Margaret Gilpin Reid: A Manitoba Home Economist Goes to Chicago." *Feminist Economics* 2, no. 3: 1–16.

Forget, Evelyn L. 2004. "Dorothy Stahl Brady." In *A Biographical Dictionary of Woman Economists*, edited by Robert W. Dimand, Mary Ann Dimand, and Evelyn L. Forget. London: Edward Elgar.

Foucault, Michel. 2008. *The Birth of Biopolitics: Lectures at the College de France, 1978–1979*, translated by Graham Burchell. New York: Picador.

Friedman, David. 2014. Unpublished interview with Jennifer Burns, Stanford University, October 16.

Friedman, Milton. 1957. *A Theory of the Consumption Function.* Princeton, N.J.: Princeton University Press.

Friedman, Milton, with the assistance of Rose D. Friedman. 1962. *Capitalism and Freedom.* Chicago: University of Chicago Press.

Friedman, Milton, and Rose Friedman. 1980. *Free to Choose: A Personal Statement.* New York: Harcourt, Brace, Jovanovich.

Friedman, Milton, and Rose Friedman. 1998. *Two Lucky People: Memoirs.* Chicago: University of Chicago Press.

Friedman, Milton, and Simon Kuznets. 1945. *Income from Independent Professional Practice.* New York: NBER.

Friedman, Milton, and Anna Schwartz. 1963. *A Monetary History of the United States, 1867–1960.* Princeton, N.J.: Princeton University Press.

Goldin, Claudia. 2021. *Career and Family: Women's Century-Long Journey toward Equity.* Princeton, N.J.: Princeton University Press.

Grier, David Alan. 2005. *When Computers Were Human*. Princeton, N.J.: Princeton University Press.

Grossbard, Shoshana. 2006. "The New Home Economics at Columbia and Chicago." In *Jacob Mincer: A Pioneer of Modern Labor Economics*, edited by Shoshana Grossbard, 37–49. New York: Springer.

Grossbard-Shectman, Shoshana. 2001. "The New Home Economics at Columbia and Chicago." *Feminist Economics* 7, no. 3: 103–30.

Harberger, Arnold C., and Sebastian Edwards. Forthcoming. "The Department of Economics at the University of Chicago, 1947–1982." In *The Palgrave Companion to Chicago Economics*, edited by Robert A. Cord. Cham: Palgrave. https://ssrn.com/abstract=3827490.

Hershfield, Dale. 1985. "Who Is That Lady, and What Is She Doing?" *Chicago Business*, May 15.

Hynes, Allan. 1998. "The Emergence of the Neoclassical Consumption Function: The Formative Years, 1940–1952." *Journal of the History of Economic Thought* 20, no. 1: 25–49.

Iowa State University Economics Department. 1986. "Dorothy Brady." Biography for Plaza of Heroines. http://www.las.iastate.edu/archive/plaza/one_name.php?id=4313.

Keynes, John Maynard. 1964. *The General Theory of Employment, Interest, and Money*. New York: Harcourt.

Kiss, D. Elizabeth, and Andrea H. Beller. 1999. "Hazel Kyrk: Putting the Economics in Home Economics." *Kappa Omicron Nu Forum* 11, no. 1: 25–42.

Klein, Daniel B., et al. 2013. "Symposium: Why Is There No Milton Friedman Today?" *Econ Journal Watch* 20, no. 2: 157–216.

Kuznets, Simon. 1934. *National Income, 1929–1932*. Washington, D.C.: US Government Printing Office.

Kuznets, Simon. 1942. "Uses of National Income in Peace and War." Occasional Paper 6: March. New York: National Bureau of Economic Research.

Mirowski, Philip. 2002. *Machine Dreams: How Economics Became a Cyborg Science*. New York: Cambridge University Press.

Modigliani, Franco. 1986. "Life Cycle, Individual Thrift, and the Wealth of Nations." *American Economic Review* 76, no. 3: 297–313.

Nelson, Edward. 2020. *Milton Friedman and Economic Debate in the United States, 1932–1972*. 2 vols. Chicago: University of Chicago Press.

Peixotto, Jessica B. 1927. *Getting and Spending at the Professional Standard of Living: A Study of the Costs of Living an Academic Life*. New York: Macmillan.

Reid, Margaret. 1953. "Random Variations in Income and Their Effect on Income Expenditure Curves." Paper presented to panel "New Approaches to the Individual and Aggregate Consumption Function," *1953 Program of Annual Meetings*, American Economic Association, December 30, p. 81. https://www.aeaweb.org/Annual_Meeting/assa_programs/ASSA_1953.pdf.

Reid, Margaret. 1987. "Dorothy Stahl Brady." In *The New Palgrave: A Dictionary of Economics*, edited by John Eatwell, Murray Milgate, and Peter Newman, 1:272. London: Macmillan.

Roosevelt, Franklin. 1932. "Radio Address to the Business and Professional Men's League throughout the Nation," October 6. https://www.presidency.ucsb.edu /documents/radio-address-the-business-and-professional-mens-league-throughout -the-nation.

Rossiter, Margaret. 1993. "The Matthew Matilda Effect in Science." *Social Studies of Science* 23:325–41.

Shoup, Carl, Milton Friedman, and Ruth P. Mack. 1943. *Taxing to Prevent Inflation: Techniques for Estimating Revenue Requirements*. New York: Columbia University Press.

Stapleford, Thomas A. 2007. "Market Visions: Expenditure Surveys, Market Research, and Economic Planning in the New Deal." *Journal of American History* 94, no. 2: 418–44.

Thomas, J. J. 1989. "The Early Econometric History of the Consumption Function." *Oxford Economic Papers*, n.s., 41, no. 1: 131–49.

Tobin, James. 1951. "Relative Income, Absolute Income, and Saving." In *Money, Trade, and Economic Growth—in Honor of John Henry Williams*. New York: Macmillan.

Ullrich, Polly. 1976. "The Other Economist in the Friedman Household." *Sunday Sun-Times*, October 31.

Yi, Yun-Ae. 1996. "Margaret G. Reid: Life and Achievements." *Feminist Economics* 2, no. 3: 17–36.

Two "Two Ostrom" Problems

Marianne Johnson

1. Introduction

In 2009, Elinor Ostrom became the first woman to receive the Nobel Prize in Economic Sciences, recognized for her work on governing the commons.[1] Reactions ranged from surprise to confusion to disparagement. "To say that she was a dark horse . . . is an understatement" declared the *New York Times* (Rampell 2012).[2] Some of the bewilderment centered on the fact that Ostrom was not an economist but instead a political scientist (Levitt 2009). That she was not the first political scientist to win the prize—Herbert Simon did so in 1978—mattered little to those on the

Correspondence may be addressed to Marianne Johnson, Department of Economics, College of Business, University of Wisconsin–Oshkosh, Oshkosh, WI 54901 (johnsonm@uwosh.edu). I would like to thank John Singleton, Evelyn Forget, Cléo Chassonnery-Zaïgouche, Béatrice Cherrier, Erwin Dekker, Pavel Kucheř, Maxime Desmarais-Tremblay, Steven Medema, and two anonymous referees for helpful comments and suggestions.

1. Known as "Lin" to family, friends, and colleagues, Ostrom shared the prize with Oliver Williamson, their work linked by an interest in nonmarket institutions and economic governance.

2. Thomas Karier (2010: 297) declared that "it was clear from the moment of the announcement that Lin Ostrom . . . did not represent Nobel business as usual." Another scholar of the prize speculated that "the Ostrom prize was out of character for the Nobel Committee and was probably a panic reaction to the financial crisis" (Avner Offer to author, email, December 22, 2020).

History of Political Economy 54 (annual suppl.) DOI 10.1215/00182702-10085629

Economics Job Market Rumors (EJMR) website, where the superior insularity often associated with economists' opinions of the other social sciences was well in evidence.[3] Another, darker stream of commentary fixated on Ostrom's gender, casting the prize as a feeble and misguided attempt at inclusivity. "But if instead of she, it was he, would he have won? The answer . . . is a most certain 'no'" (EJMR 2013). Some of the more vulgar comments led Avinash Dixit to bemoan "some of the things said about her in blogs and other media were so ignorant and in such bad taste that I felt ashamed on behalf of the economics profession" (quoted in Rampell 2012).

Regardless of popular or professional reactions, the Nobel Prize presents a significant inflection point in any career (Frandsen and Nicolaisen 2013; Offer and Söderberg 2016). Often, the next several years are taken up by invitations to universities and institutions around the world. Scholars shift from pursuing new projects to efforts to define and protect their legacy. As the first woman to win the prize, the demands Ostrom faced were especially steep. Yet, in many ways, she was not very different than the other women in this volume. Like Barbara Bergmann and Rosario López, Ostrom faced gender-biased hurdles to higher education and academic employment; like Rose Friedman and Dorothy Brady, Ostrom married a colleague, risking that her contributions would be subsumed by those of her husband.

In academe, the "two-body problem" refers to the difficulty that life partners face in establishing two successful and independent careers in proximate location to each other. In physics, the "two-body problem" is to predict the motion of two large objects, where the force of one acts on the other. This article considers two distinct but interrelated "two Ostrom" problems. When Lin married her professor Vincent Ostrom while in graduate school, it was not clear what sort of academic career she might achieve. Nor was it evident she would gain fair recognition for her contributions to their shared research program. The difficulty of the assignment of credit between spouses is a theme that runs throughout the historiographical literature considering women's contributions to economics (Burns, this volume; Gouverneur 2019; Hirdman 2006). Examining how

---

3. One critic wondered, "Not sure how that's possible as political scientists, since they have s**tty training. Also, I'm suspicious as to why they would not have a PhD in economics in the first place." Another asked, "So Simon and Ostrom weren't smart enough to get into an Econ program but won the Nobel Prize? Something is weird" (EJMR 2018).

Ostrom negotiated the gravitational pull of her husband's orbit illuminates important aspects of the mutually constitutive relationship between individual gender experiences and the larger social-cultural environment. Her experiences highlight the many, and often hidden, constraints women have faced navigating academic careers in the social sciences.

Any attempt to assess Ostrom's career faces a second "two Ostrom" problem—the problem of gauging the contributions of the Lin Ostrom who was a multidisciplinary scholar of the commons with those of the Lin Ostrom who was a winner of a Nobel Prize. Although Ostrom worked in areas as diverse as game theory, experimental design, environmental economics, and new institutional economics, I examine her engagement with the field of public choice. Ostrom's work in this field spanned the entirety of her career, from her first solo-authored paper in 1968 to her last publications in 2012. Exploring her trajectory in public choice over a half century makes apparent the remarkable force a Nobel Prize exerts on appraisals of a career. What is different in the case of Ostrom is that as the first woman to win the prize, the award has also served to obscure many of the gender-biased experiences and constraints that Ostrom shared with other women of her generation.

2. Becoming "the Ostroms"

There is no doubt that Ostrom's professional choices were circumscribed by her gender, something she readily recognized. "Certainly, gender affected the initial days very substantially" (Ostrom, quoted in May and Summerfield 2012: 32).[4] Born in 1933, Ostrom received her formative education during the 1950s. Though excelling in high school, her parents refused to support collegiate studies. Ostrom paid her way through school with part-time jobs, graduating in three years from the University of California, Los Angeles, with a degree in political science. Although she had initially considered majoring in economics, she was deterred by an academic adviser who thought she would not be able to master the necessary mathematics. Ostrom married Charles Scott almost immediately after graduation, and like many women of her generation, she delayed

---

4. Ostrom (2014: 11) explained that her "early years in the profession were not unusual for women social scientists in the 1960s and 1970s. You were very lucky to be admitted to graduate school. Finding an appointment as an assistant professor was difficult even if your dissertation was awarded an academic prize."

further education in assistance of her husband's. Ostrom spent the next three years supporting Scott through his studies at Harvard Law School.[5]

After her first marriage ended in divorce in 1957, Ostrom began part-time graduate study for a master's in public administration while working in the public personnel department at UCLA. The next year, she undertook to enroll in a PhD program. Again, discouraged from studying economics, Ostrom found a path in political science.[6] In the year she matriculated, she was one of only four women accepted for the forty spots that included a stipend. Many faculty fought the allocation, opposed to wasting resources on women who would not be able to get good academic positions and might therefore harm departmental rankings (Ostrom 2010b). At that time, there were no women on the faculty in political science at UCLA, and there had not been for decades. This was not atypical. In the years after the Second World War, men supported by the GI Bill flooded American universities, pushing women back into more traditional roles (Laskaridis, this volume). The number of women doctorates in most fields fell precipitously—in economics, women doctorates fell from 8 to 4 percent (Forget 2011). The situation was similar in political science; only 12 percent of doctorates awarded in the year Ostrom graduated went to women, down from approximately 20 percent before the war (May and Summerfield 2012).

Ostrom's first assistantship was with the Bureau for Governmental Research; there, she became involved with an interdisciplinary working group focused on water rights. The connection allowed her to take some courses taught by economists, including seminars by Jack Hirschleifer and Charles Tiebout (Ostrom 2011). Vincent Ostrom's seminar required all students to engage in fieldwork. Lin was assigned "how water producers were coping with or ignoring overdrafts" in the West Coast Basin (Ostrom 2017: 391). Intrigued by the extragovernmental systems developed by users, her dissertation examined water as a common resource, drawing on work by Vincent Ostrom and Jack Hirschleifer (Hirschleifer, DeHaven, and Milliman 1960; Ostrom 1962) as well as the newly

---

5. Biographical details can be found in Ostrom 2009, 2010b; Clark 2019.

6. "My initial discussions with the Economics Department at UCLA about obtaining a Ph. D. in Economics were, however, pretty discouraging. I had not taken mathematics as an undergraduate primarily because I had been advised as a girl against taking any courses beyond algebra and geometry in high school. While the Economics Department encouraged me to take an outside minor in economics for my Ph. D., they discouraged any further thinking about doing a Ph. D. in economics" (Ostrom 2009).

published *Calculus of Consent*, by James M. Buchanan and Gordon Tullock (1962). Comparing her analysis of the West Coast Basin with other studies led Ostrom to conclude that communities could design effective institutional arrangements to share common-pool resources. Eventually, she would challenge Garrett Hardin's (1968) conclusion regarding the inevitability of the "tragedy of the commons" based on such examples.

Lin married Vincent Ostrom in 1963 and defended her doctoral thesis in 1965. Vincent was fourteen years her senior, a full professor in the political science department at UCLA, and already held a notable reputation in the field. Traditionally, in many such academic pairings, wives took on the roles of personal secretary, editor, research assistant, and translator (Gouverneur 2019). The Ostroms deliberately chose a different route; the archival and autobiographical evidence indicates they took her career as seriously as his. Carving out an independent career for Lin contributed to the choice to move to Indiana University in 1964. Unlike UCLA, Indiana had no formal antinepotism restrictions, allowing for the possibility that Lin could secure some sort of position. As part of his package, Vincent negotiated physical space on campus for Lin, explaining that

> my wife and I share a number of intellectual interests, and I shall be pursuing some of my work in collaboration with her. She also has some other interests . . . which are quite independent of my own interests. . . . I would hope that there would be no serious institutional constraint to our collaboration in projects that might be funded in grants to the university or that she would not be precluded from pursuing independent professional interests in teaching or research at Indiana University. She would want to be judged on her own credentials and in relation to her own merit.[7]

Lin remembered being offered a visiting appointment at Indiana by agreeing to staff a 7:30 a.m. introductory class for the political science department at the last minute. Others thought she had been hired as a trailing spouse.[8]

7. V. Ostrom to Byrum Carter, December 21, 1963, box 281, folder "Personnel Files Indiana University Dept. of Government Position," Elinor Ostrom Papers, Indiana University.

8. See Allen 2013 or Cole and McGinnis 2015: "She came here as part of the deal . . . got a position, probably would not have gotten a position on her own in that set up" (quoted in Clark 2019: 43).

Concern for her career also led the Ostroms to forgo children; she advised her own students similarly, declaring "a woman could have a career, or a woman could have a child."[9] Vincent had two children from his previous marriage. Custody sharing allowed Lin some semblance of traditional family life but with far fewer demands. She would build a second, extended family from graduate students, colleagues, and visiting faculty, regularly hosting meals, holidays, weekend workshops, and "family" reunions for them (Herzberg and Allen 2012). Upon her death, it would be remembered that "all of Ostrom's substantial parental instincts went into the nurturing of her students and younger colleagues" (Arrow, Keohane, and Levin 2012). This no doubt contributed to the quality of her students' work and the long coauthoring relationships Ostrom enjoyed with them.

After her first year at Indiana, some in the department sought to convert Ostrom's visiting position into a permanent one. This was not without tension; the initial faculty vote to confer the position was rescinded by the chair, who claimed, "well 20 years from now someone might ask if you had been appointed because you are Vincent's wife and I don't think that should happen, so to protect you I am not going to appoint you." Reflecting on the incident, Ostrom remembered that she "couldn't say anything. I was in shock, but later decided . . . I would continue and see if I cannot show him that I'm being appointed on my own."[10] She won the war by leveraging a subsequent proposal to become the graduate adviser into a tenure-track position in 1966. In 1969, she received tenure.

Teaching a full load of classes and serving as the adviser for incoming classes as large as ninety left Ostrom (2010b) with little time to develop an independent research program. In these years, Vincent served as her mentor as well as her coauthor and spouse. Of Lin's first nine publications, seven were coauthored with Vincent. Most notable was Ostrom and Ostrom 1971, which argued for a public choice approach to the study of public administration by outlining an intellectual tradition that ran from Woodrow Wilson through Herbert Simon to the new work in "nonmarket

9. Interview of Harini Nagendra, quoted in Clark 2019: 55. Elsewhere, Ostrom recounted that "I made the decision not to have a family, because, in earlier times, that would have been a very, very difficult thing to accomplish" (quoted in Auffret 2009: 25).

10. Elinor Ostrom, interview by Kirsten Monroe, box 178, folder "Publicity-Interviews given Transcript Nov. 6, 2000," Elinor Ostrom Papers.

decision making" by Buchanan and Tullock. The paper anchored what would become the Bloomington School of public choice.[11]

Ostrom first solo-authored paper appeared in *Public Choice* in 1968. In it, she applied the constitutional decision-making model developed by Buchanan and Tullock (1962) to explain "the seemingly perplexing proclivity of individuals in metropolitan areas to constitute so many independent, overlapping, special purpose, local districts" (Ostrom 1968: 87). This was not far afield from the collaborative work she had been doing with Vincent or Vincent's own work on polycentric government structures (Ostrom, Tiebout, and Warren 1961). Ostrom explained that although Buchanan and Tullock's model predicted that communities should constitute a new public enterprise each time the collective benefits exceeded the costs for a clearly defined, publicly shared endeavor, this rarely happened. Ostrom's background in political science combined with her fieldwork experience allowed her to juxtapose actual community decision-making against Buchanan and Tullock's stylized model. The result was a more complicated representation that incorporated uncertainty, individual error, and learning. In the ensuing years, she would elevate this approach, devising increasingly sophisticated empirical tests and refining theoretical models of community behavior.

3. The First "Two Ostrom" Problem

3.1. Separated Spaces

The gender-biased discrimination that women experience in economics has been well documented from the earliest years of the profession through to the present (Committee on Equity, Diversity, and Professional Conduct 2019; Forget 2011; May 2022). Women have generally responded by adopting one of three strategies: super-performance, subordination, or separatism (Forget 2005; Madden 2019). The tactics are not mutually exclusive, as Ostrom demonstrates. By any measure, Ostrom was a super-performer: she amassed nearly four hundred publications, tens of millions of grant dollars, and tens of thousands of citations over her career. Yet subordination can explain Ostrom's willingness to delay her education for that of her first husband and to later accept a lower-status position at

11. On the Bloomington School and the importance of the Tocqueville-Wilson-Simon intellectual tradition, see Cole and McGinnis 2015; Aligică, Lewis, and Storr 2017; Herzberg 2015; Lemke and Tarko 2021; Mitchell 1988; Tarko 2017.

Indiana University, having followed her second husband there. However, the strategy that best encapsulates Ostrom's approach was separatism.[12] Whether by choice or by chance, Ostrom's work at the boundaries of different social sciences meant she "didn't fit in anywhere" (Korten 2010: 10). While this allowed greater freedom to pursue unconventional projects using unconventional methods, it also generated risks for publishing and career advancement.

Ostrom created separated spaces for herself in both a literal and a figurative sense. She and Vincent built their house outside Bloomington; later, they built a log cabin on Manitoulin Island in Ontario to which they escaped every summer (Ostrom 2010b). Ostrom built separated professional space as well, with the Workshop in Political Theory and Policy Analysis (the Workshop). By 1969, the Ostroms had become dissatisfied with the direction being taken by the political science department at Indiana. They felt their colleagues' view of political science was too narrow and their multidisciplinary interests had been marginalized.[13] After much jostling and growing frustration, they identified a potential outlet. In November 1972, the Ostroms formally proposed establishing an interdisciplinary workshop. Conceived as a colloquium series to bring students and faculty together from across various disciplines for "serious discourse about the structure of diverse political economies, the incentives they generated, and the patterns of outcomes" (Ostrom 2010b: 17), the Workshop was quickly institutionalized with physical space, course work, and seminars independent of the political science department.

The functioning of the Workshop and its significance for the Ostroms' research program has been well studied (Allen 2013; Cole and McGinnis 2015; Dekker and Kuchař 2021; Locher 2018; Sabetti 2011; Wilson and Eckel 2013). The earliest years of the Workshop were funded by the university. To guarantee independence, the Workshop committed "to provid[ing] an institutional mechanism that would facilitate grant applications and highlight the continuity of research undertaken by students and

---

12. Kirsten Madden (2019: 252) characterized other ways separatism can manifest: working in women's colleges, niche areas, or outside mainstream economics; moving to related academic disciplines; or choosing careers in government. Successful separatists can become innovators.

13. E. Ostrom to Dina Zinnes, February 13, 1970; see also Ostrom to Zinnes, October 21, 1969; Ostrom to Zinnes, February 24, 1970. All in box 360, folder "Dina Zinnes," Elinor Ostrom Papers.

participating faculty" (Jagger, Walker, and Bauer 2009: 1). By 1984, the Workshop was self-sufficient, having secured grants from the National Science Foundation, the National Institute for Mental Health, and the Department of Justice as well from the Ford, MacArthur, and Earhart Foundations.[14] The funds provided Ostrom with a high degree of autonomy at Indiana, largely freeing her from departmental and disciplinary constraints.

Over time, the Workshop evolved into a massive, entrepreneurial science team. Ostrom corralled workshoppers to increased coproductivity by teaching much of the core curriculum and supervising most dissertations. Although Vincent initially held the heavier teaching schedule, by the mid-1970s, Lin's courses in the methodology of fieldwork, quantitative analysis, and game-theoretic modeling came to occupy a central space (Sabetti 2011: 74). Similarly, while dissertations produced out of the Workshop were supervised roughly equally by the Ostroms in the 1970s, by the 1980s, Lin sat on 90 percent of the defenses and served as dissertation chair for most. Her investment paid off in a cadre of well-trained research assistants.[15] The Ostrom archives contain boxes and boxes of student work organized under the larger headings of Lin's own projects. For her, collaboration made "it possible to spread the costs of data collection while retaining comparability" (Poteete, Janssen, and Ostrom 2010: 118). Students collected, coded, and analyzed data; they conducted surveys, built case studies, and generated bibliographies. For *Governing the Commons* (1990), Ostrom tasked research assistants to produce case studies in their areas of expertise. The lengthy preface to the book outlines the contributions by collaborators and students. With her former students Roy Gardner and James Walker, Ostrom devised experiments to support the analysis in *Governing the Commons*. From this followed *Rules, Games, and Common-Pool Resources* (1994), which delved into new aspects of coordinating public goods provision.

The family ethos and productive functionality of the Workshop led Ostrom to decline formal offers from Harvard and Duke along with

---

14. Grants are reconstructed from the folders listed in the Ostrom Papers finding guide, additionally informed by Locher 2018.

15. Students of the Workshop produced 135 dissertations between 1968 and 2019 in fields as diverse as fisheries, agriculture, water resources and irrigation, forestry, global commons, social organization, and urban commons (Dekker and Kuchař 2021).

consideration for prestigious positions at Minnesota and Arizona.[16] Nowhere did Ostrom feel that she could replicate the structure, effectiveness, and interdisciplinarity of the Workshop. Judged based on the volume and quality of output—grants, publications, databases, models, and awards—the Workshop was a highly successful academic enterprise. The Workshop also served another role, providing an insulating barrier for Ostrom, an incubator in which to test ideas and pursue novel lines of research without encountering the hostile atmosphere often found in hypercompetitive and frequently sexist academic seminars. "I would never have won the Nobel but for being part of that enterprise," declared Ostrom (quoted in Korten 2010). Indeed, the Workshop provided Ostrom with a similar sort of freedom that Buchanan had gained at Virginia Tech and Vernon Smith had found at Purdue and later Arizona State—space in which they had free rein to pursue their interests outside traditional disciplinary boundaries.

Beyond the physical spaces created by Ostrom, she also carved out separate intellectual space at the intersection of economics, political science, public administration, and ecology. Her first choice had always been to study economics; throughout her career, she did so by approaching economics from its boundaries with other fields. Instead of top-tier disciplinary journals, Ostrom published in interdisciplinary journals such as *Public Choice, Land Economics, Ecological Economics, Rationality and Society, World Development, Science,* and *Ecology and Society.*[17] The roots of this choice can be found in Ostrom's work on policing in the 1970s, which took her into new territory at the intersection of academic research and practical policy; finding publication outlets for these projects pushed her outside the usual political science and public administration journals. Her willingness to consider niche or interdisciplinary journals likely received a boost from her collaboration with Reinhard Selten, who

16. "Given the research program underway here, I just cannot consider a move at this time," Ostrom concluded to Sara Evans (March 6, 1996, box 172, folder Ostrom, Elinor 2 of 9, Elinor Ostrom Papers). It was only declining the offer from Harvard and the opportunity to work with her friend Ken Shepsle that generated "considerable agony" (Ostrom to William Mishler, April 28, 1996, box 172, folder Ostrom, Elinor 2 of 9, Elinor Ostrom Papers).

17. While the archives contain a significant amount of correspondence between Ostrom and various journals and book publishers, there is no evidence to suggest that Ostrom attempted to publish in top-tier economics journals and was rejected. Alternatively, Ostrom may have simply tossed the rejection letters.

was known for his choice to publish in venues that would not ask for revisions.[18]

Ostrom was acutely aware of the risks of working at the edge of different social sciences (Ostrom 2009; Poteete, Janssen, and Ostrom 2010). Her solution was volume, but with a careful eye to preserving her independence as a researcher. Between 1965 and 2014, Ostrom averaged more than six publications a year, roughly half of which were coauthored (55 percent). Ostrom's publications were divided almost evenly between book chapters (151) and journal articles (169). Although roughly substitutes in terms of time and effort, Ostrom found book chapters generally came with fewer editorial and referee restrictions, thereby allowing more latitude for mixed methods and disciplinary boundary crossing. This level of productivity was sustained by a web of coauthors, nearly all of whom were students or alumni of the Workshop.[19] The sheer variety of coauthors—more than fifty over her career—highlights Ostrom's ability to achieve independence through teambuilding and leadership, even while sharing the Workshop with Vincent.

3.2. Separating "the Ostroms"

Disentangling individual credit for intellectual work produced by married couples has long been a problem for historians of economics. Virginie Gouverneur (2019) illustrated the idiosyncratic nature of such relationships by examining how partnerships with eminent economists affected the careers and contributions of Harriet Taylor Mill, Mary Paley Marshall, and Beatrice Potter Webb. Gunnar and Alva Myrdal provide an example of a couple who worked closely together for a decade before their interests diverged; Alva, however, frequently complained that despite equal effort, their collaborations rarely resulted in equal credit (Hirdman 2006). In this volume, Jennifer Burns reconstructs Rose Friedman's contributions to the

18. Later in life, Ostrom embraced her status as an "offbeat" economist, notably at a 2011 symposium in honor of Bruno Frey. In earlier years, as a "proponent of new theories . . . and methods," she felt that she faced "an existential fight for recognition and survival" (Poteete, Janssen, and Ostrom 2010: 11).

19. Publication counts and coauthor lists were generated from Ostrom's (2021) vitae. Before the 1990s, all Ostrom's coauthors were affiliated with the Workshop. Marco Janssen and Whitaker were more frequent coauthors than Vincent. Other recurring coauthors included T. K. Ahn, Gardner, Nagendra, and Parks. Although all became notable scholars in their fields, they were first Ostrom's students.

consumption function and considers the pathway by which Milton Friedman received full credit for the idea. In the case of the Ostroms, Lin's tendency to conflate her work with that of her husband complicates forming a clear picture of her as an individual scholar, especially early in her career.[20] As such, it is not surprising that previous studies emphasized their shared intellectual tradition, comingling her contributions with those of Vincent (Clark 2019; Lemke and Tarko 2021; Sabetti 2011; Tarko 2017).

Tenure provided Ostrom with the freedom to pursue larger projects with indeterminant timelines and outcomes. Simultaneously, she began to separate her research agenda from that of her husband. While they continued to share an interest in polycentric governance, Lin was increasingly interested in devising fieldwork studies to test the hypotheses they had developed. Vincent remained focused on theoretical work (e.g., Ostrom 1973, 1976). From the mid-1970s on, Lin's collaborations with Vincent became an exception, characterized by occasional points of overlap between their now largely distinct research programs. After coauthoring seven papers with Vincent between 1961 and 1972, she would produce only eight more with him over their lifetime. Lin's projects routinely followed a set trajectory. Ostrom would launch the topic with a theoretical paper, often solo-authored. This would be followed by empirical studies designed to test the theory, coauthored with students and colleagues. The project would culminate with a solo-authored theoretical paper or book by Ostrom presenting the refined theory.[21]

Lin likely sought to decouple her work from Vincent's for several overlapping reasons. A savvy scholar of institutions, Ostrom understood academic awards and additional promotions would rest on individual accomplishments (Poteete, Janssen, and Ostrom 2010: 15).[22] Further, by

20. The anecdote runs that when Ostrom received the phone call from the Nobel committee informing her of the award, she responded by shaking her husband. "Wake up, honey," she said. "We have won a prize" (Sabetti 2011: 73).

21. The policing studies commenced with Ostrom 1972. It was followed by eleven coauthored papers testing theories of police and local government service provision between 1972 and 1983. The project culminated in Ostrom 1983. Work on the commons began with Ostrom's dissertation and efforts in the early 1970s with Vincent on water rights (Ostrom, Ostrom, and Whitman 1970). It was reborn with Bloomquist and Ostrom 1985, but more important was Ostrom 1986b, which set out to define necessary terms and laid out a set of hypotheses. More than twenty coauthored studies on the commons and irrigation and nearly as many solo-authored papers followed, forming the basis of Ostrom's *Governing the Commons*.

22. See Ostrom's long-running correspondence with Zinnes, including the letters cited in footnote 14. See also her reflections on career building in Poteete, Janssen, and Ostrom 2010.

the mid-1970s, Ostrom had the time and experience to expand her research agenda. And while explorative fieldwork—including riding around in police cars at all hours to collect data—might be exciting for someone in their late thirties with an interest in empirically testing hypotheses, the appeal would likely have been considerably less for a scholar in his fifties focused on theoretical work. Last, some of the divergence may be attributable to the philosophy of the Workshop and the Ostroms' belief that "research is not very productive unless informed by theory and that theory is not very useful unless it can stand the test of experience."[23] Their desire to create a whole from two halves may have encouraged specialization. Alternatively, Lin may have sought to carve out her own half from the whole by focusing on empirical studies.

In 1980, Vincent took a leave of absence to join a project at the Center for Interdisciplinary Research at Bielefeld University in Germany. Lin arranged a sabbatical to accompany him. The year in Germany would prove transformative, as she gained a new mentor in Selten and a new methodology in game theory.[24] Lin returned to Bielefeld in 1982, 1984, and 1988. This was an especially productive period for her as an individual scholar, with solo-authored papers outnumbering her collaborative efforts by a factor of two to one. She excitedly characterized her new approach as "straddling the academic disciplines of political science and economics" (Kiser and Ostrom 1982: 179).

Game theory provided Ostrom with new insights into problems that had long been on her radar, including managing common pool resources. It also added an important theoretical component to Ostrom's work that brought her more in line with then-contemporary trends in economics and public choice that prioritized theoretical-mathematical modeling of situations verified by experimental testing.[25] Of her papers classified as "economics," all were published after 1982. "The way game theorists think about strategic possibilities in social settings strongly influences the way I analyze central questions," Ostrom (1990: xiv) declared. The approach is

---

23. E. Ostrom and V. Ostrom to L. N. Rieselback, November 1, 1972, box 109, folder "Interdepartmental Communication," Elinor Ostrom Papers.

24. Selten was a cowinner of the Nobel Prize in Economics in 1994 along with John Harsanyi and John Nash. He is best known for his work in game theory and experimental economics, particularly bounded rationality.

25. For example, consider the empirical work of Shepsle, Peter Ordeshook, and William Riker in the 1970s on political decision-making in various governmental institutions (Mueller 2003).

evident in her *Public Choice* articles from the period. Ostrom (1986a) out-
lined a new agenda for the study of institutions based on game theory.
Gardner and Ostrom (1991) introduced the idea of "rules reforms" as a
method to reach improved Pareto outcomes. Though highly theoretical,
the paper was anchored in actual examples of fishing rights revisions.

Armed with new knowledge from her theoretical explorations into
game theory, Lin shifted back to common-pool resource problems in the
late 1980s. Her research program now shared very little with Vincent,
except its origin in water rights. Her new efforts produced *Governing the
Commons* (1990), which launched the global era for the Workshop. Now
underwritten by grants from international economic development organizations, the United Nations, and the US Agency for International
Development, Lin directed a vast research program on the commons as
related to problems of resource use and ecology in economic development. Interest by economists in her work began to intensify. This was
most obvious in the fields of game theory, environmental economics, and
new institutional economics. The public choice literature was largely
indifferent to her game-theoretic turn, despite two coauthored publications in *Public Choice* on games, prisoner's dilemmas, resource use, and
collective action remedies (Ahn et al. 2001; Ahn, Ostrom, and Walker
2003).

4. The Second "Two Ostrom" Problem

4.1. Ostrom's Nobel Prize

Women prize winners in economics are few. To date, out of eighty-four Nobel
laureates, two have been women. Of the forty-three John Bates Clark Medal
recipients, five are women.[26] Two women have been cowinners of a Frisch
Medal for research published in *Econometrica*, both within the past decade.
In each case, their coauthors were men. Proportions of women award winners
were roughly the same a century ago; between 1907 and 1932, eleven of the
fifty-three monographs awarded the Hart, Schaffner, and Marx Prize were
authored by women. Kirsten Madden (2019) argues this is problematic
because discipline-based merit awards have important career implications.
First, the awards may stimulate new entrants and/or encourage those already

26. The John Bates Clark Medal, given by the American Economic Association, recognizes
economists under the age of forty who have made significant contributions to the field. Initiated
in 1947, it took sixty years for the first woman to receive a medal (Susan Athey in 2007).

in the field to greater productivity—women winners serve as role models of success for the next generation. Second, the awards confer status within the discipline, boosting citations and opening new routes for publications and influence. The paucity of women award winners should therefore be understood as both a result of the gender discrimination that has impeded women's progress in economics and a cause of fewer women choosing to study economics.

Ostrom's Nobel Prize was accompanied by more second-guessing and critical response than usual. Some of it was simply overt discrimination and harassment. Some of it was the more subtle discrimination that women economists report in judgments regarding their choices of employment, research topics, and methodology (Committee on Equity 2019).[27] Did she "deserve" a Nobel Prize? Her nomination and the committee's deliberations will long remain opaque under the fifty-year embargo of Nobel archival materials. Four years previously, however, Smith (2005) had presciently speculated on a prize for Ostrom, noting "there are deserving others yet to be recognized for their contributions to the study of behavior, e.g., Charles Plott (Caltech) and Lin Ostrom (Indiana)." Indeed, the prima facie case for Ostrom is good. Summarizing what the decision committee generally sought, Nobel insider and prize founder Assar Lindbeck (1985) stressed a desire to award specific achievements, not outstanding persons. One committee member, Tomas Sjöström, explained that members "have this in the back of our minds that the prize should go to groundbreaking contributions that have impacts not just in academia, but on society as a whole" (quoted in Zhang 2015). Though serving on the committee for more than a decade, the example he provided was that of Ostrom.

Several studies suggest that citation counts can predict "scientists of Nobel class" (Moed 2005: 235; see also Chan et al. 2016; Offer and Söderberg 2016). Comparing citations prior to award, Ostrom fares as well in aggregate as laureates working in similar areas, such as Buchanan, Smith, Ronald Coase, and Douglass North;[28] however, Ostrom had notably fewer citations than other laureates if we restrict the analysis to economics journals. By any metric, *Governing the Commons* was

27. For an example of how different forms of implicit discrimination can coalesce, consider this comment: "She always does come off as a very nice and likable woman, just a nice and likable woman that really didn't deserve a Nobel Prize" (EJMR 2013).

28. The ideological affinities between Ostrom and these previous winners may also have played a role (Offer and Söderberg 2016).

Ostrom's most cited work. Yet, in its first decade, the book averaged fewer than twenty citations per year in economics journals.[29] In 2000, citations to *Governing the Commons* began to increase swiftly, leveling out only very recently. Alexandre Truc et al. (2020) explain that this was part of a broader trend in which economics became more open to external influences. Their bibliometric analysis illustrates that the nexus between economics and natural and biological sciences has been one of the most active areas of cross-fertilization since 2000 (Truc et al. 2020). Terence Chong, Cally Choi, and Benjamin Everard (2009) developed a model to predict Nobel winners in economics based on citations, age, nationality, and affiliation with the University of Chicago. It is not without irony that gender was excluded from the model for lack of significance. They predicted Williamson, Ostrom's corecipient, had a 75 percent chance of receiving a Nobel Prize. Ostrom did not make their list of 184 economists to evaluate for two reasons: she was not sufficiently highly cited in the field of economics based on metrics compiled by the Institute for Scientific Information (ISI)/Clarivate, and she never won a John Bates Clark Medal.[30]

Also holding important sway are the sociological and institutional features of the Nobel selection process. For many of her Nordic colleagues, Ostrom was a familiar figure. In 1999, she received the Johan Skytte Prize from Uppsala University—known as the "Nobel Prize in Political Science." She was affiliated with the Beijer Institute of Ecological Economics of the Royal Swedish Academy from the early 1990s; she served on its board for six years and was named a fellow in 2007. She had received honorary doctorates from Luleå University of Technology (2005), Uppsala University (2007), and the Norwegian University of Science and Technology (2008). She served on the board of directors for the Stockholm Resilience Center (2007–12) and for the Expert Group on Development Issues (EGDI) of the Ministry of Foreign Affairs in Stockholm (2003–4). In the decade prior to her award, Ostrom gave at

---

29. Counts from Web of Science. The book recorded almost 40 citations in 2001; this rose to 60 by 2006, 80 in 2008, and 100 in 2009, with the upward trajectory maintained through Ostrom's death in 2012. Google Scholar records a similar trend for annual citations across all disciplines, from 598 in 1995 to 2,154 in 2000 to 4,323 in 2005 to more than 7,000 in 2009. Post-Nobel years record 10,000 to 18,000 annually, with the peak in 2018. Annual citation counts have since declined slightly each year.

30. Chong, email to author, December 23, 2021.

least nine seminars at Scandinavian universities.[31] Her deep connections to Swedish efforts on sustainability meant that once nominated, she was likely to fare well under the broad scrutiny of the Royal Academy of Sciences. That the 2007–8 financial crisis had recently called into question economists' perspicacity on markets may also have contributed to the committee's decision to favor those with an alternative narrative of social-economic organization.

In the press conference following the announcement of the Nobel Prize on October 12, 2009, the first question Ostrom faced was how it felt to be the first woman to receive the prize. Surprisingly, she "hadn't realized that was the case" (Prize Announcement 2009). She also had no idea how the prize would dramatically alter the remaining three years of her life.[32] Ostrom received hundreds of invitations to honorary degrees, guest lectures, and interviews.[33] The vast majority were university lectures such as commencement speeches and convocations, public lectures, or addresses to environmental, international, and governmental groups. Ostrom's files record no economics seminars and more talks to law schools than economics groups. For Ostrom, the main advantage of the prize was that "rather than having to pound on the doors of bureaucrats to get them to listen, now governments sent ambassadors to her home to invite her abroad" (Wilson and Eckel 2013: 490).

4.2. Post-Nobel Ostrom: "Nobody Now Should Say Lin Who?"

Ostrom's Nobel award was followed by a significant repositioning of her work in the field of public choice, so much so that we can identify two distinct Lin Ostroms, the Ostrom who was a multidisciplinary scholar of the

31. An abbreviated list: Uppsala University (2007), Ersta Skondal University College (2005), EGDI of the Swedish Ministry of Foreign Affairs (2004), the Swedish International Development Association (2000), the University of Fothenburg (2003), the Workshop on Management of Common Resources (2001), the Skytte Foundation (1999), Luleå University (1999), Goteborg University (1999), the Beijer Institute (1999, 2005), and the Experience Workshop on Capacity Building of Environmental Economics in Developing Countries (1996). She also spoke at the University of Oslo (2007), the European Public Choice Society meeting in Bergen, Norway (1988), and attended several meetings of the Tampere Club in Finland (1995, 2004, 2006). She was a member of the United States–Sweden Cooperative Science Program (1987) and worked with Umea University on various projects (1984–85).

32. Ostrom was diagnosed with pancreatic cancer in October 2011. She died on June 12, 2012, at the age of seventy-eight. Vincent would live only seventeen days longer, dying on June 29 at the age of ninety-two.

33. "Trip Logs," boxes 125, 172, Ostrom Papers.

commons and the Ostrom who won a Nobel Prize.[34] The first Ostrom's contributions ranged broadly across questions of the commons, resource use, local public goods, and the voluntary provision of public goods. These topics constituted the theoretical basis of her optimal policing studies and reflected the influence of Buchanan's thinking on club goods and of Charles Tiebout on sorting (Ostrom 2011). This work, along with her engagement with the Public Choice Society throughout the 1970s, resulted in her election as its first woman president (1982–84).[35] Ostrom emphasized these deep and long-running ties in the introduction of her Nobel address (2010a).

The strong presence of both Ostroms in the formative years of public choice reflected their belief in the usefulness of "the application of concepts from economics to the study of intergovernmental relationships" (Ostrom and Ostrom 1971: 138). They chose to anchor their Workshop in "the public choice and political economy traditions" (Jagger, Walker, and Bauer 2009: 1) and required a yearlong course of all participants as "a way of getting everyone to share this common language" (Wilson and Eckel 2013: 491). Over time, their efforts contributed to the perception of a distinct Bloomington School of Public Choice (Herzberg 2015; Ostrom 2014), though its existence has not always been obvious.

> Even though both Ostroms have served as President of the Public Choice Society and Vincent Ostrom is, himself, a "founding father" of the Society, few consider Bloomington a center of positive theory or public choice. Bloomington simply does not have the notoriety of the other two places [Virginia and Rochester]. This is due, partly to the ideas and ideals but also to the roles played by its leaders. (Mitchell 1988: 110)

That the Ostroms were "gentle, inconspicuous, and unassuming" midwesterners—not to mention political scientists—contributed to their being overlooked by economists (110). Another difficulty was combining into a coherent paradigm Vincent's view of public choice as a philosophical problem with Lin's focus on the empirical testing of theoretical propositions. A third reason for the hesitancy to name Bloomington a school

34. The quotation in the section heading is from Smith 2005.

35. The Ostrom archives document Lin's attendance at every Public Choice Society meeting prior to her election, with the possible exceptions of 1973 and 1981, for which there is no information. The only other woman to have served as president is Ostrom's student Roberta Herzberg (2014–16).

was the diffuse nature of their projects over time. In the end, William Mitchell lukewarmly concluded that although on policy issues and normative orientation, Bloomington was "in basic accord with the Virginians," there were perhaps sufficient differences of methodology and intellectual tradition for Bloomington to constitute a separate locus (112). Additional references to a "Bloomington School" in the published literature would not come until after Ostrom's Nobel.[36]

Lin's work was always well received by the public choice community. Tullock (1980) lauded her efforts on metropolitan reform. Randall G. Holcombe (1993) found her analysis of self-governing irrigation systems insightful. In turn, she appreciated the Public Choice Society, and particularly Buchanan, for support at the beginning of her career.

> Buchanan has affected my life in many ways. First and foremost, his scholarship has affected my thinking and research throughout my career. . . . [Buchanan's] graciousness has also been appreciated on many occasions. Especially, early in my career when women faculty members were not always treated graciously, Jim Buchanan was an incredible colleague who did not deal with me in any way that differed from how he dealt with Vincent Ostrom. I deeply appreciated his collegiality at the time and continue to do so today. (Ostrom 2011: 370)

Ostrom regularly refereed articles and contributed book reviews for *Public Choice*; she served on the journal's editorial board and the society's executive council for many years. She also contributed to various disciplinary projects, including a chapter for Dennis C. Mueller's classic handbook on public choice (Ostrom and Walker 1997).

Yet, although Ostrom made notable contributions, she was not at the epicenter of the field. Before 2009, citations to her work in the public choice literature are relatively infrequent. For example, Ostrom published six articles before her Nobel in *Public Choice*. Yet she was cited only eleven times between 1968 and 2009 in the journal—twice by Vincent.[37] In contrast, the twelve years post-Nobel would bring fifty-one citations.

36. There are two exceptions. Peter Boettke and Christopher J. Coyne (2005: 147) declared "the 'Bloomington School' is recognized as one of the three main schools associated with the development of public choice theory"; they suggest that the Ostroms share an underlying set of themes with Frank Knight, Friedrich Hayek, and Ludwig von Mises. In his comment on their paper, Paul Dragoş Aligică (2005) also refers to the Bloomington School.

37. She received an additional nine miscellaneous mentions in the journal during this period (e.g., thanks to reviewers, call for papers).

Similarly, although her contributions to the field were noted in textbooks and compendiums, it was generally only with passing mention (e.g., Shughart and Razzolini 2002: 37–38, 61, 67, 76–77, 504).[38] Ostrom received no mention in Mueller's *Public Choice II* (1995) and fared only slightly better in the revised and expanded edition (Mueller 2003: 202, 206). She was excluded from the first edition of *Readings in Public Choice* (2004), rating a mention neither as a "founding father" nor as "public choice trailblazers versus the tyranny of the intellectual establishment" (Rowley and Schneider 2004). In the subsequent edition, Mueller added the volume's single reference to Ostrom in his introduction (2008).

Many readily recognized that Ostrom only sometimes worked on topics related to public choice. As Roger Congleton (2007: 509) explained,

> Lin Ostrom's work has always been both multidisciplinary and multi-methodological. . . . This makes her research unusual within both the public choice and new institutionalist traditions. . . . Although she uses mathematical models . . . she also does experimental work, historical research, and field work on real institutions. This has created a rich and well-known body of work that is widely read and widely cited in many separate fields.

In fact, assessments of the pre-Nobel Ostrom's role in the field of public choice are sparse. So are her thoughts on her own career. While one might expect to find some reflections in her many award speeches before 2009, Ostrom instead chose to use such opportunities to drive home particular points, whether it be the "danger of self-evident truths" (Ostrom 2000) or the importance of constitutions as mechanisms to constrain threats and optimize opportunities (Ostrom 2006).[39]

The second, post-Nobel Ostrom was someone who "made a foundational contribution to the Public Choice movement and to the rise of the new institutionalism and has been a key figure in the resurgence of political economy" (Aligică and Boettke 2017). *Governing the Commons*

---

38. That Ostrom was focused on govern*ance* (either formal institutional or extrainstitutional) and public choice on govern*ment* can go some way to explaining why Ostrom was not especially well cited in that literature prior to her Nobel Prize. Much of the recent work being done at George Mason as it relates to Ostrom is to extend traditional public choice thinking to questions of governance (Boettke 2010; Herzberg 2015; Lemke and Tarko 2021).

39. Awards included the Galbraith Award (2008), the William H. Riker Prize in Political Science (2008), the James Madison Award (2005), and the John Skytte Prize in Political Science (1999).

became "one of the best pieces of work on public choice" (Smith 2012).[40] Unlike many laureates for whom the prize came close to the peak of citation impact (Offer and Söderberg 2016), Ostrom's trajectory was more like that of the mathematician Robert Aumann (Frandsen and Nicolaisen 2013). For both, their work witnessed a sudden and dramatic increase in citations in economics after the prize. Tove Faber Frandsen and Jeppe Nicolaisen (2013) suggest two reasons why citations may explode post-Nobel. First, the award directs attention to a particular problem or set of problems; citations increase as more people decide to work on closely related topics. Second, a Nobel Prize can spark a chain reaction of citations through the bandwagon effect—in effect, the prize acts as an arbitrator of what is fashionable or of interest to economists.

Some of the bandwagoning focused on cementing the Bloomington School's credentials as an independent tradition in public choice and institutional analysis (Cole and McGinnis 2015; Lemke and Tarko 2021; Herzberg 2015). The salient features of the Bloomington School were identified as (1) a willingness to learn from different fields and different perspectives, (2) an emphasis on the usefulness of multiple or mixed methods, and (3) a belief in the necessity of direct community engagement (Lemke and Tarko 2021). One could add to this a belief in situational specifics over grand general theories.

What becomes apparent is that Ostrom's contributions to public choice have been both widened and narrowed. They have been narrowed to focus predominantly on her demonstration that individuals can efficiently coordinate the use of common-pool resources, such as fisheries or forests, without resorting to either privatization or government management. Her contributions have been widened in that the "neither markets nor states" solution has been found to apply to a multitude of economic situations beyond common-pool resource problems. This theme is particularly evident in the Austrian public choice scholarship associated with economists at George Mason University and its Mercatus Center (e.g., Aligică and Boettke 2011, 2017; Aligică, Lewis, and Storr 2017; Boettke 2010; Boettke, Palagashvili, and Lemke 2013; Herzberg 2015; Lemke and Tarko 2021; Smith 2012; Tarko 2017). In the traditional public choice literature, the necessity for government to provide guardrails against anarchy was weighed against the countervailing dangers of technocracy and Leviathan.

---

40. On citation patterns post-Nobel, see Boettke, Fink, and Smith 2012; Frandsen and Nicolaisen 2013; Offer and Söderberg 2016.

The solutions provided by individuals such as Buchanan or Richard Wagner were small government, local government, and a maximum direct democratic input. Ostrom's work provided an escape from this balancing act—governance without government. As such, Ostrom's work built "a bridge" from Friedrich Hayek to present Austrian public choice analysis (Aligică 2010: 96). Beyond extrastate solutions, these scholars emphasize Ostrom's faith in democratic institutions over expert authorities and a belief that bigger is not necessarily better when it comes to collective decision-making (Boettke, Palagashvili, and Lemke 2013).[41]

5. Conclusion

In physics, one way to escape the two-body problem is to treat one object as an immobile source of force in its actions on the other. As such, it might very well have been the case that historians of economics would not have taken up Lin Ostrom without her Nobel award, or they would have done so with a markedly different focus and intent. It is the central role of the prize in the profession that demands historians take up the winners—to historicize them, to judge their work, and to place them in one of many various intellectual traditions. And it was through the pathway of the award that Ostrom became an influential economist, in many ways distinct from her prior existence as multidisciplinary scholar of the commons.

However, the prize has had another effect. For the first woman to win a Nobel prize, the award has complicated and obscured the degree to which gender-based discrimination constrained many of Ostrom's career choices, and in fact, her ability to work as an economist—hurdles include what were considered appropriate fields of study for women in the 1950s, the ability of women to secure tenure-track jobs in academe, and the ability of women to achieve proper recognition for their contributions in collaborative research. With entry barred to formal economic study, Ostrom chose to approach economics from its boundaries with other disciplines. She studied aspects of political science and public administration that overlapped with public economics. Her strategic choices regarding graduate course work, dissertation topic, and assistantships allowed her to

41. Ostrom shares with Buchanan an optimism that better political-economic decision-making can result through local democratic process, placing trust in civic engagement and civic education.

enroll in economics courses that would otherwise have been closed to her. Early in her career, she opted to work in public choice, a newly established field that sought to apply economic methods to the problems of collective choice usually associated with political science studies. Later, Ostrom mastered game theory, bringing her into theoretical and methodological concert with mainstream economic practices. Like James Buchanan, her work included important contributions to public goods and collective decision-making. Like Douglass North and Ronald Coase, Ostrom pushed the economic study of institutions in new and vital directions. Like Reinhard Selten and Vernon Smith, she developed novel experiments and games to elucidate complicated economic choices.

References

Ahn, T. K., Lin Ostrom, David Schmidt, Robert Shupp, and James Walker. 2001. "Cooperation in PD Games: Fear, Greed, and History of Play." *Public Choice* 106:137–55.

Ahn, T. K., Lin Ostrom, and James Walker. 2003. "Heterogeneous Preferences and Collective Action." *Public Choice* 117:295–314.

Aligică, Paul Dragoş. 2005. "Institutional Analysis and Economic Development Policy: Notes on the Applied Agenda of the Bloomington School." *Journal of Economic Behavior and Organization* 57, no. 2: 159–65.

Aligică, Paul Dragoş. 2010. "Lin Ostrom—Nobel Prize in Economics 2009." *Economic Affairs* 30, no. 1: 95–96.

Aligică, Paul Dragoş, and Peter Boettke. 2011. "The Two Social Philosophies of the Ostroms' Institutionalism." *Policy Studies Journal* 39, no. 1: 29–268.

Aligică, Paul Dragoş, and Peter Boettke. 2017. "Lin Ostrom (1933–2012)." *The New Palgrave Dictionary of Economics*. https://link.springer.com/referenceworkentry /10.1057%2F978–1-349–95121–5_2923–2.

Aligică, Paul Dragoş, Paul A. Lewis, and Virgil Henry Storr. 2017. "Austrian Economics and the Bloomington School: An Introduction and Overview." *Advances in Austrian Economics* 22:i–xxi.

Allen, Barbara. 2013. "Working Together, in Memoriam: Lin Ostrom." *Commons Digest* 13, no. 14: 7–11.

Arrow, Kenneth, Robert O. Keohane, and Simon A. Levin. 2012. "Lin Ostrom: An Uncommon Woman for the Commons." *Proceedings of the National Academy of Sciences of the United States of America* 109, no. 35. https://www.pnas.org/content /109/33/13135.

Auffret, Sarah. 2009. "Collective Action, Singular Accomplishment." *ASU Magazine*, March, 22–27.

Bloomquist, William, and Lin Ostrom. 1985. "Institutional Capacity and Resolution of the Commons Dilemma." *Policy Studies Review* 5, no. 3: 383–94.

Boettke, Peter. 2010. "Is the Only Form of 'Reasonable Regulation' Self Regulation? Lessons from Lin Ostrom on Regulating the Commons and Cultivating Citizens." *Public Choice* 143:283–91.

Boettke, Peter J., and Christopher J. Coyne. 2005. "Methodological Individualism, Spontaneous Order, and the Research Program of the Workshop in Political Theory and Policy Analysis." *Journal of Economic Behavior and Organization* 57, no. 2: 145–58.

Boettke, Peter, Alexander Fink, and Daniel Smith. 2012. "The Impact of Nobel Prize Winners in Economics: Mainline vs. Mainstream." *American Journal of Economics and Sociology* 71, no. 5: 1219–49.

Boettke, Peter, Liya Palagashvili, and Jayme Lemke. 2013. "Riding in Cars with Boys: Lin Ostrom's Adventures with the Police." *Journal of Institutional Economics* 9, no. 4: 407–25.

Buchanan, James M., and Gordon Tullock. 1962. *The Calculus of Consent.* Ann Arbor: University of Michigan Press.

Chan, Ho Fai, Bruno S. Frey, Jana Gallus, Markus Schaffner, Benno Torgler, and Stephen Whyte. 2016. "External Influence as an Indicator of Scholarly Importance." *CESifo Economic Studies* (May): 170–95.

Chong, Terence Tai-leung, Cally Choi, and Benjamin Everard. 2009. "Who Will Win the Nobel Prize?" *Economics Bulletin* 29, no. 2: 1–10.

Clark, Sara. 2019. "Lin Ostrom: A Biography of an Interdisciplinary Life." PhD diss., University of Michigan.

Cole, Daniel, and Michael McGinnis. 2015. Introduction to vol. 2 of *Lin Ostrom and the Bloomington School of Political Economy*, edited by Daniel Cole and Michael McGinnis. Lanham, Md.: Rowman and Littlefield.

Committee on Equity, Diversity, and Processional Conduct. 2019. "AEA Professional Climate Survey: Final Report." American Economic Association. https://www .aeaweb.org/resources/member-docs/final-climate-survey-results-sept-2019.

Congleton, Roger. 2007. "Lin Ostrom, *Understanding Institutional Diversity.*" *Public Choice* 132:509–11.

Dekker, Erwin, and Pavel Kuchař. 2021. "The Ostrom Workshop: Artisanship and Knowledge Commons." *Revue d'économie politique* 4, no. 131: 637–64.

Economics Job Market Rumors (EJMR). 2013. "Three Years Later, Did Ostrom Deserve a Nobel Prize?" https://www.econjobrumors.com/topic/3-years-later-did -ostrom-deserve-the-nobel.

Economics Job Market Rumors (EJMR). 2018. "Was Lin Ostrom as Political Scientist?" https://www.econjobrumors.com/topic/was-Lin-ostrom-a-political -scientist.

Forget, Evelyn. 2005. "American Women Economists, 1900–1940: Doctoral Dissertations and Research Specialization." In *Women of Value: Feminist Essays on the History of Women in Economics*, edited by Mary Ann Dimand, Robert Dimand, and Evelyn Forget, 25–38. Brookfield, Vt.: Elgar.

Forget, Evelyn. 2011. "American Women and the Economics Profession in the Twentieth Century." *Œconomia* 1, no. 1: 19–31.

Frandsen, Tove Faber, and Jeppe Nicolaisen. 2013. "The Ripple Effect: Citation Chain Reactions of a Nobel Prize." *Journal of the American Society for Information Science and Technology* 64, no. 3: 437–47.

Gardner, Roy, and Lin Ostrom. 1991. "Rules and Games." *Public Choice* 70 (May): 121–49.

Gouverneur, Virginie. 2019. "Harriet Taylor Mill, Mary Paley Marshall, and Beatrice Potter Webb: Women Economists and Economists' Wives." In *The Routledge Handbook of the History of Women's Economic Thought*, edited by Robert Dimand and Kirsten Madden, 73–89. New York: Routledge.

Hardin, Garrett. 1968. "Tragedy of the Commons." *Science* 162, no. 3859: 1243–48.

Herzberg, Roberta. 2015. "Governing Their Commons: Lin and Vincent Ostrom and the Bloomington School." *Public Choice* 163, nos. 1–2: 95–109.

Herzberg, Roberta, and Barbara Allen. 2012. "Lin Ostrom (1933–2012)." *Public Choice* 152:263–68.

Hirdman, Yvonne. 2006. *Alva Myrdal: The Passionate Mind*. Bloomington: Indiana University Press.

Hirschleifer, Jack, James DeHaven, and Jerome Milliman. 1960. *Water Supply: Economics, Technology, and Policy*. Chicago: University of Chicago Press.

Holcombe, Randall G. 1993. "Review of Crafting Institutions for Self-Governing Irrigation Systems by Lin Ostrom." *Public Choice* 75, no. 4: 399–401.

Jagger, Pamela, James Walker, and Jacqui Bauer. 2009. "Thirty-Five Years of Scholarship at the Workshop in Political Theory and Policy Analysis." Workshop in Political Theory and Policy Analysis. https://citeseerx.ist.psu.edu/viewdoc /download?doi=10.1.1.169.8358&rep=rep1&type=pdf.

Karier, Thomas. 2010. *Intellectual Capital: Forty Years of the Nobel Prize in Economics*. New York: Cambridge University Press.

Kiser, Larry, and Lin Ostrom. 1982. "The Three Worlds of Action: A Meta-Theoretical Synthesis of Institutional Approaches." In *Strategies of Political Inquiry*, edited by Lin Ostrom. Beverly Hills, Calif.: Sage.

Korten, Fran. 2010. "Common(s) Sense Wins One." *Yes!* 52 (Spring): 13.

Lemke, Jayme, and Vlad Tarko. 2021. *Elinor Ostrom and the Bloomington School: Building a New Approach to Policy and the Social Sciences*. New Castle on Tyne: Agenda Publishing.

Levitt, Steven. 2009. "What This Year's Nobel Prize in Economics Says about the Nobel Prize in Economics." *Freakeconomics*, October 12. https://freakonomics .com/2009/10/12/what-this-years-nobel-prize-in-economics-says-about-the-nobel -prize-in-economics/.

Lindbeck, Assar. 1985. "The Prize in Economic Science in Memory of Alfred Nobel." *Journal of Economic Literature* 23, no. 1: 37–56.

Locher, Fabien. 2018. "Historicizing Lin Ostrom: Urban Politics, International Development and Expertise in the U.S. Context (1970–1990)." *Theoretical Inquiries in Law* 19, no. 2: 533–58.

Madden, Kirsten. 2019. "Women Economists of Promise? Six Hart, Schaffner and Marx Prize Winners in the Early Twentieth Century." In *The Routledge Handbook of the History of Women's Economic Thought*, edited by Robert Dimand and Kirsten Madden, 250–71. New York: Routledge.

May, Ann Mari. 2022. *Gender and Professionalization in the Dismal Science: Women in the Early Years of the Economics Profession*. New York: Columbia University Press.

May, Ann Mari, and Gale Summerfield. 2012. "Creating a Space Where Gender Matters." *Feminist Economics* 18, no. 4: 25–37.

Mitchell, William C. 1988. "Virginia, Rochester, and Bloomington: Twenty-Five Years of Public Choice and Political Science." *Public Choice* 56:101–19.

Moed, Henk. 2005. *Citation Analysis in Research Evaluation*. Dordrecht: Springer.

Mueller, Dennis. 1995. *Public Choice II*. New York: Cambridge University Press.

Mueller, Dennis. 2003. *Public Choice III*. New York: Cambridge University Press.

Mueller, Dennis. 2008. "Public Choice: An Introduction." In *Readings in Public Choice and Constitutional Political Economy*, edited by C. Rowley and F. Schneider, 31–46. Boston: Springer.

Offer, Avner, and Gabriel Söderberg. 2016. *The Nobel Factor: The Prize in Economics, Social Democracy, and the Market Turn*. Princeton, N.J.: Princeton University Press.

Ostrom, Elinor. 1965. "Public Entrepreneurship: A Case Study in Ground Water Basin Management." PhD diss., University of California, Los Angeles.

Ostrom, Elinor. 1968. "Some Postulated Effects of Learning on Constitutional Behavior." *Public Choice* 5:87–104.

Ostrom, Elinor. 1972. "Metropolitan Reform: Propositions Derived from Two Traditions." *Social Science Quarterly* 53 (December): 474–93.

Ostrom, Elinor. 1983. "A Public Choice Approach to Metropolitan Institutions: Structures, Incentives, and Performance." *Social Science Journal* 20, no. 3: 79–96.

Ostrom, Elinor. 1986a. "An Agenda for the Study of Institutions." *Public Choice* 48:3–25.

Ostrom, Elinor. 1986b. "Issues of Definition and Theory: Some Conclusions and Hypotheses." In *Proceedings of the Conference on Common Property Resource Management*, ed. National Research Council, 597–615. Washington, D.C.: National Academy Press.

Ostrom, Elinor. 1990. *Governing the Commons: The Evolution of Institutions for Collective Action*. New York: Cambridge University Press.

Ostrom, Elinor. 2000. "The Danger of Self-Evident Truths." *PS: Political Science and Politics* 33, no. 1: 33–44.

Ostrom, Elinor. 2005. *Understanding Institutional Diversity*. Princeton, N.J.: Princeton University Press.

Ostrom, Elinor. 2006. "The 2005 James Madison Award Lecture: Converting Threats into Opportunities." *PS: Political Science and Politics* 39, no. 1: 3–12.

Ostrom, Elinor. 2009. "Biographical." Nobel Media. https://www.nobelprize.org/prizes/economic-sciences/2009/ostrom/biographical/.

Ostrom, Elinor. 2010a. "Beyond Markets and States: Polycentric Governance of Complex Economic Systems." *American Economic Review* 100, no. 3: 641–72.

Ostrom, Elinor. 2010b. "A Long Polycentric Journey." *Annual Review of Political Science* 13:1–23.

Ostrom, Elinor. 2011. "Honoring James Buchanan." *Journal of Economic Behavior and Organization* 80:370–73.

Ostrom, Elinor. 2014. *Lin Ostrom and the Bloomington School of Political Economy*, edited by Daniel H. Cole and Michael D. McGinnis. Lexington, Ky.: Lexington Books.

Ostrom, Elinor. 2017. "Learning from the Field." In *Lin Ostrom and the Bloomington School of Political Economy: A Framework for Policy Analysis*, vol. 3, edited by Daniel H. Cole and Michael D. McGinnis. Lanham, Md.: Lexington Books.

Ostrom, Elinor. 2021. Vitae. https://ostromworkshop.indiana.edu/pdf/CVs/eostrom _vitae.pdf.

Ostrom, Elinor, Roy Gardner, and James Walker. 1994. *Rules, Games, and Common-Pool Resources*. Ann Arbor: University of Michigan Press.

Ostrom, Elinor, and Vincent Ostrom. 1971. "Public Choice: A Different Approach to the Study of Public Administration." *Public Administration Review* 31, no. 2: 203–16.

Ostrom, Elinor, and Vincent Ostrom. n.d. Papers, ca. 1889–2012. Lilly Library, Indiana University. https://iucat.iu.edu/lilly/14513217.

Ostrom, Elinor, Vincent Ostrom, and Ira Whitman. 1970. "Problems for Institutional Analysis of the Great Lakes Basin." In *Proceedings: Thirteenth Conference on Great Lakes Research*, 156–67. Toronto: International Association for Great Lakes Research.

Ostrom, Elinor, and James Walker. 1997. "Neither Markets nor States: Linking Transformation Processes in Collective Action Arenas." In *Perspectives in Public Choice*, edited by Dennis Mueller. New York: Cambridge University Press.

Ostrom, Vincent. 1962. "The Political Economy of Water Development." *American Economic Review* 52, no. 2: 450–58.

Ostrom, Vincent. 1973. "Can Federalism Make a Difference?" *Publius* 3, no. 2: 197–237.

Ostrom, Vincent. 1976. "The American Contribution to a Theory of Constitutional Choice." *Journal of Politics* 38, no. 3: 56–78.

Ostrom, Vincent, and Elinor Scott. 1961. "Prediction and Planning: Some Problems in the Study of Political Behavior." *Western Political Quarterly* 14, no. 3: 49–50.

Ostrom, Vincent, Charles Tiebout, and Robert Warren. 1961. "The Organization of Government in Metropolitan Areas: A Theoretical Inquiry." *American Political Science Review* 100, no. 3: 641–72.

Poteete, Amy, Marco Janssen, and Lin Ostrom. 2010. *Working Together: Collective Action, the Commons, and Multiple Methods in Practice*. Princeton, N.J.: Princeton University Press.

Prize Announcement. 2009. "Nobel Prize Outreach," August 11. https://www .nobelprize.org/prizes/economic-sciences/2009/prize-announcement/.

Rampell, Catherine. 2012. "Lin Ostrom, Winner of Nobel in Economics, Dies at Seventy-Eight." *New York Times*, June 12. https://www.nytimes.com/2012/06/13 /business/Lin-ostrom-winner-of-nobel-in-economics-dies-at-78.html.

Rowley, Charles, and Fredrich G. Schneider. 2004. *Readings in Public Choice and Constitutional Political Economy*. Boston: Springer.

Sabetti, Filippo. 2011. "Constitutional Artisanship and Institutional Diversity: Lin Ostrom, Vincent Ostrom, and the Workshop." *Good Society* 20, no. 1: 73–83.

Shugart, William, and Laura Razzolini. 2002. *The Elgar Companion to Public Choice*. Northampton, Mass.: Edward Elgar.

Smith, Vernon. 2005. "A Second Nobel for Selten?" *Wall Street Journal*, October 15. https://www.wsj.com/articles/SB112933680480669501.

Smith, Vernon. 2012. "From One Nobel Prize Winner to Another: Vernon Smith on Lin Ostrom's Contributions to Economics." Competitive Enterprise Institute, June 12. https://cei.org/blog/from-one-nobel-prize-winner-to-another-vernon-smith-on -Lin-ostroms-contribution-to-economics/.

Tarko, Vlad. 2017. *Lin Ostrom: An Intellectual Biography*. Lanham, Md.: Rowman and Littlefield.

Truc, Alexandre, Olivier Santerre, Yves Gingras, François Claveau. 2020. "The Interdisciplinarity of Economics." https://papers.ssrn.com/sol3/papers.cfm ?abstract_id=3669335.

Tullock, Gordon. 1980. Review of *Metropolitan Reform: An Annotated Bibliography*, by Paul C. Baker, Lin Ostrom, Robert Goehlert. *Public Choice* 35, no. 5: 365.

Wilson, Rick, and Catherine Eckel. 2013. "Lin Ostrom: 'A Magnificent and Irreplaceable Treasure.'" *Southern Economics Journal* 79, no. 3: 486–95.

Zhang, Weini. 2015. "Professor Details Dual Role as Nobel Prize Committee Member." *Daily Targum*, January 21. https://dailytargum.com/article/2015/01 /professor-details-dual-role-as-nobel-prize-committee-member.

Climbing the Obelisk: The Trajectories of Five Women Economists in Colombia, ca. 1950–70

Andrés Guiot-Isaac and Camila Orozco Espinel

The economist Cecilia López's fiancé, who was her (senior) economics professor, was "not planning to marry Mrs. Robinson." This was what he replied when she told him she was planning to take a particularly heavy load of credits for the second term of her first year in economics. López, who later became minister of agriculture and of environment in Colombia, director of the National Planning Department (Departamento Nacional de Planeación), and a presidential candidate, missed the reference and replied that she was too young to be compared to the protagonist of the 1967 movie *The Graduate*. Her future husband was referring to the British economist Joan Robinson. Soon after López got married, she put her studies on hold and spent two years in the United States, where she had her first daughter while her husband completed a master's degree in development economics at Vanderbilt University, fully funded by the Rockefeller Foundation. López never contemplated the possibility of abandoning her career. Yet, although she was more proficient in English than her husband, pursuing graduate studies in the United States was not an option for her.

Correspondence may be addressed to andres.guiotisaac@bnc.ox.ac.uk and camila.orozco-espinel@univ-reims.fr. We thank our interviewees for their time and openness to share their experiences with us. We also thank Jimena Hurtado, Verónica Montecinos, Gabriel Misas, Erich Pinzón-Fuchs, and the participants of the 2021 HOPE conference for their helpful comments on various drafts of this article. An earlier version was presented at the Seminario CID at the Universidad Nacional.

History of Political Economy 54 (annual suppl.) DOI 10.1215/00182702-10085643

Her "role as a caregiver was taken for granted," as she realized during our interview. After the couple returned to Colombia, López continued her studies and had an outstanding career. But her lack of international credentials always haunted her. Indeed, during the 1950s, 1960s, and 1970s, postgraduate degrees obtained in universities in the United States or Europe opened for economists a fast track to decision-making positions, particularly in the public sector (Guiot-Isaac 2022). López was a brilliant student, and she gravitated toward the circles where contacts with universities abroad and grand opportunities existed. Nevertheless, she never headed in this direction. When asked why, she replied, "My second child was born, I could not leave the country."

We study in this article the professional trajectories of five women economists in Colombia who graduated between the 1950s and the 1970s. María Elvira Santos (b. 1930), Lucía Cruz (b. 1940), Martha Fernández (b. 1940), Cecilia López (b. 1943), and Clara Elsa Villalba (b. 1944) had, by contemporary standards, exceptionally successful careers in academe, the state, the private sector, and multilateral institutions. However, because of their gender, nationality, and nonacademic profiles, the careers of women economists like them rarely capture the attention of historians of economics. The experience of women economists, particularly those coming from the Global South, is generally absent in the literature about the professionalization of economics (Coats 1981; Fourcade 2009). When biographies and life stories are used as a tool of historical analysis, the literature has focused, with notable exceptions (Dimand, Dimand, and Forget 2000), on the professional trajectories of the few male economists who came to play a prominent role in economic theory and policymaking. This focus on great men (here, we mean this as a category) leaves in obscurity how the economics profession structured the opportunities for men and women in different national contexts, and the strategies that women economists employed to succeed in the profession. By studying the trajectories of the first women economists in Colombia from a gender perspective,[1] this article attempts to correct this historiographical bias.

While we focus on a specific set of historically and contextually situated cases, our analysis considers how gender issues at an individual scale intersect larger demographic patterns, sociocultural conditions, and

---

1. Here we understand gender perspective as an approach that focuses on how differences between women's and men's experiences structured both professional individual trajectories and institutions such as professions.

international trends in the professional development of economics. Hence, by contrasting the successful trajectories of our focus women and placing them in context, this article also yields insights into broader "institutional structures" (Forget 2002: 236), such as professions. Rather than addressing the narrower question of what made it possible for (some) women to professionally succeed as economists, we aim to shed light on broader questions regarding the professionalization of economics. How did differences between women's and men's experiences structure the process of becoming and working as economists? Which role did these differences play in shaping the professional opportunities for women during the early development of economics in Colombia? To what extent did the conflicts and constraints that successful women economists in Colombia faced resemble those that women economists encountered elsewhere?

This research angle informed our decision to focus on the trajectories of women with remarkably long and successful professional careers— rather than on those whose trajectories were interrupted at different stages. The group of women that we study belonged to the first generation of women professionals in Colombia. They became economists at a time when new educational, occupational, and political spaces were opening for women in Colombian society (Wills 2004), even if these were, across Latin America, still predominantly male environments structured by patriarchal values (Paulson 2016; Chaney 1980). Simultaneously, they belonged to the first generation of academically trained economists in the country. Their dual status as first-generation women professionals *and* economists not only shaped the opportunities available for them but also gave historical specificity to their professional experiences. In our period of study, the participation of women in the economics profession in Colombia could be depicted as a tall thin obelisk, where despite a low proportion of women overall, some did rise to the top. This characterization contrasts with the pyramidal shape of the gendered infrastructure of the social sciences in the United States during the same period (Rossiter 1997). While we cannot ignore the fact that the demands of family relationships constrained certain aspects of their professional attainment and recognition (Blau and Winkler 2017) in all five case studies, their social and economic capital also allowed them to navigate these constraints.

Our selection of cases emerged organically as our research progressed. While most women who started their training in economics during our period later disappeared from the historical records, the focus group we study in this article appeared frequently and consistently in archival and published sources as well as in oral testimonies. We therefore arranged semistructured interviews with López (11/4/2020), Cruz (12/5/2020), Villalba (12/2/2020), Fernández (12/16/2020), and Santos's eldest son, Aldo Buenahora (10/30/2020). Other women who figured in the historical records and whose experiences could have complemented our analysis we were unable to reach. Before conducting our interviews, we gathered biographical information on our interviewees and prepared question sheets based on previous research on a wide variety of primary archival and published sources, which include the institutional archives of the Gimnasio Moderno, the Universidad de los Andes, and the Universidad Nacional in Bogotá, as well as the Grants and Fellowship Files of the Rockefeller Foundation, the Ford Foundation, and the Population Council archives. We then selected a framework of themes to be explored during our conversations that covered issues related to our interviewees' socio-economic backgrounds, their experiences navigating masculine environments (mentors and masculine support were key), and marriage and parenthood. The interviews were a dialogical process, where we noticed how our interviewees connected these themes—sometimes with surprise or resistance—to their professional trajectories and the different demands and expectations that Colombian society of the time had about women and men. We also had access to around two dozen interviews with peers, colleagues, and mentors of these women, conducted between January 2020 and January 2021 for the doctoral thesis of one of the coauthors of this article. Finally, we triangulated the information gathered during our interviews with written sources.

1. The Inclusion of Women in Secondary and Higher Education in Colombia

In Colombia, only during the 1930s were women legally allowed to complete secondary education conducive to a university degree and professional credentials.[2] The watershed enactment of decree 227 of 1933

---

2. This process took place during a period of expansion of the political and economic inclusion of women in the country (Wills 2004). In 1932 a law granting women the right to freely dispose of their assets, independently contract debts, and carry out financial transactions passed. In 1936, women acquired the right to hold public office. Women's suffrage was granted in 1954, but the right to vote was exercised for the first time in 1957. All these rights were achieved after extended political campaigns led by women and feminist activism (Luna and Villarreal 1994).

allowed women to attend secondary schools conferring the high school degree (*bachiller*), which was required to access higher education. Before, women's secondary schooling took place primarily in normal schools (*escuelas normales*), which prepared primary school teachers, or technical secondary schools for women, mainly private schools of commerce. Although the 1930s and the 1940s were decades of educational liberalization and expansion, obtaining secondary schooling was a privilege of the few. Within the general precarity of the schooling system, women were clearly underrepresented. In 1942, out of 1,469 high school graduates (1.5 per 10,000 inhabitants), only 213 (1 for every 6 men) were women (Helg 1984: 98–100, 151, 118, 267). During the 1940s and 1950s in Colombia, as in many other countries (Vicedo 2009, 2011; Weiss 2000; Plant 2010; Bernard-Powers 1992), the provision of secondary education for women was framed, especially in culturally "conservative" circles, as contributing to their preparation for marriage and motherhood (Luna 2004: 57).

The shy expansion of female secondary education in the late 1940s did not translate into a proportional enrollment of women in universities, but it gradually allowed a small proportion of women to access higher education, albeit under special conditions. Mirroring the experiences of women's colleges in the United States, the first women who received higher education in Colombia did it at the special academic units for women (*secciones femeninas*) created within the main local universities during the 1940s. The degrees of women's units did not have the same status of those granted by "regular" units for men (Wills 2004: 319). It was not until 1944 that the first woman, Gabriela Peláez, obtained a professional degree (in law) from the special unit for women of the Universidad Nacional. Women were given access to regular academic programs in the 1950s, but by the end of that decade they represented less than 20 percent of all university graduates in Colombia (table 1).[3] Likewise, a significant horizontal segregation (Horning 2002; Key and Sumner 2019; Preston 1994) characterized the first years of the decade of women's inclusion in higher education. The first systematic data of university enrollment available by program and sex reported in 1957 suggest that while only a handful of women obtained degrees that year in the traditional professions, such as law and

3. By regional standards, the participation rates of women in higher education in Colombia remained low until the 1980s. In 1975, women made up 14 percent of all students enrolled in higher education in Colombia and Peru, while Salvador and Uruguay reported 23 percent for the same year and Argentina 39 percent (Wills 2004: 243).

Table 1. Distribution by sex of graduates from Colombian universities, 1944–65

	Men		Women	
Year	N	%	N	%
1944	402	97	11	3
1948	740	91	74	9
1950	737	85	128	15
1955	1,087	82	232	18
1958	1,357	81	318	19
1960	1,391	73	515	27
1965	2,784	75	915	25

Source: Wills 2004: 278.

engineering, women graduates were overrepresented in the emerging programs in the humanities and the social sciences (DANE 1957).

Unlike in the United States (Cookingham 1987), there was no tradition of home economics in Colombia. Women were instead exposed to the economics discipline in the feminized academic environments that saw the emergence of the social sciences in Colombia. As a training center for high school teachers, an occupation mainly exercised by women, the Escuela Normal Superior was the entry point of women to social science research. Women who pioneered studies about the social condition of women in Colombia graduated from its interdisciplinary specialization in social sciences, which included a course in economics and another one in the history of economic doctrines (Jaramillo Jiménez 2009: 392, 405–6). Notable alumni from the Escuela Normal Superior include the anthropologist Virginia Gutiérrez de Pineda, who teamed with women sociologists and economists trained in the 1960s to produce the landmark volume that inaugurated gender studies in Colombia (León de Leal 1977). Additionally, throughout the 1940s law students at the Universidad Nacional, both men and women, took classes in political economy, public finance, economic geography, economic history, and the history of economic doctrines (Consejo Académico de la Universidad Nacional 1945, minute 26, agreement 15). Therefore, the absence of home economics degrees did not mean that women did not receive training in economics before they could enroll in economics departments. Just like their male peers, the first generation of women who had access to higher education received some economics training by taking courses in law and the social sciences during the 1940s.

2. Women in the Emergence of Economics as a Profession in Colombia

Economics emerged as a profession in Colombia only after World War II. The structural transformation of postwar economies and the adoption of interventionist policy agendas under the new international order created an unprecedented demand for economic specialists in government (Coats 1981: 4). In Latin American countries, new patterns in the transnational circulation of economics shaped communities of national experts that challenged existing traditions of nonprofessionalized economic thought and practice (Valdés 1995; Babb 2001). In the early postwar years, only a handful of Colombians had received formal training in economics, mainly in British and North American universities. This changed with the creation in 1943 of the Facultad de Economía Industrial y Comercial in the Gimnasio Moderno, an elite high school for boys.[4] Two years later, the Universidad Nacional opened its own program in economics. This institutionalization of economics in the university system occurred rather late, if compared with the Anglo-American world (Fourcade 2009). Nevertheless, the Colombian experience is arguably more representative of what happened beyond English-speaking countries in the global North (Coats 1996).

Before World War II, the teaching of economics in Colombia resembled, and followed closely, the French example (Alcouffe 1989). Since the nineteenth century, faculties of law and of engineering taught economic-related subjects such as political economy, public finances, and industrial economics. Throughout the first half of the twentieth century, locally trained lawyers and engineers ran key decision-making institutions, such as the Ministry of Finance, the Central Bank, the General Comptroller, and *gremios* (corporate economic associations). When local universities began to grant degrees in economics in the mid-1940s, the emerging economics profession had to negotiate its jurisdictions within the prevailing system of professions. Throughout the 1950s and 1960s, the conflation of economics with business management was particularly salient. Despite

4. Initially created to train managers for public and private industrial firms, this program merged in 1954 with the Faculty of Economics of the Universidad de los Andes.

efforts to delimit the frontiers of economics by the Colombian Economists Society (Sociedad Colombiana de Economistas) (1958) and the Colombian Association of Universities (Asociación Colombiana de Universidades) (1961), the hybridization with business management, law, and engineering persisted in universities and workplaces (Mayor and Tejeiro 1993).

What was the representation of women in this emerging profession? Archival and published sources suggest, as we show below, that women went from being an exception in the 1950s to forming a minority in the 1960s and early 1970s. This progression mirrors the broader national trends in higher education represented in table 1. During our period of study, economics was undoubtedly a profession dominated by men. However, as the trajectories of our interviewees exemplify, women economists strategically navigated their way to the top in this emerging profession.

María Elvira Santos's trajectory illustrates both the opportunities and the challenges of being a pioneer economist in the 1950s. Santos was, as far as we can tell from the archival record (Gimnasio Moderno 1952), the only woman who obtained a degree in economics in Colombia between 1945 and 1957.[5] Born in 1930 in a provincial town in Colombia's northeastern region of Santander, Santos received a scholarship from Colombia's national airline (Avianca) to enroll in economics at the Gimnasio Moderno in 1950. Graduating at the top of her class in 1954, the Central Bank sponsored Santos to take a course in economic statistics in Chile, where she stayed for an additional year to work at the UN Economic Commission for Latin America (CEPAL). Upon her return to Colombia, she married a mechanical engineer who had completed postgraduate studies in France. Shortly after, she gave birth to the first of their four children. Due to her role as a wife and a mother, she quit the job that she secured at the Central Bank after returning to Colombia. A few years later, she resumed her career as chief of staff of the budget office of the Water Supply and Sewerage Company of Bogotá (Empresa de Acueducto y Alcantarillado de Bogotá), where she worked for ten years before

5. Ninety-seven economists graduated during this period from seven faculties of economics, according to a lecture delivered at the first national conference of Colombian economists organized by the Colombian Economists Society (SCE 1958: 5). The society reported three women in its member list, but there is no evidence that they obtained a degree in economics. The records distinguish between *egresados* and *graduados*. The former referred to those who completed the coursework in the pensum and the latter, those who completed the additional requirements (i.e., thesis) needed to obtain the degree. We consider the figures for *graduados*.

Table 2. Women graduates in economics from the Universidad de los Andes and the Universidad Nacional, 1960–89

Years	Universidad de los Andes		Universidad Nacional	
	N	%	N	%
1960–69	12	4.84	27	19.85
1970–74	32	28.07	49	27.84
1975–80	59	38.31	17	17
1980–85	94	39.66	80	30
1985–90	82	36.28	106	33.65

Note: For the Universidad Nacional, the statistics of graduates by sex are available only from 1966.
Sources: Calculations based on data supplied by Admisión y Registro (n.d.) and published in Oficina de Planeación (1966–89).

moving in the late 1960s to the Concesión Salinas, the national salt-production state monopoly. She worked for the Concesión Salinas, then administered by the Central Bank, until she retired. In both of her jobs, Santos was reportedly the only woman with technical functions and the only one in a managerial position. As a pioneer, Santos advanced her career in a masculine profession without the companionship and support of other women economists.

With the expansion of the university system in the 1960s, more women obtained degrees in economics as the student body became more diverse, albeit to a certain extent. According to the data collected by the Universidad Nacional and the Universidad de los Andes, around 450 students graduated during the 1960s from the economics departments of these universities, the most influential in the country. As table 2 shows, only twelve women graduated in economics from the Universidad de los Andes between 1961 and 1969, accounting for 4.38 percent of the total. The proportion of women increased sixfold between 1970 and 1974 (up to 28 percent). In Universidad Nacional, thirty-five women graduated between 1966 and 1969 (19.1 percent), while forty-three obtained a degree between 1970 and 1974 (26.67 percent).

While in the 1960s women took advantage of new educational opportunities, cultural factors such as the persistence of women's social roles as wives and mothers played against their professional advancement. The distribution of professions according to their affinity with cultural representations of masculine and feminine attributes (Gutiérrez de Pineda 1977: 357–58) may have also prevented more women from entering economics. By the late 1980s, according to the data supplied by the Universidad Nacional and the Universidad de los Andes, women accounted for more than one-third of all graduates in the two main economics programs in the country, capitalizing on the ground gained by previous generations.

Although women gradually gained access to economics education in local universities during our period of study, their opportunities to receive advanced training abroad were comparatively more limited. Having access to, or dealing with the absence of, international credentials was a subject of concern for the women economists who graduated between the 1950s and the early 1970s, as the professional experiences of our interviewees suggest. In Colombia, like in other Latin American countries during the same period (Montecinos 1996), transnational networks mediated the professionalization of economics and structured both the educational and the career opportunities for local economists.

In the 1950s, very few local economists pursued graduate degrees abroad; this was a privilege restricted to those with the financial capital to afford it. Instead, young economists attended the short courses that multilateral agencies such as CEPAL, the World Bank, and the Organization of American States (OAS) offered to train public servants from Latin American countries (Ellis, Cornejo, and Escobar Cerda 1960: 66–67). As a case in point, the short course on financial and commercial statistics that Santos attended in 1953 at the Universidad de Chile was sponsored by the OAS.

Postgraduate university degrees became more accessible in the 1960s and gradually displaced technical diplomas as the sign of international credentials. Philanthropic foundations based in the United States, such as the Rockefeller Foundation, the Ford Foundation, and the Population Council, appropriated grants to Colombian universities to strengthen local economic programs and research centers on economic development. These grants included scholarships for Colombian economists to pursue graduate degrees abroad, mainly in North American universities. Another funding source for graduate studies in economics was the US Agency for International Development (US AID), which together with the Ford Foundation granted fellowships to the staff of the National Planning Department between 1965 and 1968. Table 3 shows the degrees that Colombian students pursued (not completed) and their main source of funding. Most students returned to Colombia with an MA or as PhD candidates. Only two fellows obtained PhD degrees.

Table 3. Fellowships granted to Colombian economists by philanthropic foundations, 1959–70

Funding body	Local institution	Dates granted	Fellowships	
			Master's	PhD
Rockefeller	Universidad de los Andes	1959–64	6	5
Rockefeller	Universidad del Valle	1963–66	3	8
Population Council	Universidad de los Andes	1965–67	2	3
Ford/US AID	National Planning Department	1965–68	4	8
Ford	Universidad Nacional	1968–70	0	8
Subtotal			15	32
Total			47	

Sources: Calculations based on multiple sources from Rockefeller Foundation Records, Fellowship Files (RFR), Record Group (R.G.) 10.1, Series (S.) 311, box 7; Population Council Records, Grant Universidad de los Andes, R.G. IV3B4. 3a, S. 2, box 60, folders 92–93; FFR n.d.b.

Family life intersected these new academic opportunities. As a case in point, nine out of the twenty-two students the Rockefeller Foundation sponsored to pursue graduate degrees in economics in the United States filed requests for family allowances (RFR n.d.: box 7). In some cases, students' spouses had to abruptly interrupt their studies. This never occurred the other way around. The only woman whom the philanthropic foundations sponsored in this period was Nohra Peñaranda, a graduate from the Universidad del Valle. In her application to pursue a master's in economics at the University of Pittsburgh, she reported that she was single and had no dependents (RFR n.d.: box 151, folder 2389). Besides assessing their academic performance, funding bodies considered candidates' marital status and proficiency in English because they viewed those personal details as common predictors of desertion.[6] Peñaranda completed her degree and joined the new faculty of economics at the Universidad del Valle. Although US-based philanthropic foundations had an enormous influence in the professionalization of economics in Latin America during

6. Considerations about candidates' marital status and English proficiency were included in the selection procedures developed in 1967 by the National Planning Department, Ford, and US AID to prevent desertion. See "Note on the Selection Process for Planeación's Foreign Training Candidates and the Harvard Mission's Coordinating Role," November 24, 1968 (FFR n.d.b).

the 1960s (see, e.g., Fernandez and Suprinyak 2019), they did not appear to have a direct impact on the advancement of women economists' careers, at least in the Colombian case. To the best of our knowledge, Peñaranda was the only woman sponsored by those foundations to study abroad during this period.

Alternatively, some young Colombian women received financial support to specialize abroad from local and regional bodies. Two of our interviewees, Martha Fernández and Lucía Cruz, completed graduate programs in the United States with scholarships from the OAS and Colombia's institute for studies abroad, ICETEX. Cruz and Fernández were among the first women who obtained a degree in economics from the Universidad de los Andes. Although Cruz was two years Fernández's senior, they became lifelong friends during their university studies. Their lives drifted apart when Cruz left for Michigan State University in 1961 to complete an MBA, as part of the Universidad de los Andes's teacher training program with public funds administered by ICETEX. One year later, Fernández got a scholarship from the OAS to read international relations at Johns Hopkins University. Both at the Universidad de los Andes and in the United States, Cruz and Fernández were "rare flowers" (*raras flores*) in a garden full of men, as Cruz described in our interview her situation and that of other women she encountered during her studies.[7]

The contrast between Cruz's and Fernández's life experiences shows how new educational opportunities in economics allowed for some degree of social mobility. While Cruz was born to a family with high cultural and social capital, Fernández self-identified in our interview as being raised in a "lower-middle class" household in Bogotá. Not only did Fernández's parents not have university degrees, but she was the first among her cousins to access higher education, thanks to a scholarship from the Central Bank. Cruz, on the other hand, was the daughter of a renowned expert in public finances who headed the Ministry of Public Works from 1938 to 1940. Following in the footsteps of her two eldest sisters, Cruz enrolled in the university after completing high school at a secular private institution. Their different social backgrounds notwithstanding, both Cruz and Fernández had successful careers as economists after completing postgraduate studies in the United States. In the late 1960s, Cruz directed the agricultural unit of the National Planning Department, becoming the

---

7. All our interviews were conducted in Spanish. Unless we indicate otherwise, the translations are ours.

first woman to run a technical unit, and worked as an adviser to the Ministry of Agriculture. She then moved to the private sector, becoming the chief of the planning division of SOFASA, the car assemblage subsidiary of Renault in Colombia. Fernández developed her career in international institutions concerned with economic development in Latin America. After conducting research for the Brookings Institution, she worked for twenty years in project management for the OAS in Washington, D.C. As Cruz's and Fernández's experiences illustrate, the internationalization of the economics profession during the 1960s opened new educational and career possibilities for women economists from peripheral countries like Colombia.

However, the internationalization of the discipline also posed specific dilemmas for women economists from the global peripheries. As the life stories of Cecilia López and Clara Elsa Villalba exemplify, the value that the economics profession in Colombia attached to international credentials amplified the difficulties that women economists experienced more generally while attempting to balance their aspirations in the professional and the domestic realms. Facing a trade-off between advancing their careers and conforming to their expected social roles as mothers and wives, López and Villalba decided not to seize the opportunities the internationalization of the discipline offered. Yet their professional trajectories showcase how some women economists successfully navigated their way to the top despite lacking the international credentials of their male peers with postgraduate experience abroad.

López did not obtain a postgraduate degree abroad, but this did not stop her from having a successful academic and public career as an economist in Colombia. Born in Bogotá in 1943, López was raised in Barranquilla, a port city on the Caribbean coast. Although overall her family enjoyed a good social standing, her father suffered substantial economic losses when his commercial stores in downtown Bogotá were burned to the ground during the *Bogotazo*—a violent uprising in the Colombian capital that followed the assassination of the presidential candidate Jorge E. Gaitán in 1948. Fleeing from the violent conflict that afflicted Colombia in the 1950s, her family landed in Barranquilla, where López obtained her high school degree from a private confessional school. With the support of her father, López returned to Bogotá in the early 1960s, where she enrolled in economics at the Universidad de los Andes. In the middle of her first year, she interrupted her studies to join her husband in Nashville, where she gave birth to the first of their two children. Upon her return to

Colombia, she resumed her studies at the Universidad de los Andes and graduated top of her class in 1970. As López acknowledged in our interview, she declined offers to specialize abroad to take care of her children. Despite lacking international credentials, she developed a successful career, first in academe and—after obtaining her divorce in 1977—in the public sector. She headed the agricultural unit (1978–80) and the project evaluation division (1980–82) of the National Planning Department, which she directed between 1997 and 1998. She worked in two government administrations, as vice minister (1982–84) and minister of agriculture (1996–97). Her performance in public office gained her the reputation of a social reformist with technical credentials. In 2006 she was elected senator for the Liberal Party, which nominated her as the party's candidate for the 2010 presidential elections. Throughout her career as scholar, public official, and politician, López spearheaded research projects, policies, and legislative agendas that addressed the economic situation of women in Colombia.

Villalba's professional career was equally remarkable. This is even more significant if we consider that she probably was, among our interviewees, the least endowed with social and economic capital. She was born in 1944 in Vélez, a small town in the northeastern region of Colombia. Her father was a cattle rancher and her mother administered small family-owned businesses. Villalba finished high school in a public institution and was the first one in her family to attend university. She was also the first woman accepted to study engineering at her regional university, but she decided to enroll in economics at the Universidad Nacional in Bogotá. Villalba graduated with honors in 1967, which gained her access to a small working group that gathered around the reputed economist and New Dealer Lauchlin Currie at the Universidad Nacional and its new Development Research Center (Centro de Investigaciones sobre Desarrollo). In the early 1970s, Villalba had multiple opportunities to pursue a postgraduate degree abroad, but these coincided with the birth of her first two children. In 1971 she joined the labor division of the National Planning Department and was promoted to lead the social development unit (1971–75). Villalba then worked at the planning office of the national institute of technical training, SENA, which she directed between 1988 and 1990. As assistant to the comptroller general (1982–87) and president of Telecom (1992–94), she was a key player in the implementation of "decentralization" in public finances and telecommunications. Like López, Villalba entered politics after three decades of working for the state in technical duties. She was the first woman appointed governor of Santander, a department infamous for its macho culture, between 1990 and 1992.

The focus group of women studied in this article received training in economics when this was only an emergent profession. Their professional trajectories illustrate both the opportunities and the challenges women economists experienced as they went from being an exception in the profession in the 1950s to constituting a minority in the early 1970s. At the peak of this period, women represented less than 30 percent of all graduates in economics. In Colombia, as was probably the case in other peripheral countries, the economics profession increasingly attached greater value to international academic credentials, the obtention of which confronted women with dilemmas concerning trade-offs between career advancement and family life. The next section explores the strategies that women economists used to succeed in this male-dominated world.

3. Professional Strategies in a Male-Dominated World: From the Exception to a Minority

In masculine environments, men are the main holders of resources. Both in the rather culturally conservative Colombian society where they grew up and during their studies and professional lives, Santos, Cruz, Fernández, López, and Villalba resorted to masculine support, which is central to explaining their outstanding trajectory. Empirical evidence suggests that, by structuring access to resources and opportunities, the support of fathers and mentors plays a key role in the professional achievements of women (Berg and Ferber 1983).

The moral and material support from their fathers played a particularly important role in the lives of Santos and López. The fathers of these two women, as reported in our interviews, had extremely positive perceptions of their daughter's intellectual capacities and more generally treated them as gifted from a very young age. This perception translated into the material support that made possible their access to elite higher education but also shaped Santos's and López's self-image, which notably influenced their confidence in their ability to undertake whatever they wanted to do. As López told us, "My father always saw me as a very special person. He always thought that I was different and that I must study, in a moment when access to higher education was not entirely open for women and was almost unaffordable for our family. This left a really deep mark on my personal confidence."

Paternal support, although important, was not a sine qua non condition for women economists' academic and professional success. Indeed, paternal support may play a key role especially when other resources, particularly economic and social means, are scarce. Cruz, who was arguably the best endowed with social and economic capital of the five women who are the focus of our study, presented her relationship with her father as "good but distant." Cruz never mentioned during our interview her father's connection to the economics profession, neither as an influence that informed her decision to study economics nor as a leverage for her professional career. Of the five women we interviewed, Cruz was also the most modest about her academic and professional achievements. She repeatedly highlighted her hard-work capacity over her intelligence as the main determinant of her career's achievements: "I have always been a hard worker; I have not been brilliant, but rather a hard worker" (Yo siempre he sido moledora; no he sido brillante, pero sí moledora). In Villalba's case, her mother was the main moral and financial supporter. Her mother had conspicuously more years of education than her father and was economically active and independent throughout her life.

Mentors' support is also a key explanatory factor of women's professional achievements in masculine environments. Although the role of female mentors may be critical for the success of women in certain academic and professional communities (Berg and Ferber 1983; Johnson, this volume), the women who are the focus of our study had neither women professors during their studies nor senior women colleagues during their professional lives. Furthermore, as Burns (this volume) and Laskaridis (this volume) show in relation to Milton Friedman and Paul Samuelson, in contexts where senior male figures work as gatekeepers, women depend on their support to secure opportunities and recognition. All our interviewees described instances in which the encouragement and advice of male faculty and senior male colleagues influenced their career choices. Similar to paternal support, developing close relations with professors and collaborators had an impact on both women's self-confidence about their career plans and the resources they could use to bring them about.

Villalba's experience is particularly illustrative. As she told us, her close relationship with Roberto Arenas, director of the Development Research Centre (CID, in Spanish) at the Universidad Nacional when Villalba was a junior researcher there (1968–70), gave her access to professional opportunities: "Dr. Arenas throughout his life continued to be a close friend of mine, he appreciated me very much. I obtained my first professional position as a research assistant at CID when he was the director of that research center. Regarding my last position, he took me there, to the European Union Embassy, when he was appointed ambassador. He valued me a lot and had great confidence in me."[8]

Although fathers and mentors were certainly a source of opportunities for our focus group, the role they played in these women's professional advancement was not unambiguous. As Laskaridis (this volume) illustrates with Margaret Garritsen de Vries's relationship to Samuelson, male support for women's careers can be selective. It is also influenced by social biases. For instance, Santos's father encouraged her to study economics instead of civil engineering, according to her son Aldo Buenahora, because he did not want to see his daughter "surrounded by construction workers" and wearing a "helmet and rubber boots." Given its novelty and its diffusely defined jurisdictions, economics was perceived during the 1950s and 1960s as being more suitable for women than other established professions. This perception of economics as less masculine compared with other established professions helped explain the relatively rapid growth of the proportion of women with economic degrees. The shift in the proportion of women in the profession, from an exception in the 1950s to a minority in the late 1960s, is a key element to understand how the women in our focus group mobilized and adapted their social, economic, and academic resources to develop successful careers as economists.

As Margaret Rossiter's (1997) research about scientific communities shows, the proportion of women in a subdiscipline is the single most important indicator of their experiences in their field. Rossiter's typologies of slightly overlapping levels of feminization conceptualize how women across generations face different sorts of challenges as female representation changes in their fields. Studying in a context where less than 8 percent of practitioners were women, Santos, Cruz, and Fernández were "rare flowers" (to borrow Cruz's expression) in what Rossiter describes as "peripheral fields." Access to training and jobs is the chief difficulty at this stage. As Rossiter (1997: 171) suggests, in fields in peripherical stages, "numerous bans and taboos [exist] as to what women could and could not do." Being an "intrepid soul" (Rossiter 1997: 171) and having a developed

8. Villalba joined the National Planning Department's staff when Arenas was appointed director in 1970.

sense of challenge could come in handy here, as was Fernández's case. When a fellow student, Roberto Villaveces, recognized her outstanding academic performance but asserted, according to Fernández's recollection, that women were "just not made for mathematics," she challenged him with a bet: whoever got the best grade in mathematics at the end of the year won. They both finished top of the class with the same grade. Social norms of gender segregation also influenced how some faculty members welcomed women in their classes. For instance, Fernández remembers that her professor of economic history once started his lecture by sharing his joy for having "two beautiful ladies" in a class of around fifty men, after which he expressed his sorrow for having to see them go by the end of the year because "women were just not born for studying." This "welcoming," Fernández told us in our interview, was an important driver for her to work hard throughout the academic year.

Villalba and López faced slightly different contexts as, in the mid-1960s, the proportion of women graduates passed the 15 percent threshold. Rossiter categorizes fields in this second stage of feminization as "marginal." At this stage women are no longer the "first" and have more possibilities—such as a wider range of career choices. They face new dangers—such as limitations related to advancement and recognition and the threat of ghettoization in employment areas designated as "womanly" (Zacchia 2020). As both gatekeepers of their field and trustees of their protégées, male mentors may reinforce that process of professional ghettoization. When Fernández was choosing which graduate program to enroll at in the United States, she received guidance from Oscar Gómez, a Harvard graduate who directed the Universidad de los Andes's economics department at that time. Fernández could have applied to leading programs in economics in the United States. She was at the top of her class and was part of a select group that received intensive preparation for studying abroad. In spite of this, she did not receive from Gómez the same type of support that he gave to some of her male peers. While Gómez wrote an enthusiastic letter of recommendation in support of Villaveces's application to Harvard (RFR n.d.: box 161, folder 2495), he oriented Fernández to a more *female-friendly program*:

> Obviously, I wanted to apply to Harvard or MIT, or something like that. But he [Gómez] told me: "Martha, there are so few women. And the weather is so harsh. Moreover, you would have to walk four blocks to find a women's restroom. It will be much more difficult for you. I think

Washington would be a best fit for you, it would be kind of friendlier." So, he kind of guided me [to select Johns Hopkins]. Of course, he knew better than me, I had never left the country and he was someone who had traveled a lot. He helped all the students of my cohort who had plans to study abroad to make the best possible decision. . . . While I was in Washington, I visited my friend, the one with whom I had met before, when he was at Harvard. I don't know, it was definitely a lot easier for me, as a woman, to have gone to Johns Hopkins's School of International Studies.

After graduating with an MA from Johns Hopkins, Fernández returned to Colombia, where she quickly experienced the advantages associated with her new graduate credentials, international experience, and command of English. "A lot of opportunities opened when I came back," Fernández told us during our interview. Nevertheless, back in Colombia she also experienced a paradoxical situation. Being a single, well-educated, and economically independent woman fell into a category that the Colombian society still struggled to demarcate. Hence Fernández's place in society was undetermined. Against her desire for independence, she went back to live at her parents' house. In the workplace, the ongoing joke among her colleagues, and former fellow students at the Universidad de los Andes, was that she had returned "with the Master, [but] without the Mister" (con el Master, sin el Mister).

As the five women in our study advanced in their professional careers, increasingly more women joined the profession, building on the ground gained by the first generation of women economists. By the late 1970s and early 1980s economics in Colombia might have reached what Rossiter calls the "participatory" stage, in which between 15 percent and 40 percent of the practitioners are women. Once women gained access to the profession, however, they faced the challenge of harmonizing their career advancement with their expected social roles as housewives.

4. Marriage, Motherhood, and Career Advancement: Balancing Professional and Domestic Life

Through their example, Cruz, Santos, López, Villalba, and Fernández challenged the notion that women pursued education to become better wives and mothers. In the context of postwar Colombia, they were pioneers, not only because they were among the first women to obtain the degree in economics, but also because they managed to climb the professional ladders to the top of the obelisk. Their success stands out if they are compared with those whose trajectory was cut short.

Santos's peer and Cruz's sister, Silvia Cruz, deserted the economic program at the Gimnasio Moderno shortly after marrying a fellow classmate. Denise Castillo, Fernández's only female classmate, never attempted to apply for a scholarship in the United States, although their professors encouraged her to do so. In our interview with Fernández, she contrasted her decision to Castillo's: "She got married and did not want to go abroad to study. I did." After a successful career in the Central Bank and the Ministry of Finance, Nohra Pombo, who graduated from the economics program at the Universidad de los Andes shortly after López did, decided to quit public service when her husband, Roberto Junguito, was appointed minister of finance.[9] Although women began to value education as a "liberating force," especially after a critical mass of Colombian women accessed universities in what López (2005: 328) dubbed their "educational revolution," this aspiration conflicted with their expected social roles as wives and mothers. During our period of study, well-off educated women in Colombia had to grapple with rather conservative representations and prejudices about their place in society. Hence first-generation women professionals—and economists in particular—necessarily had to strike a balance between their career advancement and marriage and motherhood.

Women experienced higher stakes in that trade-off as international degrees became increasingly necessary to advance in the economics profession. As the top students in their class and close collaborators of influential professors with PhDs abroad, Villalba and López were in a good position to apply for scholarships. Villalba explicitly acknowledged that marriage and maternity considerations influenced her decision to reject places in top universities:

> The opportunities I had to go abroad were multiple. Dr. [Miguel] Urrutia was going to send me to Duke, the other was sending me somewhere else. . . . But I never did it. Every time I had the opportunity to go abroad, personal situations came about. Dr. Urrutia even got me a place in the University of Sussex in England, it was practically all set up, but I was married and had one child at that moment. And I was pregnant with my second daughter.

9. Written communication between the authors and Gabriel Misas, contemporary of Pombo and colleague of Villalba at the Universidad Nacional.

López was the most adamant in recognizing the impact that not having international degrees had on her career. When López's mentor—Álvaro López Toro, a PhD in economic demography from Princeton (1960), one of the first Colombians to pursue doctorate studies, and visiting professor at the Woodrow Wilson School of Public and International Affairs (1965–67) in that university—encouraged her to pursue further studies on demography with Nicole Tabard in Paris,[10] she rejected this offer on the grounds that she had two small children to take care of.

In the late 1960s, women economists could only reject opportunities for obtaining international credentials at a high cost. López remembered the first years after graduating from the Universidad de los Andes as difficult times. Her first research experience was in the population studies center that López Toro directed at that university, where she recalled being exposed to the "highbrow attitude" of the PhD candidates who had recently arrived from the United States. "The 'degrees issue' has been costly for me," López told us in our interview. I would even say that I have interiorized that more than the discrimination by gender, which I am now conscious about." Of the five women in our study, López was the most vocal about and the most professionally engaged with gender issues in the profession, as well as in the Colombian and Latin American societies (López 1977; López and Pollak 1992). When we asked her if she saw any relationship between the discrimination by level of educational attainment she experienced and gender discrimination, López was surprised by the question. She replied, "I don't know if both things came together. But, in my case, they did." López was the only one among our interviewees who considered the profession was sexist. Women were in a disadvantaged position to internationalize their expertise, not only because the allocation of scholarships was mediated by gender biases but also because family life implied higher social responsibilities for them than it did for their male counterparts.

The lack of international credentials was not an unsurmountable obstacle for women economists. They strategically made use of other resources, such as mentorship relationships, to advance their career. As we mentioned in the previous section, strategies that mobilize masculine support, such as establishing close relationships with male faculty and colleagues,

10. French statistician, the author of a groundbreaking study about the marginal costs of childbearing and the effects that family subsidies had on household consumption in France (Tabard 1967).

open opportunities for women. López's and Villalba's collaboration with reputed male economists partly compensated for the absence of postgraduate degrees. López expressed this idea when she disclosed that "the confidence that I would have lacked with all those PhDs, Álvaro López Toro gave it to me." López Toro supervised her undergraduate thesis and gave her a symbolic master's in demography. "That is the thesis with which I graduated my students in Princeton," López Toro allegedly told her. Cecilia López's thesis, published as an outcome of the Universidad de los Andes's economics research center (López de Rodríguez 1970), together with subsequent publications about fecundity and the demographic transition, positioned her as a local expert in social economics.

Similarly, Villalba considered that her research experience with reputable professors like Currie and Miguel Urrutia at the Universidad Nacional was "almost, really, like a master's." After graduating from that university, Villalba took advanced courses with visiting professors sponsored by the Ford Foundation. Simultaneously, she worked for her alma mater's Development Research Center. This center also received financial support from the Ford Foundation, upon a request put forward by Currie when he was dean of the economics department (FFR n.d.a). Villalba was Currie's student and participated in the economic *tertulias* (coteries) he spearheaded in the Fundación de Investigación de Estudios Sociales y Económicos, an independent economic think tank. Of its fourteen founding members, Villalba was the only woman. At the Development Research Center, she worked with Urrutia, with whom she coauthored pioneering studies in economic history and income distribution (Urrutia and de Sandoval 1971a, 1971b).

In all five case studies, women interrupted their professional career to fulfill their social role as wives and mothers. In some cases, like Santos's, this decision had to do with the husband's professional choices. Shortly after Santos got married, she quit her job at the Central Bank and took their son to the very remote town of Belencito, where her husband found a job in the national steel plant, Acerías Paz de Río. When Santos resumed her professional career, she opted for a well-paid job in Bogotá's Water Supply and Sewerage Company to provide their children with a good education. Santos's decision showcases how, even when women economists resumed their professional career after having children, motherhood considerations influenced their career choices. But this experience also reveals the subtle balance women must reach between being an "intrepid soul" (Rossiter 1997: 171) and developing a sense of pragmatism as they navigate masculine environments.

Women economists' decisions about how to allocate time to motherhood and to their career advancement were also conditioned by the share of household labor that fell on their shoulders. Those who counted on their husband's support in the household expressed less remorse about their choices. Although Cruz quit the direction of the agricultural division of the planning department when she gave birth to her first son, she quickly resumed her professional career. She joined the technical staff of the Ministry of Agriculture, where she collaborated with other women[11] in the elaboration of economic reports for the United States Department of Agriculture. According to Cruz, her husband's "domestic" character helped her balance her domestic and professional lives, as both a mother and a full-time technical government employee: "Also, my husband was a very domestic man, so once he left the [Central] Bank he went home diligently to stay with the kids. Sometimes he even arrived before I did, as occasionally my meetings went beyond working hours. He, in turn, was absolutely inflexible and diligently arrived home to stay with the kids."

Male support in household labor was particularly important for women economists who, like Cruz, worked for the state in the late 1960s. During this decade, not only Colombian economists received an unprecedented degree of backing from the president in policymaking bodies, but they were also the interlocutors between the national government and international financial institutions. According to multiple interviews with government employees at that time, an intense work ethic thus prevailed among economists working for the state (Guiot-Isaac 2022). As Cruz's statement suggests, it was not uncommon for her to stay after hours at work.

Facing these constraints, our interviewees made different job choices in their early careers to combine motherhood and professional advancement. While Cruz opted for full-time employment with the state, López decided to take a more flexible job at Fedesarrollo, an independent think tank. At Fedesarrollo, López reported having a "special" arrangement that allowed her to work part-time so that she could spend the afternoons with her children. This ad hoc arrangement was facilitated by the nature of her job, which consisted in conducting research and consultancy projects, and editing Fedesarrollo's quarterly journal. While women economists found in state institutions economic and professional stability, research and

---

11. María Teresa Méndez, María Teresa Berry (Albert's wife), Nohora Mosquera, and Nubia de la Roche.

consultancy positions gave them more flexibility to balance their professional and domestic lives.

Regardless of the sector in which they worked, all five women employed domestic workers to alleviate their share of household labor. Given Colombia's high levels of socioeconomic inequality,[12] paid domestic laborers have been historically accessible and relatively inexpensive for urban professional classes. Our interviewees highlighted the centrality that domestic workers played in their professional advancement, revealing how their privileged position in the broader Colombian society helped mitigate the gender inequalities they encountered in the profession. While López hired the woman who had worked in her parents' house to take care of her children when she was at work, Villalba employed her aunt, a former teacher in an elementary school, who was single and did not have children. The testimonies of our interviewees support the findings of cross-country surveys conducted with women business executives in Latin America (Eagly et al. 2014: 15–16), according to which access to paid domestic labor was critical for the professional success of women in the second half of the twentieth century.

Fernández's experience is illustrative of the multiplicity of intersectional relations that made it possible for women to advance their careers. As a project manager at the OAS, her job required traveling constantly to Central America to supervise development interventions. When we asked her what it was that made it possible for her to travel so often, considering that her husband had a full-time job in academe, she answered that she had the advantage that the OAS allowed her to "bring someone [to Washington], to get her a visa, and to have her working at her home; hence, that was why I could travel." Fernández's high-skilled job in a multilateral institution allowed her to access similar privileges to those that other woman economists enjoyed in Colombia. Furthermore, her status as professional migrant contrasted with that of her domestic worker. Fernández employed an "educated woman" from Chile who was exiled in the United States after Augusto Pinochet's coup in 1973. This case reveals a sour reality. The surprising success of a few women, as well as the self-confidence that this success entails, brings to the fore the persistent problems of many other women (Ehrenreich and Hochschild 2004).

---

12. Since 1991, when the Gini coefficient was first measured in Colombia, the country has consistently ranked as one of the most inequal (by income) in the world (World Bank 2021).

5. Conclusion

As we showed in this article, gender distinctions are significant for studying comparatively the economics profession, since men and women economists in given societies have dissimilar resource endowments and face different sociocultural constraints. The late professionalization of economics in Colombia created specific opportunities and challenges for women economists. If access to the profession was facilitated by the hybridization of economics and business management and the diffusely defined jurisdictions of economics, the relative importance that international credentials had to accessing positions of influence in the state and academe often conflicted with the roles as mothers and wives that the Colombian society expected from well-off women. In this context, the transnational character the profession adopted with the so-called "post-1945 internationalization of economics" (Coats 1996) added an additional layer to the obstacles that women economists faced to advance their careers in the global North.

Yet a few Colombian women economists did manage to circumvent those difficulties by constantly negotiating between their professional aspirations and the social roles that Colombian society assigned to them. The focus group of women studied in this article successfully climbed to the top of the obelisk. To do so, they resorted to a mix of professional strategies. They managed to mobilize resources in favor of their career advancement by securing the support of male figures, such as fathers and mentors. To successfully harmonize professional and domestic life, our interviewees struck a delicate balance between displaying an intrepid character and developing a sense of pragmatism. Given the privileges of belonging to an emerging professional class in a highly unequal society, they were also able to delegate part of the care and domestic tasks that were expected of them to other women less endowed with economic, social, and cultural capital.

We shed light on the important degree to which broader cultural values determine how academic and professional settings are organized. For example, gendered models inform decisions regarding the choice of graduate programs, the type of labor contracts, and the employment sector. These mechanisms of horizontal segregation within the profession are even more effective, since most of the time they remain invisible to the individuals they affect. This was clear throughout our interviews. With the exception of Cecilia López, none of them thought economics is a sexist profession or reported having ever been victims of gender discrimination. Almost immediately, however, they all provided some nuance to this claim by providing examples that they nevertheless presented as isolated cases.

References

Admisión y Registro, Universidad de los Andes. "Serie histórica de graduados de la Facultad de Economía." Unpublished spreadsheet, registrar's office, Universidad de los Andes.

Alcouffe, Alain. 1989. "The Institutionalization of Political Economy in French Universities." *History of Political Economy* 21, no. 2: 313–44.

Asociación Colombiana de Universidades. 1961. *Estudios para el planeamiento de la educación superior: Primer seminario de economía.* Vol. 3. Bogotá: Fondo Universitario Nacional.

Babb, Sarah L. 2001. *Managing Mexico: Economists from Nationalism to Neoliberalism.* Princeton, N.J.: Princeton University Press.

Berg, Helen M., and Marianne A. Ferber. 1983. "Men and Women Graduate Students." *Journal for Higher Education* 54, no. 6: 629–48.

Bernard-Powers, Jane. 1992. *The "Girl Question" in Education: Vocational Education for Young Women in the Progressive Era.* London: Falmer.

Blau, Francine D., and Anne E. Winkler. 2017. "Women, Work, and Family." In *The Oxford Handbook of Women and the Economy,* edited by Susan Averett, Laura M. Argys, and Saul D. Hoffman, 395–424. New York: Oxford University Press.

Chaney, Elsa M. 1980. *Supermadre: Women in Politics in Latin America.* Austin: University of Texas Press.

Coats, A. W. 1981. *Economists in Government: An International Comparative Study.* Durham, N.C.: Duke University Press.

Coats, A. W., ed. 1996. *The Post-1945 Internationalization of Economics.* Supplemental issue to vol. 34 of *History of Political Economy.* Durham, N.C.: Duke University Press.

Consejo Académico de la Universidad Nacional. 1945. "Actas del Consejo Académico." Archivo Central Histórico de la Universidad Nacional de Colombia.

Cookingham, Mary E. 1987. "Social Economists and Reform: Berkeley, 1906–1961." *History of Political Economy* 19, no. 1: 47–65.

DANE. 1957. "Estadísticas Culturales." Bogotá.

Dimand, Robert W., Mary Ann Dimand, and Evelyn L. Forget. 2000. *A Biographical Dictionary of Women Economists.* Cheltenham: Edward Elgar.

Eagly, Alice, Elvira Salgado, Walkyria Goode, Lidia Heller, Kety Jauregui, Nathalia Quirós, Naisa Gormaz et al. 2014. "Latin American Female Business Executives: An Interesting Surprise." *Gender in Management* 29, no. 1: 2–24.

Ehrenreich, Barbara, and Arlie Russell Hochschild, eds. 2004. *Global Woman: Nannies, Maids, and Sex Workers in the New Economy.* New York: Henry Holt.

Ellis, Howard S., Benjamín Cornejo, and Luis Escobar Cerda. 1960. "La enseñanza de la economía en La América Latina." Washington, D.C.: Unión Panamericana, Secretaría General de la Organización de Estados Americanos.

Fernandez, Ramón Garcia, and Carlos Eduardo Suprinyak. 2019. "Manufacturing Pluralism in Brazilian Economics." *Journal of Economic Issues* 53, no. 3: 748–73.

FFR (Ford Foundation Records). n.d.a. Development of Economics Training and Research- Universidad Nacional. Reel 3402, Rockefeller Archive Center, Sleepy Hollow, NY.

FFR (Ford Foundation Records). n.d.b. Technical and Training Assistance in Economic Development Planning in Colombia. Grants HK, Reel 4661, Rockefeller Archive Center, Sleepy Hollow, NY.

Forget, Evelyn L. 2002. "A Hunger for Narrative: Writing Lives in the History of Economic Thought." *History of Political Economy* 34, no. 5: 226–44.

Fourcade, Marion. 2009. *Economists and Societies: Discipline and Profession in the United States, Britain, and France, 1890s to 1990s*. Princeton, N.J.: Princeton University Press.

Gimnasio Moderno. 1952. "Libro de Matrículas," Matrícula No. 206. Unidad de Administración Documental, Universidad de los Andes (UADA).

Guiot-Isaac, Andrés M. 2022. "The Emergence of an Economic Technocracy in Colombia, 1948–1974." PhD diss., University of Oxford.

Gutiérrez de Pineda, Virginia. 1977. "Status de la mujer en la familia." In *La mujer y el desarrollo en Colombia*, edited by Magdalena León de Leal, 318–94. Bogotá: Asociación Colombiana para el Estudio de la Población.

Helg, Aline. 1984. *Civiliser le peuple et former les élites: L'éducation en Colombie, 1918–1957*. Paris: L'Harmattan.

Horning, Lilli, ed. 2002. *Women at Research Universities*. New York: Plenum/ Kluwer.

Jaramillo Jiménez, Jaime Eduardo. 2009. "La Escuela Normal Superior: Un semillero de las ciencias humanas y sociales." In *República liberal: Sociedad y cultura*, edited by Rubén Sierra Mejía, 557–603. Bogotá: Universidad Nacional de Colombia.

Key, Ellen M., and Jane Lawrence Sumner. 2019. "You Research Like a Girl: Gendered Research Agendas and Their Implications." *PS: Political Science & Politics* 52, no. 4: 663–68.

León de Leal, Magdalena. 1977. *La mujer y el desarrollo en Colombia*. Bogotá: Asociación Colombiana para el Estudio de la Población.

López, Cecilia. 1977. "El trabajo de la mujer." In *La mujer y el desarrollo en Colombia*, edited by Magdalena León de Leal, 186–228. Bogotá: Asociación Colombiana para el Estudio de la Población.

López, Cecilia. 2005. "La mujer en la vida nacional: Tres revoluciones recientes 1970–2005." *Coyuntura Económica* 35, no. 2: 327–34.

López, Cecilia, and Molly Pollak. 1992. "La incorporación de la mujer en las políticas de desarrollo." In *Género y mercado de trabajo en América Latina: Procesos y dilemas*, edited by Cecilia López, Molly Pollack, and Marcela Villareal, 9–24. Santiago de Chile: Organización Internacional del Trabajo.

López de Rodríguez, Cecilia. 1970. *Tasas específicas de mortalidad y fecundidad para Bogotá, 1964*. Bogotá: Universidad de los Andes, Facultad de Economía, CEDE.

Luna, Lola G. 2004. *El sujeto sufragista, feminismo y feminidad en Colombia: 1930–1957*. Cali: Ediciones La Manzana de la Discordia / Universidad del Valle.

Luna, Lola G., and Norma Villarreal. 1994. *Historia, género y política: Movimientos de mujeres y participación política en Colombia 1930–1991*. Barcelona: Seminario Interdisciplinar Mujeres y Sociedad, Universidad de Barcelona.

Mayor, Alberto, and Clemencia Tejeiro. 1993. "La profesión de economista en Colombia: Entre el autodidactismo y el entrenamiento académico." In *Cambio Técnico, Empleo y Trabajo en Colombia*, 109–22. Bogotá: FESCOL.

Montecinos, Verónica. 1996. "Economists in Political and Policy Elites in Latin America." In *The Post-1945 Internationalization of Economics*, edited by A. W. Coats. *History of Political Economy* 34 (supplement): 279–300.

Oficina de Planeación de la Universidad Nacional. 1966–89. "Boletín de Estadística."

Paulson, Susan. 2016. *Masculinities and Femininities in Latin America's Uneven Development*. London: Routledge.

Plant, Rebecca Jo. 2010. *Mom: The Transformation of Motherhood in Modern America*. Chicago: University of Chicago Press.

Population Council Records. Grant Universidad de los Andes. Record Group IV3B4. 3a, Rockefeller Archive Center, Sleepy Hollow, N.Y.

Preston, Anne E. 1994. "Why Have All the Women Gone? A Study of Exit of Women from the Science and Engineering Professions." *American Economic Review* 84, no. 5: 1446–62.

Rockefeller Foundation Records (RFR). n.d. Fellowship Files, Social Sciences/ Humanities. Record Group 10.1, Series 311, Rockefeller Archive Center, Sleepy Hollow, NY.

Rossiter, Margaret W. 1997. "Which Science? Which Women?" *Osiris* (*Bruges*) 12:169–85.

Sociedad Colombiana de Economistas (SCE). 1958. *Primer Congreso Nacional de Economistas: Memoria*. Bogotá.

Tabard, Nicole. 1967. *Les conditions de vie des familles*. Paris: Centre de recherches et de documentation sur la consommation.

Urrutia, Miguel, and Clara Elsa de Sandoval. 1971a. *El sector artesenal en el desarollo colombiano*. Bogotá: Universidad Nacional de Colombia.

Urrutia, Miguel, and Clara Elsa de Sandoval. 1971b. *Politica fiscal y distribucion del ingreso en Colombia*. Bogotá: Universidad Nacional de Colombia, Centro de Investigaciones para el Desarrollo.

Valdés, Juan Gabriel. 1995. *Pinochet's Economists: The Chicago School in Chile*. Cambridge: Cambridge University Press.

Vicedo, Marga. 2009. "Mothers, Machines, and the Morals: Harry Harlwo's Work on Primate Love from Lab to Legend." *Journal of the History of the Behavioral Sciences* 45, no. 3: 193–218.

Vicedo, Marga. 2011. "The Social Nature of the Mother's Tie to Her Child: John Bowlby's Theory of Attachment in Post-War America." *British Journal for the History of Science* 44, no. 3: 401–26.

Weiss, Jessica. 2000. *To Have and to Hold: Marriage, the Baby Boom, and Social Change.* Chicago: University of Chicago Press.

Wills, María Emma. 2004. "Las trayectorias femeninas y feministas hacia lo público en Colombia (1970–2000): ¿Inclusión Sin Representación?" PhD diss., University of Texas at Austin.

World Bank. 2021. "World Bank Poverty and Equity Database." https://databank .worldbank.org/source/poverty-and-equity.

Zacchia, Giulia. 2020. "What Does It Take to Be Top Women Economists? An Analysis Using Rankings in RePEc." *Review of Political Economy* 33, no. 2: 170–93.

"Writing History as a Way of Life": The Life and Work of Margaret Marie Garritsen de Vries

Christina Laskaridis

1. Introduction

The name of Margaret Marie Garritsen de Vries may not be the first that pops into people's minds when thinking about the International Monetary Fund. It is through her work, as the long-standing official Fund historian, that those interested in the Fund's history will travel. Trained as an economist, on a journey to becoming a historian, she is most remembered for her histories of the Fund and her role as a mentor to women in the economics profession. Although she left no personal papers, through published works, others' personal correspondence, and institutional archives, this article explores the life and work of Margaret Marie Garritsen de Vries.[1]

Correspondence may be addressed to Christina Laskaridis, Open University, UK (christina .laskaridis@open.ac.uk). My gratitude and thanks to the volume editors—Cléo Chasson-nery-Zaïgouche, Evelyn Forget, and John Singleton—for the invitation to participate in the project and the support and enthusiasm along the way. Special thanks to two anonymous refer-ees for helpful and encouraging comments, to the participants of the HOPE 2021 conference, and to Sofia Valeonti. I benefited from communication with James Boughton and Roger Back-house, and others who responded to my queries, including the archivists at the International Monetary Fund, MIT, and Bristol University. My deepest gratitude to Chris de Vries, one of Margaret Garritsen de Vries's children, for our communications.

1. In retirement, Garritsen de Vries (hereafter referred to as Garritsen) started writing her memoirs, provisionally titled "Economics in My Backyard," that was never published (Chris de Vries, daughter, personal correspondence with author).

History of Political Economy 54 (annual suppl.) DOI 10.1215/00182702-10085668
Copyright 2022 by Duke University Press

The difficulties facing women in the economics profession have come to light through a series of works that point to distinct phases of women's representation in economics during the twentieth century (Dimand et al. 1995; Forget 2011; Madden 2002). An early phase, up to the late 1930s, saw relatively higher numbers of degrees and publications by women, followed by a prominent decline at midcentury in women's participation and subsequent growth following the efforts of the Committee on the Status of Women in the Economics Profession. Garritsen studied and received her PhD during the relatively more adverse period and received growing recognition for her achievements during and after the third phase. She worked as an economist until 1959, reaching the position of chief of the Far Eastern Division, the first woman to gain this status, one that no woman received again until the 1970s, and at a time where divisions were highly important (AEA CSWEP 2003). She returned to the Fund in 1963 as a consultant to write the Fund's history, alongside the principal author, Keith Horsefield, taking over his role on his retirement. By the time Garritsen retired in 1987, she had authored seven volumes and spent forty-one years at the IMF. The movement between two distinct spheres of professional expertise—economist and historian—was not one of preference and resulted from the career choices she faced.

She was an inspiration for improving the status of women in the economics profession in and out of the academy. In 1987, the managing director of the IMF, Michel Camdessus, on receiving notice that Garritsen was honored with the Outstanding Washington Women Economist, congratulated her.[2] "This award is richly deserved. Your pioneering work here at the Fund and the great distinction with which you served as the Fund Historian are an inspiration for us all."[3] In 1998 the American Economic Association's (AEA) Committee on the Status of Women in the Economics Profession (CSWEP) inaugurated the Carolyn Shaw Bell Award to commemorate women who furthered the status of women in economics in a

2. Washington Women Economists was set up in 1979 and brought together academic economists, like Barbara Bergmann, of the University of Maryland, and government economists, like Lucy Falcone (AEA CSWEP 1979).

3. Camdessus to Margaret Garritsen de Vries (hereafter cited as Garritsen), November 23, 1987, Paul A. Samuelson Papers, Correspondence Series, 1935–2010 and undated, box 75, DeVries, Margaret, 1944–2005 (hereafter cited as PAS Archive), David M. Rubenstein Rare Book & Manuscript Library, Duke University.

number of ways.[4] In 2002, the award went to Garritsen.[5] Upon request for academic support to solicit her nomination, Paul A. Samuelson, her former PhD supervisor, promptly wrote to the AEA to second her nomination and described how "the road was not smooth for a woman scholar hoping to follow a career in economic research at the frontier" (de Vries 2003).

This article contributes to the recent scholarship on the tensions and compromises that women navigate in professional contexts (see Chassonnery-Zaïgouche, Forget, and Singleton, this volume). Centering on the life of Garritsen complements histories and knowledge of the Fund, and it adds to scholarship on its role in gender and women's employment. While existing work on the representation of women in the economics profession has largely focused on academic economists, this article shines a light on women economists in international organizations during the mid-twentieth century, at a time where policy positions in international finance remained overwhelmingly male dominated, including at the IMF.

2. Early Years

Driving across Detroit, Garritsen's father took her, aged eight, to see what the Depression had brought. People had lost their homes and were out of work, while just an avenue or two away were the "most beautiful houses you'd ever seen," belonging to the executives of the automobile industry (de Vries 2003: 10). Born in Detroit in 1922, with the images from the Great Depression imprinted from an early age, her aspiration was to become an economist who would work in public service. But this was not an obvious choice for the daughter of immigrant parents—her father was a tradesman in Detroit in the construction sector, and both her parents had only grade-school educations. No one in their family circle had been to college or had any other advanced degree. But the other reason economics was not the obvious choice was, in her words, "I was a girl, and the girls

---

4. For more on CSWEP, see Chassonnery-Zaïgouche et al. 2019.

5. At the time, the chair of the Bell Award Committee was Barbara M. Fraumeni, and Joan G. Haworth was the chair of CSWEP (AEA CSWEP 2002). Personal correspondence with Fraumeni confirmed that no further information was available about the nature of selection for the award. Previous award winners included Alice Rivlin of the Brookings Institution (1998), Sandra Ohrn Moose of Boston Consulting Group (1999), Eva Mueller, Professor Emerita of the University of Michigan (2000), Francine Blau of Cornell University (2001), and Marianne Ferber, Professor Emerita of the University of Illinois Urbana-Champaign (2001).

we knew were dropping out of high school to take temporary jobs, then going on to marry and start families."[6]

Faced with a lack of role models, Garritsen asked her teacher, one of the few professional women role models in her life at the time, what to do, but her teacher's only advice was to become a teacher. In high school, Garritsen tried again, this time by writing to a newspaper advice columnist, stating, "I'd like a career and the only one I can think of is teaching." But even the columnist "had no other careers to suggest" (de Vries 2003: 10). At college, while she found the ambitions for women significantly broader, they did not quite stretch as far as those of men. Thought of as researchers, even proficient ones, women still fell short of "operators negotiating with countries or as formulators of economic policy in responsible positions"—*that* was uncommon (10).

Enrolling for a degree in economics in 1939 at the University of Michigan was fitting, with its leaning in institutional economics and public service, and professors working in Washington for the New Deal (de Vries 2003). Winning a Phi Kappa Phi Fellowship in 1943, she graduated with honors, and with her mainly male classmates heading off to war, her immediate environment upon graduating was one of great uncertainty. It was at the University of Michigan where she met Pu Shan, with whom she started a long-lasting affair. With him continuing his PhD at Harvard, a place she was excluded from, she used her fellowship from Michigan to search for scholarships.[7] She was encouraged by her professors to continue her studies, and specifically to join the Massachusetts Institute of Technology, where the young Paul Samuelson was building up the economics department and PhD program.[8] Funding for her undergraduate studies at the University of Michigan and the exceptional endorsement she received secured MIT's tuition fellowship.

Garritsen was enrolled at MIT from the summer of 1943 through June 1946; of the thirty PhDs granted that year (1946), there were only two, hers and one other, that were earned by women—also in economics and social sciences.[9] She remembered the university being inspiring, with photographs of women faculty hanging on the corridor walls, and that she

6. Phi Kappa Phi newsletter, 1992, PAS Archive.

7. Chris de Vries, personal correspondence.

8. For the postwar expansion of American graduate economics education and MIT, see Duarte 2014, and for a detailed of account of the young Samuelson, see Backhouse 2017.

9. Massachusetts Institute of Technology, Office of the President President's Report 1945–1946, MIT Archive.

received equal treatment by professors and fellow students, with "no mur-
mur of surprise at my presence."[10] MIT had a certain "receptivity" to
women, an "unusual quality" that she thought was insufficiently recognized by the broader public. This was memorably not the same elsewhere—she "did not find the same acceptance at that eminent university
further up Massachusetts Avenue,"[11] where she recalled that she was even
refused admission to the Widener Library.[12] This receptivity to women
economists, remembered Samuelson, was not due to being "especially
fair-minded" but "because the War was taking most students elsewhere."
The brevity of her studies, with her PhD completed in three years, may
have been the result of the ongoing war, during which studies continued
without any summer break. Garritsen and her contemporaries, such as
Louise Freier—another of Samuelson's students with whom they
remained friends, or Ruth Gertrude Gilbert, who graduated in the same
cohort—"softened the economics community both for women and for
MIT products."[13] Garritsen was one of the first economists to receive a
PhD from MIT and one of the first women.

By the war's end, central to US macroeconomic policy was the size of
public debt. Garritsen's thesis, titled "Some Theoretical and Practical
Problems in the Management of the Federal Debt in the Post War Period,"
examined the problems the US Treasury faced in its management of public debt as of 1945. Analytically, she compared the changing tides of the
purpose of debt management policy, shifting from what had been a focus
on steady debt retirement to one that emphasized more wholeheartedly
the possible fiscal benefits of debt management policy. Empirically, she
studied in detail the market of various government securities. Her work
focused on practical issues, and she hoped her manuscript would serve as
a "basis for some constructive debt management policy recommendations."[14] Samuelson followed the thesis closely and judged it to represent
"an excellent and useful piece of work."[15]

Over the twentieth century, women wrote across a number of topics not
"stereotypically" seen as women's issues (Madden 2002). Broadly, and as

10. Letter, September 2000, PAS Archive.
11. Technology Review, July 1994, MIT Archive.
12. Letter, September 2000, PAS Archive. For a similar disparaging and discouraging
reception at Harvard, see Forget 2011 on Anne Carter's testimonies.
13. Samuelson to Garritsen, September 2000, PAS Archive.
14. Thesis chapter, PAS Archive.
15. Samuelson to M. J. Barloon, May 13, 1946, PAS Archive.

covered by Forget (2011), in the early years of the twentieth century, women economists focused on labor, economic history, and social problems. Garritsen's research was not entirely "typical" of the expertise of other women economists; nevertheless, women economists also worked in this area. Catherine Grace Ruggles, from Radcliffe College, wrote her PhD dissertation in 1937, "The Financial History of Cambridge, 1846–1935," a more or less contemporary of Garritsen's thesis (Radcliffe College 1937: 20). Anna P. Youngman, an early twentieth-century graduate from the University of Chicago, had an extensive career working in the research and policy field of public finance and monetary issues, writing "The Federal Reserve System in Wartime" in 1945, touching on topics in debt management (Dimand et al. 2012). Ursula Hicks earned her PhD in 1935 from the London School of Economics, went to work there subsequently, and made several contributions in public finance. While the attraction to this field may have been related to the inordinate pressing presence of this policy issue during this time, it may also be related to professional prospects, where women working in the area of monetary and financial history, as well as public finance, were more likely to find employment in nonacademic institutions. As noted by Forget (2011), the growth of government bureaucracy and its incentives for work created new career opportunities for women, who were discriminated against in academic environments.

While at graduate school, Garritsen taught at Tufts, but when she came to finish her PhD and applied to several academic and nonacademic positions, her search for academic posts ended in frustration.[16] She interviewed for two academic jobs, neither successfully. The first, the economics faculty at Cleveland Reserve (subsequently Case Western Reserve University), "never had a female applicant" but considered her because of the shortage of men, who were in the war. Her second interview was for a teaching job with Sarah Lawrence College, a liberal arts college in New York. Her supervisor stood behind her. "It is my belief that she has a successful career as a professional economist ahead of her," wrote Samuelson, when asked if Margaret would be suitable. He did not hold back his praise: "She is intelligent and exceedingly industrious . . . ranks very high as compared to the graduate students whom I have known

16. Susan Ye, OWWE Award, 1987, PAS Archive.

at M.I.T, Radcliffe, and other institutions. . . . She has a great deal of drive and initiative."[17]

What to wear to interviews ended up symbolizing the extent to which she would be a suitable candidate, not only in the context of gender roles but also against the background of a polarized economics profession. About Cleveland Reserve, she recalled, "I had dressed very conservatively for the interview, but not only was I a young woman (in my early twenties) among much older men but also my Keynesian economics favouring governmental intervention was too new and liberal for a traditional money and banking department" (de Vries 2003: 10). This contrasted with the women's college at Sarah Lawrence, where she "dressed the same way, in a skirted suit, but this time I was too conservative. My Keynesian economics did not go far enough for what was then their socialist planning orientation" (10).

She was to find greater success in nonacademic posts. Samuelson wrote to Edward M. Bernstein at the Treasury Department to introduce him to Dr. Margaret Garritsen, praising her exceptional work and informing him that she would like to seek a job at the World Bank or the IMF. To preempt any possible doubts about her competence, Samuelson added, "I would place her in the highest ten per cent of women graduate students whom I have known in the past in Chicago, Radcliffe, and this institution [MIT]. Where that would place her in the population of all graduate students, without regard to sex, is a problem to which I have paid insufficient attention and would not care to formulate even a provisional appraisal."[18]

With an extensive career in Washington, chief technical adviser and deputy to Harry Dexter White at the US Treasury, the principal spokesperson for the US delegation at the Bretton Woods Conference, Bernstein had also taken the position of the Fund's director of research in 1944 and held it until 1958. Later histories reflected on Bernstein's ability to spot talent. One of his greatest Fund achievements, according to a subsequent managing director, Michel Camdessus, was whom he hired. "Perhaps," Camdessus (1996) wondered, "his most lasting contribution was that he attracted many of the brightest economists of his time to work at the Fund—Sydney Alexander, Marcus Fleming, Robert Mundell, Jacques Polak, Robert Triffin, and numerous others." Garritsen should have been added to this list.

17. Samuelson to Contance Warren, April 25, 1944, PAS Archive.
18. Samuelson to Bernstein, June 26, 1946, PAS Archive.

Bernstein's ability at finding good candidates may have had something to do with his interviewing technique. He was "notorious for intensively questioning candidates, not unlike oral PhD exams. He would present the candidate with hypothetical country situations and test whether they could apply theory to real-life political situations" (de Vries 2003: 10). Bernstein wanted to know how Garritsen would have handled the management of public debt if the postwar period resulted in growing inflation, a prediction shared by Bernstein and other economists. A lukewarm recommendation letter, and a tough interview, yet Garritsen aced it. Writing to Samuelson of the "very interesting talk" he had with "Miss Garritsen" at the interview, and despite Samuelson's letter, Bernstein offered her the job right away, in July 12, 1946, requesting Samuelson to "release" her so that she could start no more than three weeks later. Garritsen later recalled that being hired on the spot was "too quick," as she was not even sure what her work would entail (de Vries 2003: 10).

Her move from Cambridge to Washington brought the next phase of her lifelong correspondence with Samuelson. Samuelson was a great mentor to Garritsen, despite meeting only occasionally after her graduation—no more than three times in close to fifty years—but they exchanged frequent letters. He often praised and commented how much he had learned from reading reports she would send, returning substantive comments and always promptly.[19] His correspondence with her revealed how he developed a personal exchange with Garritsen but also kept up his extensive professional network of acquaintances alive through Garritsen—asking her to remind him to their common acquaintances in Washington.

Although Samuelson acknowledged the difficulties along the road for a woman economist, he seemed less aware of his own role, including his position as he described it, as the "MIT patriarch."[20] When Garritsen was close to seventy, he wrote how "teachers always bask in the reflected glory of their students, attributing to their instructions, much of the merit."[21] He was often full of praise: "Certainly your successes at the IMF enable us to bask in reflected glory."[22] This was reciprocal, and in 2000 she wrote, "How envious are many colleagues, friends and new acquaintances when I tell them of my opportunity to study with you in such a minutely small

19. This concurs with the view of Roger Backhouse and Béatrice Cherrier (2019) that he was very supportive of his female students.
20. Samuelson to Garritsen, January 17, 2002, PAS Archive.
21. Samuelson to Garritsen, May 27, 1992, PAS Archive.
22. Samuelson to Garritsen, January 17, 2002, PAS Archive.

handful of students in the 40s!" When invited to Samuelson's ninetieth birthday celebration in 2005, she also expressed her enjoyment of "glory by association" given the rise to fame that the MIT Department of Economics, under his leadership, enjoyed.

At other times the evidence was mixed. While his support and mentorship remained, Garritsen received various types of discriminatory and patronizing remarks. In one of her academic job reference letters, he wrote, "Personally, Miss Garritsen is an attractive, wholesome girl, whose only possible flaw is a slight tendency to over seriousness. However, if a defect at all, this is a very minor one, and I do not hesitate to commend her to your consideration."[23] Garritsen would never fail to write to him to update him of her news and achievements. This may not have been solely to count on him for support, references, and guidance that he, on the whole, consistently provided. Through her continued exchanges, she never failed to remind him of her achievements and successes, in this way "teaching" him and subtly reversing the mentorship role with regard to women's professional success.

3. Economist at the Fund

3.1. Overview

Countries faced the devastation from war with monetary and economic systems still wrapped in wartime controls put in place to help tend to the most pressing needs. There was obvious recognition that exchange controls that protected scarce foreign currency would be kept after the war's end, preventing them from dissipating, but the Fund agreement would move countries toward the gradual removal of restrictions on current transactions. Of the Fund's foremost tasks was nothing less formidable than deciding the entire structure of exchange rates that the world's transactions would be governed by. The thirty-five countries that signed up to the Articles of Agreement, entering into force by December 1945, would gradually be approached by the Fund to communicate their par values and begin the processes of negotiations. When Garritsen began in August 1946 at the Fund, she was among the institution's earliest recruits, at a time when the staff body was growing only slowly.

---

23. Samuelson to Contance Warren, April 25, 1944, PAS Archive. Samuelson's deprecatory remarks about women made him the object of a detailed investigation into his views on the role of women in the economics profession (Backhouse and Cherrier 2019).

A more malleable system than the gold standard, the Bretton Woods system pegged exchange rates to the US dollar, which was in turn pegged to gold. But this could be adjusted, so countries could pursue domestic goals like full employment without the sacrifices of deflating their economies. The IMF's facilities could be drawn on to tide its members over during temporary payment difficulties, under various and increasingly complicated stipulations and procedures (IMF 1946). Over time, this system came to fall short of its initial promise of fostering full employment and economic growth in its members.

Of the Fund's initial members, many hesitated to send the few people with financial and economic expertise to Washington at a time of intense need to reconstruct from the devastation caused by the war. The employment and promotion of personnel at the Fund for much of its first decade of operation were driven by a greater concern for geographic scope than gender balance, reflected in the type of data collected and reported on. As the institution grew, so did the geographic scope of its employees: by the first annual meeting, there were 100 staff coming from 15 countries, and by 1947, there were 355 staff members originating from 27 countries, overwhelmingly the wealthier ones. As the number of member countries grew, so did the staff and the balance of quotas—the paid-in membership—so its activities began to expand.[24] The efforts at broad geographic recruitment were tied into new training programs offered on general international economics and balance of payment techniques, with the Fund hosting technicians from foreign ministries and central banks, setting up an extensive network of contacts, and simultaneously establishing its early work in technical assistance.[25]

3.2. Garritsen

Garritsen started as an economist in the research department, where all economists started during this period, before the area departments were established.[26] At a time when the Fund was small—the research

24. IMF Annual Reports, various years (1946–50).

25. By 1953 sixty-one trainees from forty member countries spent six months to a year in formal training at the Fund. This underscores the role of the International Monetary Fund not only in the shaping of economic expertise and policy but also in the production of experts.

26. This followed a similar approach to the organization of economic research at the World Bank, which also redirected economists into area departments when those were eventually formed. However, contrary to the Fund, economists lost the power battle to the engineers and lawyers in the World Bank, until the mid-1970s (Laskaridis 2021).

department consisted of about eighty personnel, and budget freezes prevented further hiring—Garritsen found her colleagues, and those responsible for Fund policy and practice, humble, with a deliberate policy of keeping outside the limelight.[27]

Garritsen was devoted to her work, working evenings and weekends and teaching three evenings a week at George Washington University. Her course, Public Finance and Taxation, focused on public debt and fiscal policy, and drew heavily from her work in her PhD. It was mainly attended by eager war veterans.[28] She wrote nonchalantly of the accident she was in, just two months after beginning her career at the Fund.[29] A train accident on her way to visit Pu Shan caused a fractured vertebra, hospitalizing her for two weeks; she subsequently needed to wear a steel brace for several more. Brushing it off as minor and joking about the lawsuit she would file against the railroad company, she wrote to her former supervisor about her enjoyment of working at the Fund.

In the US-Canada division, she worked in a small cohort under the direction of Irving Friedman, with whom she authored reports and worked closely.[30] He would become a friend and lifelong mentor (de Vries 2003). Her work was self-directed; besides responding to queries of the executive directors on the nature of par values and exchange controls, she spent her time studying topics she felt were pertinent. Her work was technical, drawing from government and academic sources, and at the time, she worked on dollar scarcity, the US business cycle, and the role of US exports domestically and abroad.

Central to the debates in the early days of the Fund was multiple currency practices—the ways with which countries established multiple arrangements simultaneously. The elimination of multiple currency practices along with other foreign exchange restrictions and bilateral clearing arrangements was pivotal to the Fund's Articles of Agreement, and a common requirement to gain access to Fund resources. Since its inception, the Fund viewed them as a source of instability and potentially as undermining the par value system, and during the 1950s especially, the Fund focused on reducing multiple currency practices (de Vries and

27. Garritsen to Samuelson, September 12, 1947, PAS Archive.

28. Garritsen to Samuelson, September 12, 1947, PAS Archive. A year after starting, despite her enjoyment of teaching, she considered pausing teaching to work on other issues.

29. Garritsen to Samuelson, November 10, 1946, PAS Archive.

30. Friedman worked in the Secretary of the Treasury, and was one of the IMF's earliest recruits, eventually heading the Exchange Restrictions Department. He continued his career at the World Bank from 1964 and subsequently in the private financial sector.

Horsefield 1969). Whether and to what extent these should be eliminated for contravening the Articles of Agreement, as the all-powerful legal department maintained, prompted the economists, in the also all-powerful research department, to investigate. De Vries (1967, 1969) worked on their rationale and effects extensively, and with Friedman, they worked to gradually reform the Fund's stance "from a strict legal approach to one that was more economically oriented and less insistent on their elimination" (de Vries 2003).

3.3. Traveling on Missions

When Mexican officials started considering devaluation, Garritsen was the US desk economist in the US-Canada division. Concerned about the impacts on commodity prices and trade with the United States, Garritsen was assigned to work on this issue. Mexico's postwar balance of payments crises ended up being crucial milestones in the IMF's early history (Gold 1988). The IMF's monetary approach to the balance of payments emerged from the papers and documents circulated during the Mexican experiences of devaluation (de Vries 1987).[31] The two Mexican officials who became the IMF's first executive directors later took up key positions in the central bank. Maintaining this former contact, they were keen for Garritsen to visit, and the first of many missions that Garritsen went on was to Mexico in 1949.

This was a crucial time for the Fund's development: the period of the late 1940s and 1950s was when the principle of conditionality started to gain ground, on US insistence for explicit guarantees for use of Fund resources. In the early 1950s, standby arrangements inaugurated the legal instrument for conditional loans that mimicked domestic adjustment under the gold standard, where in exchange for access to IMF resources, governments implemented deflationary fiscal and monetary policies. Theoretically, this was associated with the monetary approach to the balance of payments—the view that rapid domestic credit expansion would put pressure on the real value of countries' currency, prompting deficits and losses in reserves. The operational vehicle for rolling this out in practice was financial programming—the set of national accounting

31. Jacques Polak began his career as an assistant to Jan Tinbergen, sharing an office with him at the League of Nations, working together on empirical studies of business cycles (Boughton 2011).

calculations that would help staff identify the target policy variables, in particular ceilings of domestic credit expansion, to stem what was seen to be the monetary source of external imbalance. Garritsen was in the midst of these circumstances at the time the Fund began to betray what had been its great expectations. Programs were increasingly concentrated in Latin America during the 1950s, where the Fund developed and tested its approach most consistently in that region (Boianovsky 2012). Despite growing criticism from its members for deflationary recommendations, by the end of 1960s, this was broadly generalized across regions.

Given the role that the Fund was taking, it would not be easy to face country authorities. Garritsen went on many missions, of varying lengths, throughout her career. Travel was a formative component of her role as Fund economist. She visited a string of countries in Southeast Asia, within about two months (Thailand, Sri Lanka, Burma, India, and Pakistan).[32] Sometimes she traveled alone, as she did in Thailand in 1952. Through frequent cables and dispatches between offices of central banks, in hotels, she worked hard to fulfill the Fund's mission.

Her tasks were far from straightforward, and her role as a privileged, white, American woman in the position of an international expert was highly complicated. This partly had to do with being a functionary of a contentious institution, but there were significant challenges that came from the rarity of a woman in her role. Missions visited not only policy authorities but also large companies to gauge a sense of the foreign exchange earnings and remittances they were making. The mission to Pakistan was assigned high importance by the country's top officials, with the minister of finance and the most senior economic technician coming to the Fund meetings. "These men had never worked with a woman before, and certainly not one in her twenties," but eventually she was "accepted as the Fund's representative" (de Vries 2003: 10). In Turkey, in 1953, playing bridge with officials and the deputy director of the European Department, Ernest Sturc, was more than a way to pass the time. "After that, I had little trouble convincing them that I was smart and might know economics" (11). Garritsen participated in all the high-level meetings taking place with officials from the Central Bank and Ministry of Finance. In Sri Lanka, Garritsen was advised to clarify the figures on different entries on the balance of payments.[33] In Burma she attended a

32. Document ID 50831, p. 20, IMF Archives.
33. Document ID 50831, p. 18, IMF Archives.

conference; in Thailand her role was to confirm authorities' plans on exchange rate issues. Visiting Yugoslavia in 1955 further challenged her: she exclaimed that the country had "literally hundreds of multiple rates. The Fund's Executive Board did not understand why Yugoslavia had all those rates, and it was my job to understand the system and its rationale" (11). In the case of her two-week mission to Costa Rica, in 1951, about the multiple rates and compliance under Fund Articles of Agreement, Garritsen reported back her own understanding of economic affairs and exchange restrictions to the mission head, which was not necessarily what crystallized in the final report to the executive board.[34]

Garritsen was a dedicated Fund economist, and gradually her role was elevated. Senior staff in Washington made it clear that she was expected "to have a much more important part" in missions, which largely came from "intimate knowledge" about the Fund's "attitude" to certain policies, which was sufficient "to have her exercise judgment on the application of our department's attitude" to the issues. This emphasized the relative importance of how staff operated and carried out Fund duties—authority came from developing an understanding of *attitudes*, to a sufficient degree to be trusted to impart those to policy officials. Socialization into becoming a IMF staffer represented what came to be the malleability of Fund expertise, the "oral tradition" that characterized much of the Fund's policy work (Fine and Hailu 2000; Laskaridis 2020).

4. "Writing History as a Way of Life"

4.1. Overview

Garritsen married Barend A. de Vries in 1952, who studied under Charles P. Kindleberger at MIT, after which they both went to the IMF. Decisions about having a family fundamentally altered Garritsen's career. She and her husband signed up to an adoption service. After an extensive waiting period, they were given only one month's notice and "had to prepare for her quickly." In early 1958, they adopted a daughter.[35] Garritsen was still an economist at the Fund and on a Fund mission to the Philippines just three

34. Document ID 39438, Memo Garritsen, July 24, 1951, p. 69, IMF Archives.
35. Two years later the family adopted a son. The two children were adopted from different birth families, with the only connection being the use of the same adoption agency. Garritsen has two granddaughters, one from each child (Chris de Vries, personal correspondence with author).

months prior to the baby's arrival. However, the adoption agency prohibited her from working for any significant length of time outside the house. Raising children, with both her and her husband traveling, made working very difficult, and Garritsen stepped back from her operational career. As she later recounted, "The adoption agency insisted that Mrs. De Vries stop working full time," requiring her to quit her job. "They just said, 'Your office is going to miss you when you have to quit.' They never even asked if I would miss the IMF. The emphasis in the 1950s was on a traditional family, with a mother at home while the husband had a career" (de Vries 2003). When she left the Fund as division chief, initially on leave of absence, she did not expect to return.[36] "My hardest struggle as a woman professional was with this now-familiar 'juggling' act." On a subsequent visit to Europe, she wrote to a friend who worked in the European IMF office, "One of the disadvantages of motherhood is being grounded—as you may recall."[37] Beyond these more common challenges through which her life fundamentally changed was the additional issue of being a family with adopted children during this period.

To continue her intellectual and research pursuits, she tried to secure research funding. She kept up some teaching and prepared a research project on exchange rate systems and economic development, and she looked for funding to work from home. "Such a grant would frankly make me free from routine household duties, and thus enable me to devote 20–25 hours per week to the project," she wrote to Samuelson.[38] The Ford Foundation was the first funder that came to mind, but without much funding experience she asked for Samuelson's advice, both substantively on the project's value and about how to approach funders. While otherwise warm and supporting, his replies were curt and dismissive. He accepted to act as a reference, but doubted he could be of much use, and did not offer much on tactics, besides sharing the names and details of some contacts with whom she could liaise for further information. "It may not be easy for a woman working at home to get a grant, but I certainly wish you luck."[39]

She was not deterred and followed up with the contacts Samuelson provided, detailing her extensive experience and project proposal. Buttressed

36. Garritsen to Samuelson, March 11, 1958, PAS Archive.
37. Document ID 107144, p. 145, IMF Archives.
38. Garritsen to Samuelson, March 11, 1958, PAS Archive.
39. Samuelson to Garritsen, March 26, 1958, PAS Archive.

by references not only from Samuelson but also Kindleberger and Friedman, she had also received assurances from the dean of George Washington University that she would be hired as a consultant to have desk space, that she would have access to the libraries and collections of the World Bank and IMF and could make use of her extensive network in Washington. Despite receiving some financial support from the Ford Foundation grant (de Vries 1966) and her work arising from it appearing in academic journals, she did not receive the necessary support for the publication of her work with the oldest American university press, Johns Hopkins University Press. It appears that Samuelson, upon request to referee the manuscript by the editor, gave her work a critical review, judging it to be "the work of a lone wolf," which "of course there is nothing wrong with that" but that it needed help from established experts, such as Harry Johnson, Peter Kenen, Robert Mundell, Kindleberger, to name a few, in order to make it something more than "a marginally acceptable contribution to knowledge and scholarship."[40] Without them, Samuelson was doubtful as to her work's merits. He was also doubtful as to whether such experts would bother, as "it is not likely that an established gifted scholar like Johnson would have the time" to provide that sort of feedback.[41] Samuelson's disparaging remarks toward Garritsen's effort to make a mark as an economist in the academic field stands in contrast to his more positive encouragement of her work in a policy institution.

While working from home, she wrote for *Staff Papers*, the IMF publication established in 1950 to popularize general research by the Fund staff. Around 1963, the managing director of the Fund, Per Jacobsson, sought out authors to document and describe what was evaluated as being the Fund's successes. Through Friedman, she was recruited to help, working partly in the office, partly at home, as part of a "flexible part-time consulting arrangement" (de Vries 2003). And so began a long-term second affiliation with the IMF, as historian of the Fund—first working alongside Keith Horsefield, the IMF historian at the time, and later alone until her retirement in 1987.

Her role as historian was to "portray the evolution of the Fund and its activities in the broader setting of contemporary economic developments, and to describe its policies and their evolution against the background dialogue engaged in by professional economists and government officials."

40. Samuelson to John Gallman, July 7, 1964, PAS Archive.
41. Samuelson to Gallman, July 7, 1964.

The purpose of her historical prose was to provide authoritative accounts of Fund policies, activities, and views of key officials and member states, in a way that was seen to be "accurate, sufficiently complete, and reasonably balanced." She reminisced that "writing histories of the International Monetary Fund has been a way of life for me for over two decades," and expressed a great debt of gratitude toward her family for enabling it (International Monetary Fund and DeVries 1985: xxii).

The way official Fund history was written changed over time, as the Fund and the world changed. Initially focused on what the executive board did, as with Horsefield's early histories, Garritsen's work integrated more of the institution itself and outside issues, such as academic debates and other groups such as the Group of 24—the group that coordinates developing countries' position on monetary and development issues in Bretton Woods fora. By the time of James Boughton's later histories, Garritsen's successor, the access to Fund documents was fundamentally altered, and official histories were less "the vehicle for secret revelations" and more about putting the Fund into the setting of the world economy (de Vries 2003). These were written as "history written from the inside" but for which the Fund itself was not formally responsible, in that what emerged was not formally approved by the board or by country officials.

4.2. Becoming a Historian

After the work on his official histories that covered the period 1945 to 1965 was complete, Horsefield informed the head of legal counsel, the head of research, and other senior staff that Garritsen would stay. She would be continuing the writing of the next installment of Fund history to cover the major international monetary developments between 1966 and 1971. He requested the most senior officials to give Garritsen the same level of access he had: "notes about the true inwardness of happenings which are known to you but which do not get properly reflected in Board minutes or papers," as "Mrs de Vries' task would be made much easier if the material from which she will work was enlightened by such inside knowledge in future."[42] Horsefield was keen to ensure that, in light of proliferating informal and undocumented documents, that she was kept in the loop. He strongly urged that "special arrangements . . . be made to permit Mrs. De Vries to see all documents circulated to the Board, whether or

42. Document ID 107144, p. 189, IMF Archives.

not they are included in the regular series.'[43] In general, senior staff welcomed her, with Joseph Gold, former legal counsel and a great authority within the Fund, professing that he would be very happy to help Garritsen any way he could and encouraging Horsefield to suggest that she speak to him from time to time.[44]

The first history Garritsen worked on was the update to Horsefield's volumes. The content was decided by consultation, with topics and suggested structure of the books discussed with the managing director and deputy managing director. Any Fund history for the period 1966–71 would need to cover international liquidity, including the creation of the SDRs, currency crises, and exchange rate rigidity. Those reviewing Horsefield's volumes had commonly agreed that their main drawback was that they hadn't included the most recent financial turbulence. The problem was not one of identifying the issues but of "understanding, sorting and organizing material." By 1970, Garritsen had progressed on the writing, and during this time, her identity on official documents was described as "Historian."

How did she learn to write history? She primarily worked alongside Horsefield, who had lectured in banking at the LSE and during the war served in the Ministry of Aircraft Production. When he started at the Fund, he too worked at first as an operational economist—a division chief—and later as historian.[45] Horsefield developed into a professional mentor to whom she devotedly dedicated her solo-authored works.[46] Before the war, Garritsen was familiar with the work of British monetary and financial historians and through her writing of history began to foster relations. This was integral to how she built up her professional network and expertise in writing history. She traveled to Europe to meet with monetary historians and help prepare the way for reception of upcoming books, and she held the British school of monetary and financial history in high regard. Given the relative scarcity of international economic history at the time, and lack of discussions on methodology, she found herself a niche. Wanting to show her own voice—distinct from annual

43. Document ID 107144, p. 187, IMF Archives.

44. Document ID 107144, p. 188, IMF Archives.

45. Other female economists who worked at the Fund also contributed to the writing of the earlier histories, such as Gertrud Lovesy.

46. Besides expressions of gratitude in the printed preface, de Vries sent signed copies to her mentor. In a signed copy of de Vries 1976a and 1976b, she expressed her admiration and appreciation; in de Vries 1985, she thanks Horsefield for his example and help, and in de Vries 1986 she recalls her "fond memories" of their earlier association (Keith Horsefield Papers, box 1 and 2, Bristol University Library Special Collections).

reports, and more interesting than a dull account of operations—she turned to how British historians studied burning topics such as the UK balance of payments that was intimately part of the Fund's history during this period.[47]

Another benefit of discussions with economic historians and academics was to develop more of the outside eye—sitting "beyond the fray of current operations" and seeing what future audiences would find most interesting about the growing complexity of Fund activities. Her visits included a meeting with Donald E. Moggridge, the biographer of J. M. Keynes, who had positively reviewed Horsefield's history and who invited her to lunch with him and James Meade, and an overnight stay in college. She also met with Richard S. Sayers, who upon retiring from the LSE had taken on writing the history of the Bank of England. She wrote to several historians and economists, including Harry Johnson. In France she hoped to meet Pascal Salin, Maurice Levy-Leboyer, and Claudio Segre. The only woman she contacted during this trip to Europe was Susan Strange, at the Royal Institute of International Affairs at Chatham House, to whom she wrote a friendlier letter: "Since our pleasant meeting at the Fund in 1970 I have considered you a friend; after your most kind review of our History in International Affairs, I have regarded you with genuine affection."[48] On returning from the trip to London and Paris, Garritsen reported of the "fruitful and stimulating" encounters and warm encouragement received for her historical work.

Writing IMF history was "a job that others had found very difficult."[49] The difficulties of working with the "well-known shyness of central banks (and I include the IMF) in disclosing what goes on behind closed doors" left her satisfied with what she was able to produce in her first two-volume history. Carefully curated drafts resulted both from the deputy managing director reading and rereading drafts and being kept up to date with changes to structure, topic, and titles of chapters and sections, as well as from waiting for five months for comments by the executive directors. Usually, the sorts of comments received were either to give more space and attention to one's own country or relevant issue or to clarify technical issues. But it was also about sensitivities, such as with the 1967 devaluation of sterling and eventual IMF standby arrangement, a great cause of concern about what could or could not be said. "It has been a long haul,

---

47. Document ID 107144, p. 162, IMF Archives.
48. Document ID 107144, p. 152, IMF Archives.
49. Document ID 107144, p. 122, IMF Archives.

especially getting the material through the institution."[50] She tried to prepare for critics' comments, especially about portrayals of the Fund being seen as "overly optimistic."[51] Garritsen assumed that the audience of Fund histories wanted to know what was happening at the time. The problem with this was the "problems of writing virtually instant history."[52] She formatively shaped the institution through her writing of its history, as she moved between how history was made by those higher up, to be used by those lower down. It was a carefully curated and crafted but trusted history—one that would fulfill multiple roles. Her histories were about acquainting new staff to Fund activities and providing a narrative structure to new Fund staff.[53] They were relevant for the Fund's members and fodder for its critics.

Her academic mentor praised her highly. Samuelson wrote, "You must feel good now that the Fund history is done. Like Gibbon after his labour." Similarly, the monetarist economist Tim Congdon, on reviewing her history in the *Times Literary Supplement*, also likened her to Gibbon: "Mrs. De Vries has good claim to be the Gibbon of postwar international finance."[54] On a separate occasion, the reference point was to "Samuel Eliot Morison, official historian of the U.S. Navy during World War II," who observed naval battles to write the history. The books not only were of interest to academics but were reviewed in popular and commercial outlets such as the *Challenge*, the *Magazine of Economic Affairs*, and *Fortune Magazine*, capturing the interest of those in business and banking. She received favorable reviews from many eminent economists, and her mode of writing history "has been used as a model for histories written by other national and international institutions."[55] Important critics of the Fund also engaged with her work: Cheryl Payer and Susan Strange, mostly commenting on the critical aspects of Fund activities, rather than the author's work.

Nevertheless, the desire to return to operational work remained. "In 1977, after doing the first three volumes of the history with Horsefield and two on my own, I wanted to get back into operational work. But it was difficult to fit into the Fund's new structure" (de Vries 2003). Garritsen

50. Garritsen to Samuelson, March 14, 1977, PAS Archive.
51. Document ID 107144, p. 63, IMF Archives.
52. Document ID 107144, p. 139, IMF Archives.
53. Document ID 107144, p. 122, IMF Archives.
54. PAS Archive.
55. Susan Ye, OWWE Award, 1987, PAS Archive.

embarked on the second set of history, covering the period 1972–78, and before coming to the end of her career at the Fund, she published two more books—mini-histories—and overview pieces. Toward the end of her career, she wrote to Samuelson, "With these books out of the way, I have a real sense of completion of my work at the Fund."[56] After more than forty years of association with the Fund, Garritsen was to retire in 1987, as retirement was mandatory at sixty-five. As she prepared to leave the Fund, she observed that "in the eyes of old-timers, the Fund is no longer the same." After a career there, her reflections were mixed. Four decades were a "pleasant and mutually fruitful association." As to the switch from an operational economist to the Fund's historian, due to "personal circumstances—juggling a career and family—with a husband himself steeped in international operations and travel," she judged this to have "worked out well for both the Fund and myself." She reaped the many benefits of academic and institutional praise, joking she too was a workaholic, and that for most of her life she was "too busy."[57] She took up the piano and continued writing short pieces after retirement.

5. Awards and Furthering the Status of Women

The world's finance ministers and central bank governors gathered to attend the World Bank and IMF annual meetings with not a woman in sight. This was an obvious reminder of the dearth of women in international finance. Garritsen posited that "it's because money is considered just too important and too powerful to be entrusted to a woman." From the Fund's beginnings to the end of 1978, there was not a single woman head of department in the Fund, despite the existence of women staff members who had over twenty years' experience at the Fund. Six women, with experience of more than twenty years at the Fund, had not progressed even to the level of deputy director or director. This continued, and even after forty years of Fund existence there was not a single woman head of department (de Vries 1976b). In her damning review of the status of women in the Fund (de Vries 1976b: 1030–31), she saw the Fund's lack of diversity as a reflection of what went on in the area of international finance more generally.

56. Garritsen to Samuelson, November 19, 1986, PAS Archive.
57. Garritsen to Samuelson, November 19, 1986, PAS Archive.

Garritsen, the first women to head an operational division at the Fund, already by 1957, and although she subsequently spent a large portion of her career as a historian, was awarded multiple times for her contributions to furthering the status of women in the economics profession. In 1989 she received an award from the Washington Women Economists, having lectured on the themes of women in international finance from 1979, and was recognized as a "pioneer in the advancement of other women economists" for her role in supporting other women. She was admired by other colleagues, who recommended her to the committee for nomination. She won this award just at the time she was retiring.

In 2002 Garritsen was awarded the Carolyn Shaw Bell Award by the AEA's CSWEP in a packed room, attended by the former economic counselor and director of research, Jacques Polak, as well as former deputy managing director P. R. Narvekar, who had both sponsored her nomination.[58] In attendance were Margaret Kelly, director of the Human Resources Department and fellow pioneer of furthering the status of women in the Fund, and Robert Solomon, formerly from the Federal Reserve and sponsor of her nomination. Representatives from her educational institutions came, Professor Gary Solon, chair of the Department of Economics at the University of Michigan, and Olivier Blanchard and James Poterba from MIT (AEA CSWEP 2002).

By the time she received the award, there were many more women in senior positions in finance and monetary affairs, including at the Fund. These commendations were in recognition for serving "as a mentor for young economists, editors, librarians and archivists" and being a pioneer in advancing the status of women beyond the Fund, such as in starting Women in Economic Development, which later became part of the Society for International Development.[59] She wrote to Samuelson that "women's issues" had become one of her "retirement activities," although as stated elsewhere it was far more than this; it was really a "topic very close to her heart."[60] And so toward the eve of her retirement, when *Staff News*, an internal Fund publication, interviewed Garritsen to talk about women's issues at the Fund, it was easier to speak out. "There used to be a term called the 'double standard' and my colleagues often commented

58. Following from personal correspondence with Boughton, Narvekar was one of the male colleagues eager to support women's careers in the Fund.

59. Outstanding Washington Woman Economist award announcement 1987; PAS Archive: Susan Ye, OWWE Award, 1987.

60. IMF *Staff News*, September 1988, PAS Archive.

that I was very conscious of the fact that one standard was imposed for women and another for men. . . . My early colleagues recalled that 'Margaret was always pointing out that an unfair double standard existed.'"[61] Over time, Garritsen became more outspoken and reflexive about gender roles.

Her view of how discrimination worked in the Fund was less about explicit, deliberate acts, where men would announce "I don't want a woman in this office," but more the case of men being more comfortable working with other men, more used to the norms and what to expect. She observed the habitual nature with which they would "simply, and automatically" only recommend other men when vacancies needed filling. To the frequent complaint of it being hard to find women to fill posts, she would remind them of the quote by Juanita Kreps, who became secretary of commerce under President Jimmy Carter, that "it depends on who's doing the looking."[62] She painted the picture: "In the early days if you were making a presentation to the Executive Board, you knew you would be the only woman in the room. What man goes to the Board wondering whether he'll be the only man there? . . . We even wondered how we should dress . . . [or] what kind of suit we should wear so we would blend in."[63]

Within the Fund, Margaret had a very clear sense of how men could assist with advancing the status of women, such as eagerly trying to promote them, recommending and supporting them to take leadership roles in becoming heads of divisions and departments. She hoped her colleagues could promote and advertise why men may want women as heads, to have a "more progressive attitude in the work place." Colleagues on the whole showed some level of curiosity at these issues but "felt no personal responsibility for the situation."[64] Faced with an activist mindset, she called for pressure for change that has to come from somewhere and strongly believed this pressure could be created by advocating to senior male colleagues "to make them conscious of the need to hire and promote women." Her inclusion of the status of women in the Fund as part of her histories was precisely with this rationale—of making male colleagues aware of the situation, for them to start wondering what they themselves could do.[65]

---

61. IMF *Staff News*, September 1988, p. 6.
62. IMF *Staff News*, September 1988, p. 6.
63. IMF *Staff News*, September 1988, p. 7.
64. IMF *Staff News*, September 1988, p. 7.
65. The task of gathering data to document and monitor the extent of discrimination and

Recognized as a mentor, her advice to women was about encouragement to apply for jobs and to believe that they can do them. She commented that "women tend to lack confidence and undervalue their qualifications. Rarely do you find a man who lacks confidence. I've never seen a man who said 'I can't do this' or 'I'm not qualified for that.'" She joked how a junior male economist would probably jump on the offer to become managing director overnight, whereas a women would be in disbelief and look around asking "Who? Me?"[66]

6. Later Life

After retirement, Garritsen continued writing, in particular in the *Caravan*, the IMF's retiree's association publication.[67] She was frequently asked by former colleagues to contribute and write for anniversary events and issues, for instance, the fiftieth anniversary of Bretton Woods. She kept up her participation in scholarly activities, notably, the Duke conference held in 1995 on the post-1945 internationalization of economics, whose papers were collected in the edited volume by A. W. Coats. This was not the first of Coats's projects that she worked on; she had contributed to *Economists in International Agencies* (1986) when she was still at the Fund, when Coats explored the sociology of economic knowledge and the role of economists in government and international organizations.

In December 2001, Margaret Garritsen de Vries suffered a stroke, followed by a second one in 2004 that was more disabling than the first; she spent five weeks in the hospital.[68] Garritsen de Vries passed away on December 18, 2009, a week after Paul A. Samuelson, and was survived by her husband, Barend A. de Vries, two children, two grandchildren, and three siblings. At the time of her death, two financial funds were established to provide assistance to women who wanted to study economics. One was the Margaret Garritsen de Vries Memorial Fund set up by CSWEP. Functional from 2010, this fund has helped support doctoral students present at CSWEP-sponsored sessions at the AEA annual meetings.

---

exclusion was similar to what the newly formed CSWEP undertook on its creation in the 1970s: documenting the representation of women faculty in economics departments and the number of PhDs going to women (Forget 2011).

66. IMF *Staff News*, September 1988, p. 7.

67. Letter, February 2005, PAS Archive. James Boughton brought an earlier version of this paper to the attention of the editors of the *Caravan*, who circulated notice of it to their membership in April 2022, vol. 41, issue 2, p. 3.

68. Letter, September 2002, PAS Archive; Garritsen to Samuelson, January 2005, PAS Archive.

Several awardees have benefited from this fund, working across a range of topics.[69] The second was the Margaret Garritsen de Vries (1946) Memorial Fund set up at MIT (*Washington Post* 2010).[70] After her death in 2009, funds were donated in her name to the MIT fund every year until the latest public record in 2019.[71]

7. Conclusion

The male-dominated environment of the IMF, coupled with the obstacles in continuing a career as an operational economist while having a family, may be what motivated Margaret Garritsen de Vries to actively support, encourage, and eventually receive great praise and admiration for pioneering the inclusion of women in the economics profession. There was an issue of prestige and status across numerous aspects of her career. Coming out of her prestigious university studies, her professional role promised exciting research opportunities and a wealth of exposure to the world through travel. At the same time, working in a nonacademic setting was the result of difficulties in attaining academic employment. There may have been an issue with rising to a position of relative seniority of a regional department that was not European or American-centric. Finally, the changing professional status arising from the fundamental change in career from economist to historian was not from preference but due to the constraints of the adoption agency and her employer.

When Horsefield sent her an advance copy of his review for the *Economic Journal*, his review contained critical remarks with regard to the organization of the material and relative importance given to specific events. Garritsen did not shy away from candidly expressing her frustration at having being let down by her mentor. "I am, quite frankly, surprised—and . . . disappointed—at the thrust and tone of your review which contains none of your earlier enthusiastic responses . . . not even a reference to the fact, stated in your letter . . . that after reading Part I, you 'understood what was happening while I was still at the Fund far better than I did while I was there.'"[72] She recounted what he had mentioned in

---

69. See AEA 2010.

70. Information about the memorial fund can be found at https://giving.mit.edu/explore/student-aid/scholarships/memorial-scholarships.

71. See MIT 2020.

72. Garritsen to Keith, June 27, 1977, Keith Horsefield Papers, box 2, Bristol University Library Archive.

private in order to show its distance from his publicly expressed review, exposing injustice where she saw it.

To counter the concern that her work as a historian was somewhat lesser than the work of an economist, she never failed to send her mentor, and Nobel Prize winner, Paul A. Samuelson the glowing praise that her work received, especially when that appeared in academic journals. Despite fearing that circulating her commendations would make her seem "immodest," doing so prompted Samuelson to reveal his surprise at her success—"That is not always the fate of authors who write economic histories!"—often colored with a positive comment: "Economic scholars and historians will be lastingly in your debt."[73] Mentorship by senior men proved very important in Garritsen's career. Yet through many examples of what made her a pioneer, the mentorship relation was challenged, and at times, reversed.

References

American Economic Association (AEA). 2010. CSWEP: Margaret deVries Memorial Fund. https://www.aeaweb.org/about-aea/committees/cswep/awards/devries.

American Economic Association (AEA CSWEP). 1979. *Newsletter of the Committee on the Status of Women in the Economics Profession*, Summer. https://www.aeaweb.org/content/file?id=558.

American Economic Association (AEA CSWEP). 2002. "Dr. Margaret Garritsen de Vries, Recipient of the 2002 Carolyn Shaw Bell Award." Press release, American Economic Association. https://www.aeaweb.org/content/file?id=451.

American Economic Association (AEA CSWEP). 2003. 2003 Awards Ceremony Photos. https://www.aeaweb.org/about-aea/committees/cswep/about/awards/awards-ceremony-03.

Backhouse, R. 2017. *Founder of Modern Economics: Paul A. Samuelson.* Oxford: Oxford University Press.

Backhouse, R. E., and B. Cherrier. 2019. "Paul Samuelson, Gender Bias, and Discrimination." *European Journal of the History of Economic Thought* 26, no. 5: 1053–80.

Boianovsky, M. 2012. "Celso Furtado and the Structuralist-Monetarist Debate on Economic Stabilization in Latin America." *History of Political Economy* 44, no. 2: 277–330.

Boughton, J. M. 2011. "Jacques J. Polak and the Evolution of the International Monetary System." http://papers.ssrn.com/abstract=1876968.

73. Samuelson to Garritsen, November 25, 1986, PAS Archive.

Camdessus, M. 1996. "Statement by IMF Managing Director Michel Camdessus on the Death of Edward M. Bernstein." International Monetary Fund. https://www.imf.org/en/News/Articles/2015/09/29/18/03/nb9603.

Chassonnery-Zaïgouche, C., B. Cherrier, and J. Singleton. 2019. "'Economics Is Not a Man's Field': CSWEP and the First Gender Reckoning in Economics (1971–1991)." https://papers.ssrn.com/sol3/papers.cfm?abstract_id=3510857.

De Vries, M. G. 1966. "Trade and Exchange Policy and Economic Development: Two Decades of Evolving Views." *Oxford Economic Papers* 18, no. 1: 19–44.

De Vries, M. G. 1967. "The Decline of Multiple Exchange Rates, 1947–67." *Finance and Development*, 0004, no. 004: 297–303. https://doi.org/10.5089/9781616352882.022.

De Vries, M. G. 1969. "Multiple Exchange Rates." In *The International Monetary Fund, 1945–1965: Twenty Years of International Monetary Cooperation*, vol. 2, edited by M. G. De Vries and J. K. Horsefield. Washington, D.C.: International Monetary Fund.

De Vries, M. G., ed. 1976a. *The International Monetary Fund, 1966–1971: The System under Stress.* Vol. 1, *Narrative.* Washington, D.C.: International Monetary Fund. https://www.elibrary.imf.org/view/book/9781475530117/9781475530117.xml.

De Vries, M. G., ed. 1976b. *The International Monetary Fund, 1966–1971: The System under Stress.* Vol. 2, *Documents.* Washington, D.C.: International Monetary Fund.

De Vries, M. G. 1986. *The IMF in a Changing World, 1945–1985.* Washington, D.C.: International Monetary Fund. https://www.elibrary.imf.org/view/books/071/07050-9780939934652-en/07050-9780939934652-en-book.xml.

De Vries, M. G. 1987. *Balance of Payments Adjustment, 1945 to 1986: The IMF Experience.* Washington, D.C.: International Monetary Fund.

De Vries, M. G. 2003. "Margaret de Vries Reflects on Her Pioneering Role." *Newsletter of the Committee on the Status of Women in the Economics Profession*, Fall, 1, 10–12.

De Vries, M. G., and J. K. Horsefield. 1969. *The International Monetary Fund, 1945–1965.* Vol. 2, *Analysis.* Washington, D.C.: International Monetary Fund.

Dimand, M. A., R. W. Dimand, and E. L. Forget. 1995. *Women of Value: Feminist Essays on the History of Women in Economics.* Aldershot: Edward Elgar.

Dimand, R. W., M. A. Dimand, and E. L. Forget. 2012. *A Biographical Dictionary of Women Economists.* Aldershot: Edward Elgar.

Duarte, P. G. 2014. "The Early Years of the MIT PhD Program in Industrial Economics." In *MIT and the Transformation of American Economics*, edited by E. Roy Weintraub. *History of Political Economy* 46 (supplement): 81–108.

Fine, B., and D. Hailu. 2000. "Convergence and Consensus: The Political Economy of Stabilisation and Growth." CDPR Discussion Paper 2202. https://core.ac.uk/download/pdf/2790022.pdf.

Forget, E. L. 2011. "American Women and the Economics Profession in the Twentieth Century." *Œconomia* 1, no. 1: 19–30.

Gold, J. 1988. "Mexico and the Development of the Practice of the International Monetary Fund." *World Development* 16, no. 10: 1127–42.

IMF (International Monetary Fund). 1946. *Annual Report of the Executive Directors.* Annual Report No. 1. Washington, D.C.: International Monetary Fund. https://www.imf.org/external/pubs/ft/ar/archive/pdf/ar1946.pdf.

IMF (International Monetary Fund). 1947. *Annual Report of the Executive Directors.* Washington, D.C.: International Monetary Fund. https://www.imf.org/external/pubs/ft/ar/archive/pdf/ar1947.pdf.

IMF (International Monetary Fund). 1948. *Annual Report of the Executive Directors.* Washington, D.C.: International Monetary Fund. https://www.imf.org/external/pubs/ft/ar/archive/pdf/ar1948.pdf.

IMF (International Monetary Fund). 1949. *Annual Report of the Executive Directors.* Washington, D.C.: International Monetary Fund. https://www.elibrary.imf.org/downloadpdf/books/011/11892-9781616351618-en/11892-9781616351618-en-book.pdf.

IMF (International Monetary Fund). 1950. *Annual Report of the Executive Directors.* Washington, D.C.: International Monetary Fund. https://www.imf.org/external/pubs/ft/ar/archive/pdf/ar1950.pdf.

International Monetary Fund and M. G. DeVries. 1985. *Cooperation on Trial.* Vol. 1 of *The International Monetary Fund, 1972–1978.* Washington, D.C.: International Monetary Fund.

Laskaridis, C. 2020. "More of an Art Than a Science: The IMF's Debt Sustainability Analysis and the Making of a Public Tool." *Œconomia* 10, no. 4: 789–818.

Laskaridis, C. 2021. "Debt Sustainability: Towards a History of Theory, Policy, and Measurement." PhD diss., SOAS University of London. https://doi.org/10.25501/SOAS.00035675.

Madden, K. K. 2002. "Female Contributions to Economic Thought, 1900–1940." *History of Political Economy* 34, no. 1: 1–30.

MIT (Massachusetts Institute of Technology). 2020. Past In Memoriam Gifts. https://giving.mit.edu/past-memoriam-gifts.

Radcliffe College. 1937. *Official Register of Radcliffe College: Reports of the Officers, 1935–36.* Vol. 2, no. 5. Harvard Library. https://iiif.lib.harvard.edu/manifests/view/drs:2573642$1i.

Washington Post. 2010. Obituary for Margaret G. deVries. https://www.legacy.com/us/obituaries/washingtonpost/name/margaret-devries-obituary?id=5932487.

Appendix A

Figure A1. Photograph of Margaret Marie Garritsen de Vries speaking to the Managing Director about her retirement (February 25, 1987), negatives, box 3, ISAD(G) Reference Code 73780, Technology and General Services Department Records, TGSIMIG Retirement Photographs 1971–1989, IMF Archives, Washington, D.C.

Appendix B
List of Published Works

1. Books

1976: *The International Monetary Fund, 1966–1971: The System under Stress*, 2 vols.
1985: *The International Monetary Fund, 1972–1978: Cooperation on Trial*, 3 vols.
1986: *The IMF in a Changing World, 1945–85*
1987: *Balance of Payments Adjustment, 1945 to 1986: The IMF Experience*

2. Articles in *Finance and Development*, a joint publication with the World Bank started in 1964 to explain in short, nontechnical terms the institutions' activities

1966: "Twenty Years with Par Values, 1946–66," vol. 0003, no. 004
1967: "Trade and Exchange Policies for Economic Development," vol. 0004, no. 002
1967: "The Decline of Multiple Exchange Rates, 1947–67," vol. 0004, no. 004
1968: "The Magnitudes of Exchange Devaluation Finance and Development," vol. 0005, no. 002
1969: "Fluctuating Exchange Rates: The Fund's Approach," vol. 0006, no. 002
1969: "Exchange Restrictions: Progress toward Liberalization," vol. 0006, no. 003
1971: "Women, Jobs, and Development," vol. 0008, no. 004
1974: "International Monetary Developments and Changes in the World Economy," vol. 0011, no. 003
1985: "The IMF: Forty Years of Challenge and Change; Through the Fund Historian's Eyes," vol. 0022, no. 003
1995: "The IMF Fifty Years Later," vol. 0032, no. 002
2004: "In Brief: In New Reports, IMF Watchdog Pinpoints Policy Missteps," vol. 0041, no. 003

3. Book reviews appearing in *Finance and Development*

1984: June, Review of A. Cairncross and B. Eichengreen, *Sterling in Decline*, vol. 0021, issue 002
1991: January, Review of P. Krugman, *The Age of Diminished Expectations: U.S. Economic Policy in the 1990s*; review of Henry Nau, *The Myth of America's Decline: Leading the World Economy into the 1990s*, vol. 0028, issue 001
1997: January, Review of S. L. N. Simha, *Fifty Years of Bretton Woods*, vol. 0034, issue 002
2000: January, Review of *Historical Dictionary of the International Monetary Fund*, 2nd ed., vol. 0037, issue 001

4. Articles in *IMF Staff Papers*, a publication established in 1950 for scholars outside the Fund to access Fund economists' research

1965: January, "Multiple Exchange Rates: Expectations and Experiences," vol. 1965, issue 002
1966: January, "Fund Members' Adherence to the Par Value Regime: Empirical Evidence," vol. 1966, issue 003
1968: January, "Exchange Depreciation in Developing Countries," vol. 1968, issue 003

5. Garritsen appeared in several issues of *IMF Survey*, established in 1972, aiming to inform the public about Fund activities, reproducing official press releases and key decisions of the Board.

6. Garritsen wrote extensively in the *Caravan*, the publication for IMF retirees. It was not possible to gather her work in this publication.

7. Book chapters and contributions

1986: "The International Monetary Fund: Economists in Key Roles," in *Economists in International Agencies*, edited by A. W. Coats (New York: Praeger Press)
1996: Comment in *The Post-1945 Internationalization of Economics*, edited by A. W. Coats (Durham, N.C.: Duke University Press)
1996: "The Bretton Woods Conference and the Birth of the International Monetary Fund," in *The Bretton Woods-GATT System: Retrospect and Prospect after Fifty Years* (Armonk, N.Y.: Sharpe)
1997: "Macroeconomic Policy in Open Economies," in *Handbook of Comparative Economic Policies*, vol. 5 (Westport, Conn.: Greenwood)

A History of the Institutionalization of Feminist Economics through Its Tensions and Founders

Camila Orozco Espinel and Rebeca Gomez Betancourt

> I was a feminist before I was an economist.
> —Lourdes Benería, interview with the authors, October 20, 2019

1. Introduction

The term *feminist economics* was used by Barbara Bergmann in 1983 in an article published in *Academe*. Nevertheless, the term was not widely employed until the early 1990s, with the institutionalization of the field. At that moment, choosing the word *feminism* to name an association and a journal was risky. Since then, feminism has become a respectable word in public discourse, so much so that in 2017 *feminism* was designated "word of the year."[1] The desire of feminist economists

Correspondence may be addressed to Camila Orozco Espinel, Université de Reims Champagne-Ardenne, Regards, 57 bis, rue Pierre Taittinger, 51096 Reims, France (camila.orozco-espinel@univ-reims.fr); and to Rebeca Gomez Betancourt, Université Lumière Lyon 2, Triangle-MSH, 14 Avenue Berthelot, 69007 Lyon, France (rebeca.gomezbetancourt@univ-lyon2.fr). We gratefully acknowledge our interviewees; Kirsten Madden, Randy Albelda, Carole Boulai, Robert W. Dimand; the organizers and participants of the HOPE conference at Duke University in June 2021; the editors of this special issue; and two anonymous reviewers for their useful feedback.

1. "The 'word of the year' is defined based upon a statistical analysis of words that are looked up in extremely high numbers in our online dictionary while also showing a significant year-over-year increase in traffic" (www.merriam-webster.com).

History of Political Economy 54 (annual suppl.) DOI 10.1215/00182702-10085682
Copyright 2022 by Duke University Press

to get other scholars' attention in other fields and to be challenging to economists—they were interested in gender and equality, not just in women—explains the name of their association (International Association for Feminist Economics; IAFFE) and journal (*Feminist Economics*). They used the word *feminist* because this was precisely what the group had in common and why they were getting together, despite their differences. Indeed, like some other new research fields, feminist economics was produced by relatively diverse researchers under a single academic label.[2]

From the beginning, feminist economics questioned not just the organization of the economics discipline but its theory and methodology. In the context of second-wave feminism, the critique began with the microeconomics of the household and labor markets. Mainstream models were unable to explain the persistence of wage discrimination and the power dynamics within the household. Soon the critique spread to macroeconomics, international trade, development, and the feminization of poverty. Ultimately, feminist economics extended to all areas of traditional economic analysis.[3]

Here we aim to show the heterogeneity of the approaches that coexist under the umbrella of feminist economics and the porosity among them. We offer a picture of the field, explaining the process in which it develops and strengthens its identity through the creation of formal institutions. Our article is about the history of the institutionalization of feminist economics as seen by its foremost formal institution.[4] We take IAFFE and the journal *Feminist Economics* to be notable examples of such institutionalization. For doing this, we focus on three of the tensions faced by some feminist economists from IAFFE mainly in the United States. Although initially IAFFE meetings were held in the United States and its firsts members were based mainly in North America, from the beginning and throughout the years IAFFE has been an international organization, and feminist economics an international movement. This article is the first in

2. Feminist economics is rooted in critical work, and the concept predated the establishment of IAFFE. See, e.g., Phillips and Taylor 1980.

3. Pioneering works in the 1980s and 1990s from the Global South (see, e.g., Agarwal 1994; Deere and León 2001) insisted that development and poverty needed a gender perspective when studying wealth and asset inequalities. Also, there were some key intellectuals known in the West not calling themselves feminist economists, such as Marilyn Waring and Ester Boserup, before their research was spread to other countries.

4. On the history of other groups as feminist political economy in particular, see Rao and Akram-Lodhi 2020; Cohen 2018, 2019; Luxton and Bezanson 2006; Pietrykowski 2000; and Hartmann 1979. These histories are intertwined.

a series on how the international character of feminist economics shaped its development from the beginning and on how feminist economists formed and interacted as a community of scholars.[5]

We use interviews as our principal sources (like Emami-Olson 2002, Mata and Lee 2007, and Kim 2018), collecting in the process the oral histories of selected feminist economists. We conducted seventeen semistructured interviews (ten by video conference, six in person, and one by email) with academic feminist economists.[6] Our interviewees included authors active in the early years of the institutionalization of feminist economics, the founding editor of the journal *Feminist Economics*, and scholars based in different regions (India, Latin America, Australia, the United Kingdom).[7] Fourteen of these scholars were presidents of the International Association for Feminist Economics. The account that follows could be enriched by conducting more interviews, especially of other groups related to feminism in economics, closer to both heterodox and mainstream approaches, with little or no relation to IAFFE. Interviewing economists who are members of IAFFE but without explicit leadership responsibilities, and more widely the association's members, will also enrich our account, making even more explicit the heterogeneity and tension within the subfield.[8]

The literature on women economists has grown in recent years (e.g., Madden 2002; Dimand, Dimand, and Forget 2000; Madden and Dimand 2018), but no detailed histories of feminist economics have been written so far. The most complete study currently available is the *History of Feminist and Gender Economics*, by Giandomenica Becchio (2020), which contains a chapter on the origins of feminist economics. The only

5. Many scholars not based in the United States contributed to internationalizing IAFFE and the journal, especially organizing conferences and sessions periodically in the Global South.

6. Jean Shackelford, Myra Strober, Rhonda Sharp, Jane Humphries, Nancy Folbre, Lourdes Benería, Robin Bartlett, Edith Kuiper, Martha MacDonald, Cecilia Conrad, Joyce Jacobsen, Julie Nelson, Diana Strassmann, Carmen Diana Deere, Diane Elson, Alma Espino, and Bina Agarwal. We wish to make our interviews accessible on a website after interviewees' agreement.

7. We are currently writing an article on the international character of *Feminist Economics* in which the conference "Out of the Margin," held at the University of Amsterdam in 1993, played an important role.

8. Emami and Olson 2002, a collection of oral histories, is cohort-based, not restricted to academic economists, and focused on the personal experiences of women rather than institution building. It includes two deceased feminist economists (Marianne Ferber and Barbara Bergmann) and individuals we interviewed (Strober and Benería) but at an earlier time in this history. Our interviews are complementary.

pieces offering a history of IAFFE were written by IAFFE's first president, Jean Shackelford (1999), and founding members April Aerni and Julie Nelson (1995). Writings on feminist economics has grown, and its successes and limitations have been widely discussed by feminist economists and documented in articles and books as part of the institutionalization process (e.g., Ferber and Nelson 2003; Meulders 2001; Peterson and Lewis 1999; Barker and Kuiper 2003; Benería, Berik, and Floro 2015; Meagher and Nelson 2004).[9]

The originality of our contribution lies in telling this story based on the voices of the founders of the institution who represent the subfield. We listened and interacted with the protagonists, taking advantage of the fact that most of them well remember what still is a recent history. We recognize, however, the limits of memories and autobiographical stories for historical research (Forget 2002). We are aware of the limits of using interviews in history of economics, in particular the problem with false or wishful memories, the motives someone might have for wanting to be interviewed, and the possibility of expressing certain themes better in speech than in writing (see Jullien 2019 and Weintraub 2005). Because of this, we quoted only statements linked to our research question, and we kept out remembrances about personal relations and experiences beyond the institutionalization process. We also used as much as possible other written sources (in particular the history of other groups linked to feminist economics such as the Union for Radical Political Economics [URPE] and the recent secondary literature) to contrast and to complete the statements made by our interviewees.

Our work is also original in recognizing the importance of aspects that often remain hidden in some histories. Examples are conferences as spaces for the production of knowledge (Cherrier and Saïdi 2021); the role played by personal, social, and political values in the construction of IAFFE (Strassmann 1993); the diversity of topics and methodologies gathered under the same umbrella; and the cohesion of the community of feminist economics. These factors help explain the success of this field.

9. Information on the origins of feminist economics is scattered across personal archives in different places, mainly in the United States, Canada, and the Netherlands. There are no official available institutional archives either for IAFFE or *Feminist Economics*. Having said that, the David M. Rubenstein Rare Book & Manuscript Library at Duke University is in conversation with *Feminist Economics* about acquiring its archives.

2. Feminism and Feminist Economics: *L'air du temps*

The history of feminist economics as a subfield is closely linked with a larger history of feminism in economics. Feminism in economics existed before the subfield of feminist economics and before IAFFE.[10] In the twentieth century, there are two key historical and feminist movements for the economists who created IAFFE in the 1990s. The first is narrowly linked to the women's lib movement and the second wave of feminism starting in the late 1960s. The second arose from social science debates in the United States in the 1970s and 1980s and is linked to the creation of women's and gender studies,[11] the URPE Women's Caucus, and the Committee on the Status of Women in the Economics Profession. Both movements focused on equality and antidiscrimination.

So feminism was entirely in the air when the field's founders were young. Two important economists who were feminists were Marianne Ferber (1923–2013, PhD in 1954) and Bergmann (1927–2015, PhD in 1959). They were followed by Lourdes Benería (1937–, PhD in 1975) and Myra Strober (1940–, PhD in 1969), among others who finished their PhDs in the 1970s. They participated both orally (see ASSA conference programs) and in writing (articles and books; see the references and type of journals) in the central economic debates of their time. They were marked by the feminist movements mentioned above. Their feminism was also forged by personal readings and courses exploring the absence of women in the social sciences.[12] Some were also politically active in feminist movements, fighting for more rights for women and the family.

When we interviewed the leading founders of IAFFE, most of them explicitly affirmed they were feminists before becoming economists. They gave at least two complementary explanations for their feminism: on the one hand, their interest and engagement as feminists were the result of an intellectual process related to their education; on the other, their feminism evolved from a personal and political concern with concrete experiences. For example, Strassmann (interview with authors,

10. On the history of feminism in economics, see Pujol 1992; Albelda 1997; Mutari, Boushey, and Fraher 1997; and Cohen 2019. The history of feminism in economics was primarily based in URPE and URPE's Women's Caucus, and in the founding members of IAFFE.

11. On the link between women's studies and feminist economics, see Boxer 1998, Buker 2003, and Becchio 2020.

12. These courses started at sociology, political science, and philosophy departments before entering economics departments.

January 5, 2020) remembered reading a lot about feminism in her youth: Gloria Steinem and the feminist philosophers Helen Longino, Donna Haraway, and Sandra Harding. Shackelford as well as Strober participated in a reading group on feminist theory with some interdisciplinary scholars at her university.[13] Diane Elson (interview with authors, November 21, 2019) attributed her feminism to the education she received from a working-class mother who supported women's right to vote. Cecilia Conrad (interview with authors, January 5, 2020) stressed that "her feminism has no French influence. I was a feminist politically, I grew up in an activist family, in the context of the women's rights movement." For her, feminism was more than an intellectual approach coming from other social sciences or countries (i.e., Simone de Beauvoir); feminism was centered above all on political activism. From her youth Nancy Folbre was a political activist in favor of women's reproductive rights.

Elson encapsulates their position on feminism, explaining that being a feminist for her generation brought people together from different political backgrounds and allowed her to be part of a group: "When you're struggling for equal pay and antidiscrimination legislation, you can embrace a range of different feminist positions because antidiscrimination is something that people from a liberal position and a socialist position can unite to fight" (November 21, 2019).

These are some examples of economists who had earlier engaged feminist sociology, politics, and literature. They were also personally engaged in the fight for the rights of women and minorities, sometimes being directly affected by discrimination in their workplace. The kind of feminism that these economists represented in the 1990s was united in its criticism of the androcentric bias in society and academe. According to Sheba Tejani (2019: 99), in the beginning, as feminists, they generally adopted a social constructivist position. They retained a "notion of objectivity which they claim might be improved by high standards of social criticism, diversity, and space for the expression of alternate points of view or by utilizing women's perspectival advantage, partial though it is, in the production of knowledge" (Tejani 2019: 99).

13. Strober shared with us her personal readings on feminism: the American suffragist Elizabeth Cady Stanton, inspiring work by Simone de Beauvoir, Betty Friedan's *Feminine Mystique*, *Pride and Prejudice* by Jane Austen, and the treatment Toni Morrison gave of slavery in her novel *Beloved* (November 21, 2019; and Strober 2016).

3. How Did These Feminists and Economists Become Feminist Economists?

Although the women we interviewed shared similar feminist back-grounds, the intellectual sources of their feminist economics and their first publications seem more diverse. Before the field's institutionalization in the 1990s, the Danish economist Ester Boserup (1970) wrote a systematic study of women's wages and living conditions, documenting that women fared worse than men in both areas. This study inspired many feminist economists, including Benería, Carmen Diana Deere, Heidi Hartmann, and Folbre. Other economists built their feminist economics mainly in opposition to Gary Becker's theories; examples are Bergmann, Ferber, and Blau. All of these women finally became recognized as feminist economists whose work dealt with the "study of gender roles in the economy" and "biases in the focus and methodology of economics" (Nelson 2008).

After Boserup, the most commonly used works by our interviewees in courses and articles on women and economics were published by self-identified feminist economists; these works include Benería's *Women and Development: The Sexual Division of Labor in Rural Societies* (1982); Bergmann's *Economic Emergence of Women* (1986); Ferber and Blau's *Economics of Women, Men, and Work* (1986); and Ferber's *Women and Work, Paid and Unpaid* (1987). These books focused on development, labor, and gender economics, placing women at the center of their analysis. In 1988, Marilyn Waring published *If Women Counted: A New Feminist Economics*, which came to be considered, alongside the titles listed above, a foundational work of feminist economics. These works can be considered landmarks in the literature of feminist economics, and they were frequently referenced by the next generation of feminist economists who finished their PhDs in economics in the early 1980s and started publishing their own articles and books in the 1990s.[14]

14. These works are "foundational and landmarks" because of the number of quotations (we are currently working on this for another article) but also, as it came out from the interviews, because other feminist economists used them for pedagogical and research purposes (see interviews with Nelson, Humphries, Espino, Bartlett, on demand), and their books and articles were translated and used in many syllabi (http://www.iaffe.org/pages/resources/syllabus/).

To understand how they built feminist economics, let us consider the first tension that arose when these feminists with different economic backgrounds started meeting at ASSA conferences.

4. First Tension: The Mainstream's Rejection of Feminist Work

Some tensions contributed to the formation of IAFFE. The first tension that we found is about why and how IAFFE came into existence as the product of conflicts in the discipline of economics. The necessity to create a formal institution like IAFFE came in response to the mainstream's rejection of feminist work in economics. Feminist economists wanted more equality in all spheres of the economy and society, including children and all genders, races, and sexualities, using other methods and approaches. This tension appeared before the creation of IAFFE (1992) and the journal *Feminist Economics* (1994) and persists to some extent today.

IAFFE is a professional association that met the need and desire for an active, nonsexist organization for feminists in economics in a context in which that work was marginalized because of sexism in the discipline. In that sense, it is similar to and could be understood as a continuation of the work done by feminists to form the URPE Women's Caucus. To understand this tension, it is essential to study the role played by some young women economists in AEA meetings during the late 1980s and early 1990s and see how different factions emerged. As paradoxical as it may seem, the foremost society in mainstream economics was the place where the founders of this new institution initially met every year to exchange their critical views on the discipline (Livingstone 2003).

The first group promoting feminist work in economics in the United States, URPE's Women's Caucus, was formed in the early 1970s by URPE members, mainly Paddy Quick, Marianne Hill, Benería, Hartmann, Francine Blau, and Folbre. With other women economists and motivated by their dissatisfaction with mainstream economists, they created the Committee on the Status of Women in the Economics Profession.[15] Although CSWEP sought to improve the condition of women in the

---

15. "On 29 December 1971 a group of women calling itself the Women's Caucus brought before the Executive Committee of the American Economic Association a series of resolutions designed to equalize opportunities for women in economics" (Forget 2011). On CSWEP, see also Kim 2018 and Bartlett 1998.

profession, it was not at all interested in challenging the mainstream approach that dominated economics. As a result, some members of CSWEP began to look for a new home. Cohen (2019), Kim (2018), and recently Chassonnery-Zaïgouche, Cherrier, and Singleton (2020) tell the story of the role played by URPE's Women's Caucus in giving birth to CSWEP in the 1970s and in forming a group of feminist economists in the late 1980s. They explain that in practice, there would be no CSWEP without the URPE Women's Caucus, and it is entirely possible that there would not be an IAFFE, since many of the founding members came from URPE. Our story here is more focused on what took place during the ASSA conferences in which scholars promoting feminist work in economics could be encountered, and through which they built feminist economics and IAFEE. Meeting at conferences and finding each other through articles and collaborative projects characterized the consolidation of a knowledge base in feminist economics during the late 1980s and early 1990s, when the scholars working on feminist economics topics were scattered around the world.

When we studied the programs of the ASSA annual meetings from the 1970s until the late 1980s, we could not find any reference to feminism in the title of any panels or papers, and we found only a few references to the role of women in the profession (mainly in URPE sessions). From 1988 and until 1992, however, much of the energy given to the institutionalization of feminist economics happened in informal interactions in the hallways and rooms where the conferences took place. In the histories of IAFFE there is no mention of these panels prior to 1990. Before studying the AEA programs and interviewing these feminist economists, we could not find any explicit connection between these panels and the organization of feminist economists as a group.

Neither the internationalization of IAFFE as an organization nor the development of feminist economics as a field was a linear process, where first feminist economists from and based in the United States were active, then Europeans joined, and finally scholars from the Global South played a role. IAFFE was conceptualized from the start as an *international* association; and substantial research by feminist economists outside the United States long preceded its founding. Conspicuously, feminist development economics was well established before the founding of IAFFE.[16]

16. The workshop on the "subordination of women" at the Institute of Development Studies at Sussex University in 1978 was key for these networks both in Europe and in the Global

Likewise, in 1989 the International Economic Association Conference had numerous panels on feminist economics.[17]

4.1. Where, When, and How Did They (Future Feminist Economists) Meet?

The international conferences were the sites where theories but also tools and practices were built through bringing various intellectuals together (Cherrier and Saïdi 2021). In the interviews, they told us that if it had not been for the ASSA conferences, they would not probably have met as often they did. The December 1988 meeting, in New York, was the first meeting to feature a sizable number of sessions on gender and feminist topics. Benería reported that she met Bergmann, Blau, and Strassmann at this meeting. Benería presented a paper in an URPE session titled "Studies on Gender, Work, and Welfare." Bergmann and Blau presented in an AEA session titled "Equal Employment Opportunity for Women in the 1980s," while Strassmann gave a communication titled "Occupational Choice and Asymmetric Mobility." Then in 1989 at least two meetings reunited some of the future founders of IAFFE: the Southern Economic Association conference in Orlando and the ASSA in Atlanta, where Ferber and Nelson organized a session titled "Feminism and Economic Argument."[18]

Why was it so important to meet in the same place? These sessions and the articles presented there led to the founding book of the subfield, the so-called manifesto, *Beyond Economic Man*, by Ferber and Nelson, as well as to the creation of the association and journal, with scholars coming from different backgrounds.[19]

South. Papers at the workshop were given by Bina Agarwal, Lourdes Benería, Carmen Diana Deere, Diane Elson, and Ruth Pearson (see *IDS Bulletin* 10, no. 3, https://bulletin.ids.ac.uk /index.php/idsbo/issue/view/178).

17. As a result, the book *Women and Work in the World Economy* (edited by Nancy Folbre, Barbara Bergmann, Bina Agarwal, and Maria Floro) was published.

18. The following economists participated in the session: Nelson ("Sex, Gender, and Economic Research"), Donald N. McCloskey ("Feminine Science and the Dismal Science"), and Lisa J. Brown ("The Economics of Gender vs. Gender in Economics"). Strassmann ("Gender Roles, Discrimination, and Quit Rates"), Folbre, and Conrad also attended these ASSA meetings.

19. See interviews with Elson (22:55), Strassmann (1:28), Benería (00:43), and Folbre (00:58), who consider this book the founding work of the subfield of feminist economics. In Folbre's words (interview, January 5, 2020), "Marianne Ferber and Julie Nelson took the lead. It was an explicit kind of effort to advance the feminist economic project."

The idea of creating an international association for feminist economics was first formally discussed at the 1990 AEA conference in
Washington, D.C. In almost all the interviews we conducted, the feminist economists described the panel held on December 28, 1990, as a
foundational moment. Strassmann titled this session "Can Feminism
Find a Home in Economics?" "It was the only session at that conference with the word 'feminism' in the title and more than 100 of us
packed ourselves into the room and stood in the hall outside to hear.
Jean and I passed around a signup sheet and we went home with a list
of 87 of people interested in feminist economics" (Aerni and Nelson
1995: 1). As we saw in the program conferences they organized, feminist economists made an effort to keep up a conversation with some
mainstream economists.

Shackelford and Aerni thought that "this session would be the perfect
place where we could gather signatures from invited members of the audience to sign up for a new network with an explicitly feminist slant"
(Shackelford, interview with authors, June 17, 2020). On the same day,
URPE organized a session titled "The Rhetoric of Economics: Marxist
and Feminist Perspectives," chaired by Folbre.

The new group of feminist economists held no sessions at the ASSA in
1991; that year was dedicated to creating and developing the network.
According to Shackelford, there was no place where people who were
doing feminist and economics research could meet, could send a note, and
say "I want to present a paper"—a place where they could be heard, a safe
spot, outside the standard conferences. There was a desire for conversation with like-minded economists. A kind of division of labor appeared
among some feminist economists: some scholars who were more established in the AEA, like Nelson and Strassmann, organized sessions on
feminist economics during the ASSA meeting, and Shackelford created
the Femecon network as a (free) electronic discussion group (and the list
of members, Femecon-L); it went online in December 1991.[20] Shackelford's
initial thought was to create an international network of people interested
in discussing feminist economics during the year and between the conferences. This was before they had an organization (or even the name of an

20. The list was labeled under section J (Labor and Demographic Economics) by the AEA,
and the information for submission was (and is still) posted on the AEA webpage. The contact
person was Shackelford. After 1992, one could also join IAFFE and receive (by mail) the
IAFFE newsletter and conference announcements. See https://www.aeaweb.org/rfe/showRes
.php?rfe_id=395&cat_id=27.

organization) of feminist economists, but it was an important step that allowed instant communication around the world.[21]

In the interviews, Shackelford, Nelson, Strassmann, and Benería acknowledge that the connection they established, and the work of the previous year allowed them to participate in five sessions at the 1992 ASSA conference in New Orleans, treating some women and economics topics as well as feminist economics. These sessions were organized jointly with some feminist political economists from URPE who helped concretize IAFFE's position in the ASSA. The main topics were "Feminism and the Boundaries of Economics," "Alternative Pedagogies and Economic Education," and "The Status of Women in Changing Economies."[22] During this meeting, the Committee on the Status of Women in the Economics Profession agreed to let the group on the Shackelford list use their rooms for a first meeting. After this, they went to Ralph & Kacoo's, a southern food restaurant in the French Quarter, to choose a name for the society and brainstorm its future structure and activities.

4.2. Tensions among Economists during the ASSA Conferences

These first sessions at the ASSA conferences were crucial for the institutionalization of feminist economics. Conferences were essential to get to know other scholars and organize as a group. They were the first steps toward more formal institutions such as IAFFE and the journal.[23] For most of the feminist economists, ASSA meetings proved a propitious space to meet and work. As Béatrice Cherrier and Aurélien Saïdi (2021) argued, conferences can be weapons of mass dissemination, whereby theories and practices are sent out to colleagues, opponents,

---

21. Some published articles refer to intellectual exchanges that took place through the Femecon-L list.

22. Participants in these sessions included Ferber and Nelson, Strassmann, and Brian Cooper. They invited Robert Solow and Robert Clower as discussants. The URPE session that year was also on feminist economics with papers by Benería and Maria Floro, while the joint AEA-ACES session was on the status of women in changing economies, chaired by Ferber.

23. The benefits obtained and their experience with the ASSA meetings and the AEA were different than those of older academic societies, like URPE and AFEE (Association for Evolutionary Economics). And at the same time, the age and context were not the same for these groups (the 1960s for AFEE, the 1970s for URPE, and the 1990s for IAFFE), and also their goals differed.

and institutions. These panels also served to gain visibility, for the formation of networks and communities of like-minded scholars and also the exclusion of others. Since 1992, when created, IAFFE started to evolve as a separate institution from CSWEP but has maintained a bond with the AEA for all these years, which allows organizing panels at their meetings every year.

The debate on gender parity (CSWEP), on the one hand, and criticism of the current economic system (URPE and part of IAFFE), on the other, provide examples of what later became two distinct subfields in economics: the well-established gender in economics and the newborn feminist economics, respectively. These two groups developed separately and pursued different aims. Feminist economists were interested in promoting feminist discussions that went beyond discrimination in the economics job market between women and men, which was CSWEP's main concern. To many in the group, CSWEP was not feminist enough (Strober, interview with authors, November 21, 2019). In the words of Chassonnery-Zaïgouche, Cherrier, and Singleton (2020: 34), "As the most contentious aspect of women's research on gender-related issues moved out of CSWEP, what remained had, by the early 1990s, become more mainstream and moderate . . . as well as less central." IAFFE and more generally feminist economics followed a separate path.

4.3. Naming What They Were Doing: An International Association for Feminist Economics

After the meeting in New Orleans, feminist economists began to move away from CSWEP, and in a certain way from URPE, creating their own society. The official creation of IAFFE is marked by the organization of the first conference at American University, in Washington, D.C., by Bergmann and Shackelford in July 1992. Shackelford, who became the first IAFFE president, accepted at the beginning an enormous administrative and community-building challenge. As she told us, "I was the one everyone called if they needed anything. Barbara called me the founding president" (Shackelford, interview with authors, June 17, 2020). To officially create the society affiliated with the Allied Social Science Associations, Shackelford asked the AEA what it needed: "They said something like, 100 dues paying members and bylaws, and then you could have panels at the ASSA meetings. So, during that spring before the conference, me, Iona, April we met in Washington, and we sort of set out the bylaws" (interview with authors, June 17, 2020).[24] The first board of the society had five officers: a president, a president-elect, and three vice presidents. Enlisted representatives from many different places and selections for the first boards were easy: "Someone came up with a nomination list and so we elected them right there" (Shackelford, interview with authors, June 17, 2020). IAFFE was created as a non-profit international association dedicated "to raising awareness and inquiry of feminist economics."[25] Members of IAFFE asked later for the legal advice of lawyers to revise and create appropriate bylaws for an organization legally established in the United States but with an international scope.[26]

The year after, in January 1993, and with the help of their colleagues from URPE and CSWEP, feminist economists organized the first three official IAFFE sessions at the ASSA conference in Anaheim. Their aim to explicitly expose their views is shown by the titles of the panels: "Can Feminist Thought Improve Economic Conversations?," "What Is Feminist Economics?," and "Feminism and Postmodernism in Economics." From 1993 until now, IAFFE has organized three to four sessions every year at the ASSA meetings. IAFFE never boycotted the meetings (as URPE did) and has always held its business meeting there.[27]

Another foundational moment was the "Out of the Margin" conference held in Amsterdam in 1993 and organized by Jolande Sap, Edith Kuiper, and a group of students under the supervision of the foundation Out of the

24. "IAFFE is independent of the AEA, and open not only to female and male economists but to academics from other fields, as well as activists who are not academics" (Ferber and Nelson 2003: 7).

25. According to Becchio 2020 and Aerni and Nelson 1995, IAFFE was created in New Orleans, but the election of the first board, the vote on the bylaws, the registration of members happened in Washington, D.C., during the first conference. The IAFFE mission statement is at http://www.iaffe.org/pages/about-iaffe/miss/.

26. As part of the process of institutionalization, one of the most important sources of funding was the Ford Foundation, as well as the Swedish International Development Agency (SIDA). Part of these funds were used to encourage the presence of scholars from the Global South in IAFFE. This helped diversify IAFFE's governance and conferences from very early on.

27. "A specially memorable meeting was the IAFFE-ASSA meeting on gender equality in 1999. We had a completely full Ballroom at 8 am on a cold New York morning. As I recall Barbara saying, Gary Becker agreed to join the panel if she could ensure no one threw eggs or tomatoes at him from the audience!" (Agarwal, pers. comm., February 25, 2022). The meeting was presided over by Strassmann, and Agarwal, Arrow, Bergmann, Becker, Ashenfelter, and Folbre participated.

Margin, with board members Jolande Sap, Edith Kuiper, Rose Kuiper, and the leader of the left-wing party, Ina Brouwer. Although, as we saw with the 1978 workshop on the "subordination of women," feminist economics had already had a presence in Europe before, the Amsterdam conference served to build links between feminist economists in different European countries and was an important marker of the international character of the organization of IAFFE. Other markers were the panels organized in 1995 at the United Nations Women's Conference in Beijing with a significant presence of feminist economists from twenty-nine different countries from the South and the North.[28]

4.4. A Second Institution: The Creation of the Journal *Feminist Economics*

When Shackelford sent the first messages through the Femecon list, many people answered, saying that they wanted a journal. Strassmann took the lead for this task: "She contacted publishers, she put together a huge document, with the would-be editors, the kinds of topics that would be addressed, the reasons for having a journal, what libraries would be interested in it, etc." (Shackelford, interview with authors, June 17, 2020).

In 1994 the journal was created, with Strassmann as founding editor. The first issues of *Feminist Economics* in 1995 contained articles that clearly defined a scope for feminist inquiry well beyond the gender pay gap.

In the beginning, the journal was an open home for research on feminist economics in a broad sense while showing pressures among scholars asking for a more feminist political economy, more applied economics, more gender economics. It was instrumental in making the work of feminist economists visible and accessible. The journal was also instrumental in shaping the international character of IAFFE.[29]

The journal, the international association, and the first publications were the fruit of these encounters in conferences. Despite the differences with CSWEP, and the points in common with URPE, feminist economists formed a group and created their own field. These two institutions helped

28. Bina Agarwal set up the committee that organized these panels, organized several of them, and raised the funds that made IAFFE members' presence in Beijing possible.

29. Several members from the Global South served as associate editors, editorial advisory board members, paper writers, reviewers, and promoters of subscriptions in libraries of the Global South.

IAFFE to face this first tension in relation to the resistance of mainstream economics to accept feminism, so feminist economics started to flourish. As Nelson (2020: 223–24) wrote, "During the early 1990s, I was fortunate to be in on the blossoming of the field of feminist economics. Through articles published here and there, the circulation of working papers, sessions at various conferences, and dedicated organizing activity by a few, we started to find each other."

5. Second Tension: Feminist Economics Methodology and Feminist Critique

By the early 1990s, feminist economists were advancing a thoroughgoing critique that incorporated feminist scholarly insights from the 1980s questioning the implicit male bias of "objective" social science frameworks (Keller 1985). Mobilizing this literature, feminist economists raised epistemological and ontological questions about the mainstream's definition of the economy (as limited to the market), its central image of "economic man" (as a rational, autonomous, self-interested agent, successfully making optimizing choices), and the exclusive use of a particular set of tools (formalization, modelization, and abstraction based on mathematics) (Nelson 1993; Woolley 1993). Folbre's (1994) work on *care* exemplifies well how this epistemological and ontological critique was applied from the early 1990s to analyze economic issues. Indeed, the introduction of caring labor challenges the traditional image of "economic man" as an autonomous, self-interested individual who neither requires care nor has any inclination to provide it and, at the same time, contests the definition of the economy as limited to market interactions.[30]

In addition, feminist economists were developing a critique of mainstream empirical methods. For them, the standards for data collection and analysis in mainstream economics created difficulties in dealing with feminist concerns (MacDonald 1995). To respond to these constraints, feminist economists engaged in empirical research took two different yet overlapping paths. First was the collection of new kinds of data (such as detailed time diaries) and the measurement of previously unmeasured economic phenomena (such as women's unpaid work). Second was the use

---

30. Work on *care* should also be connected to research on *reproductive* labor carried out, during the 1970s and early 1980s, by Marxist economists who later joined IAFFE (i.e., Benería, Hartmann, and Sue Himmelweit).

of qualitative methods borrowed from other social sciences, including survey research, case studies, historical studies, and interviews. For many feminist economists, both during the institutionalization of the field and today, by following these two paths they helped create and promote adequate economic practices, whether or not the topic being studied was explicitly gender related.

Yet economists are neither trained nor rewarded for this kind of work— which could explain why feminist economics is frequently considered exclusively a heterodox approach to economics (Becchio 2020) or even as not belonging to the discipline at all, as we show in the next section. Nevertheless, feminist economics is not a homogeneous field, and feminist economists use a variety of methodologies, adapting them to their own purposes. Some feminist economists make use of traditional mainstream tools, others do not (Nelson 2008: 3). Overall, the field is characterized by the inclusion of a broader range of methods, as was often highlighted during our interviews. For instance, to describe the field, our interviewees employed metaphors such as "broad umbrella" or "big umbrella" and "Venn diagram." Moreover, this methodological heterogeneity was presented as "something good and healthy" (Jane Humphries, interview by authors, online, July 16, 2020) or even as "one of the main strengths of feminist economics" (Rhonda Sharp, interview by authors, online, January 3, 2020). Sharp compared feminist economics to a bowerbird, an Austro-Papuan bird that collects trinkets, particularly shiny objects, to put in its nest: "I think feminist economics sort of gathers up what it perceives to be good ideas from elsewhere, no matter if some of that is the mainstream at the time or not" (interview by authors, January 3, 2020).

This heterogeneity existed from the beginning of the institutionalization process of IAFFE. During the early 1990s some of those coming from a Marxist feminist tradition were hesitant to join the group. They "were concerned with how the more neoclassical approach and the more political economy approach to gender would play out" (MacDonald, interview by authors, online, July 16, 2020). As Benería, who was deeply involved with URPE at the time, told us, "I didn't join [IAFFE] at the beginning because I didn't want to join another orthodox women's group. American economists are mostly neoclassical economists and then I thought that [IAFFE] was like Barbara Bergmann, I mean interesting but orthodox and not lefty" (interview by authors, Barcelona, October 20, 2019). And yet some of them joined. Frustration about economics' resistance to including feminist perspectives played a key role here. As Folbre told us,

> We were all very different, methodologically, but that didn't matter because we shared such a common frustration with the profession's resistance to any kind of feminist theory or feminist activism. Then, we just sort of made a pact, that we were not going to insist on any one methodology or have any requirement, there's no loyalty oath or litmus test to be going to the organization and so, it was always pretty diverse. I came from a kind of Marxist feminist tradition, but most people did not, most people came from a more kind of institutional or neoclassical or postmodernist tradition. (Interview by authors, San Diego, January 5, 2020)

Identification, self-identification, and more generally typologies and labels are political in character and largely derive from interactions (Bourdieu 1980). They are all built from the outside as well as from the inside, serving different and changing purposes.

To capture the methodological heterogeneity of feminist economics—while considering how individual positions influenced both identification by others and self-identification—we can present the group along a continuum between the mainstream and the heterodoxy of economics (fig. 1). At one end—but alienated from feminist principles—we have (mainstream) economists who are feminists. These "(mainstream) economists and feminists" neither have a public presence in the feminist economics community nor identify as feminist economists. In institutional terms, members of this group are more likely to occupy positions of prestige and influence within the discipline (Conrad 2018: 126–27). We can place in this first category economists working on gender or other topics associated with CSWEP such as Carolyn Shaw Bell.

At the mainstream end of the feminist economics' spectrum, we have "feminist economists using mainstream tools." These economists could use the language and methods of mainstream economics but self-identify as feminist economists and have a public presence in the feminist economics community. For "feminist economists using mainstream tools," feminist economics analysis is an expansion of mainstream economics more than a correction (Strober 1994: 143). As Strober, who for us belongs in this category, told us, "At the beginning the main concern was the transformation of labor market policies and not of the discipline itself" (interview by authors, online, November 21, 2019).

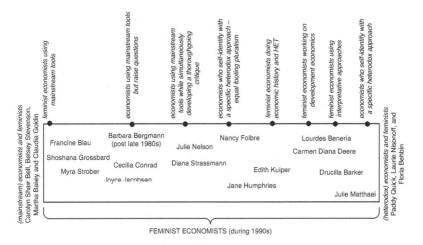

Figure 1. Methodological heterogeneity: Feminist economics spectrum, 1990s.

By associating these names with a single category, we are not implying that their work and trajectories are all alike and that we can place them on a single point of the spectrum.[31] Contrarywise, their differences illustrate the importance of using a continuum to represent the heterogeneity that characterized feminist economics during its institutionalization process (and with new nuances characterizing it still today), rather than using independent, uniform, and nonoverlapping categories. Some economists use mainstream methods for critical arguments. Likewise, the names and categories we devised are not exhaustive; there are other names and categories that might have been included. Moreover, we are conscious that no one ever fits precisely into any category; people are complex and professional trajectories are long, so positions can change over time. Perhaps more important, the people we chose as examples may not agree with our classification. We use the spectrum, the categories, and the examples we chose to highlight the different methodological positions that coexisted within feminist economics during its institutionalization process. We are aware of the fact that what is "mainstream" at one point in time may be heterodox—or vice versa—at another point in time.

For some "feminist economists using mainstream tools," using the language and the methods of the mainstream was part of a professional

31. For instance, Shoshana Grossbard's work is very close to Becker's. Blau was one of the original members of URPE's Women's Caucus but did not maintain her affiliation with URPE.

strategy in a discipline dominated by a strong mainstream—rather than the result of a deep belief in the superiority of mainstream methods. For instance, some feminist economists make use of mainstream theories or econometric models at the beginning of their careers and start using a broad set of methods and even other theoretical frameworks once they secure a tenured position.

Between the "feminist economists using mainstream tools" and the "feminist economists who self-identify with a specific heterodox approach" are two categories: "feminist economists who use mainstream tools but raise questions" about the ability of such tools used alone, and "feminist economists who use mainstream tools while simultaneously developing a thoroughgoing critique of them." Examples of the first category might be Bergmann's work from the late 1980s.[32] These feminist economists highlight fundamental problems with the underlying assumptions of econometrics and explore them from a feminist perspective, encouraging increased investigation into the social, political, and institutional structures of gender. As Conrad, who identifies as a "mainstream economist who questions the models of the dominant theory," told us, "We're still pretty much in the economics mode: you develop a theory, and you test the theory with the data and the data can be qualitative maybe, but we still have a struggle with that. This is part of what defines us as economists, we still take that approach" (interview by authors, San Diego, January 5, 2020). Likewise, these feminist economists tend to believe that pluralism, understood as a movement that acknowledges the primacy of the neoclassical tradition but also argues for multiple strands of active contraposition, is congruent with feminist economics (Jacobsen 2020: 9).

In the second category are feminist economists like Nelson. Nelson had published in the top mainstream journals while developing in parallel an ontological, epistemological, and methodological critique of mainstream economics using feminist theory. These economists have the quantitative skills that the discipline requires,[33] and in their view the discipline needs their presence; the legitimacy of their critique and work comes from the fact that they operate from inside the discipline. Another economist in this

---

32. On the evolution of Bergmann's work, see Small, this volume.

33. This does not imply that those economists who work in noneconomics departments, either because they opted out or because they were pushed out, did it on the grounds of being unskilled economists.

category might be Strassmann, who graduated from Harvard with a dissertation on pricing strategies on airlines and wrote on methodology.

The diversity among feminist economists in the more mainstream segment of our spectrum is also there on the heterodox side. Feminist economics heterodox approaches include institutionalist economics, social economics, Marxist economics, ecological economics, Post Keynesian economics, and interpretative approaches such as post-postmodernism and more recently postcolonialism. Moreover, throughout its almost thirty years of existence, IAFFE has regularly collaborated with various heterodox organizations. As we saw in the previous section, the birth of IAFFE is closely linked to URPE's Women's Caucus, and, as suggested by Jennifer Cohen (2019: 97–98), the seven special issues of the *Review of Radical Political Economy* devoted to the political economy of women established the building blocks of feminism in economics. Over the years, the two associations continued to organize joint sessions at ASSA. Likewise, IAFFE frequently organizes joint sessions in different venues with other heterodox organizations, including the Association for Social Economics, the Association for the Study of Generosity in Economics, and the Association for Evolutionary Economics.

During the early 1990s feminist economists who self-identify with heterodox approaches were very active in these heterodox associations. As one of our interviewees told us, "At the beginning of IAFFE a lot of us came through URPE, we were really involved and sort of pillars in that association" (Deere, interview by authors, San Diego, January 3, 2020). It is thus not surprising that heterodox feminist economists, on the one hand, "felt outside of mainstream economics long before [they] clearly identified as feminist economists," as Martha MacDonald, former president of IAFFE who was also close to URPE, told us; on the other hand, they did not and do not spend much energy trying to influence or criticize the mainstream. The targets of their critics are heterodox approaches themselves. Indeed, heterodox feminist economists argued that heterodox approaches were constructed with gender biases akin to those of mainstream economics (Cohen 2018, 2019).

We can separate feminist "economists who self-identify with various heterodox approaches" into two categories. The first is those who argue for a form of pluralism that encompasses, on an equal footing, all kinds of approaches under the umbrella of feminist economics. Economists in this category might be Folbre. The second is those who see any collaboration between feminist economists and mainstream economists as impossible, given the former's critique of the latter. For this last group, only within the heterodoxy can emancipatory projects such as feminism bloom. Particularly at the beginning of the institutionalization process of IAFFE, there was some push to found feminist economics on the basis of only heterodox lines of work (Matthaei 1996), but none of them really held sway. In this category of feminist economists might be Julie Matthaei.

We can place on the heterodox side of the spectrum three additional categories of feminist economists. First, "feminist economists working on development economics." Although most of the feminist economists in this category (active in the 1990s and before) self-identify with heterodox approaches (such as Carmen Diana Deere, Lourdes Benería, and Diane Elson), some use mainstream tools. Second, "feminist economists doing economic history" (such as Jane Humphries) and "history of economic thought" (such as Edith Kuiper and Michèle Pujol). Third, "feminist economists using interpretative approaches" such as post-postmodernism and more recently postcolonialism (such as Drucilla Barker, Suzanne Bergeron, and S. Charusheela).

Finally, at the heterodox edge of the spectrum—but alienated from feminist principles—we have (heterodox) economists who are feminists. While these "(heterodox) economists and feminists" do not identify as feminist economists and are not active members of IAFFE, they have closer links with IAFEE than "(mainstream) economists and feminist," and some of them have a public presence in the feminist economics community. We can place in this category for example members of the URPE Women's Caucus who never officially joined IAFFE or did it just for a single conference like Paddy Quick.[34]

6. Third Tension: Within or Out of Economics

Being a feminist affects the experiences of women academics (Edwards 2000). Feminist scholars may face a double bind: simultaneously retain a feminist ethos and build a career within mainstream academia (Jenkins 2014). Feminist economists are particularly exposed to this double bind, which can call into question their place and permanence in the discipline. On the one hand, economics is the most male-dominated of the social

---

34. The difficulty of finding members of the URPE Women's Caucus who never officially joined IAFFE is telling of the overlaps between the feminists in URPE and IAFFE, and between "feminist economics" and "feminist political economy."

sciences—as CSWEP reports from 1972 to 2020 show.[35] For many years, sexism and even misogyny have been a common experience of many women in economics (Wu 2017). On the other hand, while feminist economics—together with other feminist groups in the discipline—has worked to change (at least partially) the discourse about women and gender in economics, the more fundamental questions advanced by feminist economist have received little attention (Ferber and Nelson 2003: 11).

From the start of the institutionalization process, the feminist economics critique and its contributions had more of a hearing among the practitioners of public policy. International organizations are perhaps some of the major places where feminist economics ideas have been heard and applied (Kuiper and Barker 2006). The social sciences and the humanities have as well been an important audience for the work of feminist economists. Yet developing effective interdisciplinary collaboration between economics and other social sciences requires more than a desire. It implies overcoming certain obstacles: the disciplinary structure of academe, the insularity of economics and economists' vision of the economy as not embedded in society. Moreover, as we mention in section 4, economists have been for many decades neither trained nor rewarded for collaborating with other social scientists, especially when those collaborations involve the use of qualitative methods (Lenger 2019). While the use of qualitative methods is not common to all feminist economists, as we also showed in section 4, qualitative research techniques—as much as the challenges to the discipline that the feminist critique implies—are at the heart of the debate about whether feminist economists are a part of economics at all. Indeed, both the tendency of mainstream economists to define economics through a set of assumptions and methods (Hopkins 2012: 489–91) and their conviction that "[capturing] complex social processes through equations or clear-cut causality [is] evidence of the discipline's superior scientific commitments" (Fourcade, Ollion, and Algan 2015: 92) exclude from the discipline those questioning the assumptions and using alternative methods.

Real consequences exist for those who depart from canonical practices. It is thus not surprising that many members of IAFFE faced resistance in

---

35. See American Economic Association, "CSWEP: Annual Reports," https://www.aeaweb .org/about-aea/committees/cswep/survey/annual-reports.

their departments when they tried to research economic issues from a feminist perspective (Strober 2016). Several of our interviewees recalled experiences of harassment, bullying, not getting tenure, and even getting fired by universities because their peers considered their work as not being economics.[36] MacDonald's experience illustrates well the situation. In 1992, after becoming full professor of economics at Saint Mary's University in Canada, one of MacDonald's colleagues shared with her the resistance expressed by other members of the economics department during the tenure committee's meetings. While there was a consensus that she "had done enough work to be a Full Professor," some members of the committee were opposed to granting her the rank in economics. As she told us during our interview, "Some of my economists' colleagues didn't see the work that I have done in interdisciplinary projects and the use I made of qualitative methods as economics" (interview by authors, online, July 16, 2020).

In its early years, IAFFE was regarded as a "safe spot." As Shackelford, first president of the association, told us, "At the beginning our focus was to create a safe spot for people who were looking at economics through the feminist lens, to create a place where they could be heard and do research" (interview by authors, online, June 17, 2020). Vis-à-vis the mainstream, the institutionalization of feminist economics established the conditions that, for almost three decades, have made it possible for many economists working on gender-related issues from a feminist perspective to stay in the discipline. The creation of a venue to publish has been from the 1990s key for many feminist economists to foster their careers within economics. Indeed, the difficulties that feminist economists were having developing their careers within the discipline were closely related to the difficulties many of them were having publishing in economic journals, whether because they were using methods outside the mainstream toolbox or because they were questioning economic theory.

Strassmann saw the journal from the very beginning as a necessary step to claim that feminist work in economics was, of course, important but, first and foremost, that it belongs in the discipline. For Strassmann, who was editor for almost thirty years, during the creation process the main question was strategical: How to place the journal so that it could publish the type of feminist research frequently excluded from the

36. At least four of our interviewees (Strober, Nelson, Kuiper, and Strassmann) were discriminatory tenure cases. See Nelson 2009.

discipline yet still count as economics? More concretely, how to publish research critical for women's lives in a discipline where a tight management from the top down fostered intellectual uniformity and excluded those who questioned the canon? The journal *Feminist Economics* was intended as an intervention into the field, an intervention that certainty sought to subject standard economic theory to critical scrutiny, but whose emphasis was on being "heard by people in the mainstream," as Strassmann told us during our interview. During the early years of the journal, two elements made the intended intervention successful. The first was recruiting four Nobel Prize laureates to join the editorial board; the laureates "didn't do any substantive work; they just lent their names" to enhance the credibility vis-à-vis those who "have all the power in the discipline" (interview by authors, San Diego, January 5, 2020). The second was developing "a multipronged publishing strategy," as Strassmann called it during our interview, aiming to enhance research on gender-related topics that the mainstream had traditionally not considered important, using both standard and nonstandard methods.

Yet, for some feminist economists, in particular those placed in the *mainstream segment* of our spectrum, standard and nonstandard methods do not have the same ability to draw the attention of the mainstream to the feminist critique.[37] For Bina Agarwal (2016: 375–80), a feminist challenge to the mainstream is more likely to be effective if it uses some branch of mainstream theory as a building block and lends itself to formal modeling and empirical testing. (It is worth mentioning that since the late 1970s, Agarwal has used a distinctly heterodox approach [a political economy framework]. Her work has challenged the mainstream methodologically, empirically, and data wise.) Maintaining the journal as a venue for this kind of research has made it possible for many feminist economists to publish their work in an economics journal and have this count toward their promotion in an economics department. It has also allowed feminist economics to influence the way in which economists do research (Doss 2020).

For those occupying decision-making positions with the journal, both the fact that the journal made it easier for some feminist economist *to find a home in economics* and the influence of feminist economics on the mainstream prove the success of the journal's original strategy. For others, especially those placed in the *heterodox segment* of our spectrum, but

37. See Albelda 1997 on the impact of feminist economics in the economics discipline.

not exclusively, the journal's strategy led feminist economics to be influenced by the approach and the ideas that were originally intended to be changed, thus excluding those who disagree that the mainstream could provide useful tools for a feminist critique.

Certainty, there is an important consensus on how to define outsiders and keep them out. As a member of the editorial board and former associate editor told us regarding the differences in the articles submitted to the journal, "the worst cases are definitely those articles where the authors think that because they have a gender variable it must be feminist economics. Those get rejected straight away."[38] Nevertheless, a tendency toward publishing an increasing number of quantitative articles using standard methods has accompanied the decline of a more fundamental feminist critique. Sheba Tejani (2019) studied this tendency using the articles published in the journal during 1995–2015. Her results capture a heavy empirical tilt between the first (1995–2005) and the second (2006–15) decade. For Tejani,

> Despite its stated aims of building a more transformational feminist economics, through (but not only) the use of alternative methodologies, research published in the journal has become more consistent with the standard view of what counts as legitimate economic research. The use of statistical, and particularly econometric, methods to address a variety of empirical questions has swamped all other types of research design. A heavy emphasis on empiricism has also meant a declining engagement with theory and conceptual questions, economic methodology and history of economic thought, areas of lively debate earlier. (Tejani 2019: 110)

Many of our interviewees connected the journal's tilt toward empirical-econometric research to the transformations the discipline had experienced since the early 1990s. As Deere told us, "In the new generation, to get a job you have to be an econometrician (laughs), that's sort of a fact. In the journal, this is a big issue because we get a lot of dull papers on interesting topics, but it's all regression analysis and very little deep feminist and methodological questions" (interview by authors, San Diego, January 3, 2020).

An active debate about the usefulness and potential dangers of the journal's priority to be "heard by the mainstream" has accompanied feminist

38. Deere, interview by authors, San Diego (2020 ASSA meeting), January 3, 2020.

economics over the years. At the heart of the tensions between the different positions we identified a concern with the risk of *losing their identity*. As Folbre told us,

> It's possible to do a lot of descriptive work about gender inequality without really challenging any real underlying presumptions. I think our comparative advantage as a group is in pushing the envelope theoretically. In the beginning not many mainstream economists were doing work on gender, and we wanted to encourage all the work on gender that we could. Now a lot of them are working on gender, that's great. Now we should move on and stay ahead of the curve, that's what we're good at, being ahead of the curve. (Interview by authors, San Diego, January 5, 2020)

For those who disagree (to different degrees) with the journal's strategy, "being ahead of the curve" while still using or favoring mainstream methods keeps feminist economics in metaphorical shackles. In the words of Barbara Hopkins (2012: 492), "the epistemological strategies of the dominant community will not be successful if applied to liberate the dominated." For this group, the strategy of the journal strikes a form of "patriarchal bargain" (Kandiyoti 1988)—the compromises may allow feminist economics to survive, but they will leave intact the oppressive system that gave rise to feminist economics in the first place.[39] These different interpretations bring to the fore a key issue: while feminism functions as a point of gravity for feminist economics, a commitment to feminism means different things to different people, as feminist scholars know well (Jaggar and Rothenberg 1978; Tong 1989). Some feminists emphasize reform; some feminists emphasize transgression. Between these two poles a continuum of positions exists. In this context, some feminist economists feel "that the trade-off has gone too far toward a sort of applied micro" (Nelson, interview by authors, New York, June 22, 2019) and that this trade-off has been made at the expense of a deep critique of standard economic theory. In other words, the emphasis on "being heard by the mainstream" has made the umbrella smaller.

A long-standing tension has steadfastly persisted over the years. This tension has reached several pinnacles, putting the unity of the group in

---

39. This strategy may maximize the benefits that accrue to any individual woman, but it may also harm the group as a whole.

danger.[40] And yet, the umbrella has resisted the storms—although not without leaving some outside. Certainly, a refusal to establish a unique definition of feminist economics and a common commitment to feminism held the group together. Nevertheless, the disciplinary organization of economics around a strong mainstream may also prevent a permanent split or keep the group from dissolving. As MacDonald told us,

> Whereas my colleagues in sociology splintered into the more distinct subgroups within feminism, feminist economists have managed to stay under a single association, work together and respect each other's work, even though we're coming from some quite different perspectives. I think this has something to do with the fact that the field is so marginalized within economics. In economics there's such a dominant orthodoxy that I think more people make more effort to make their own voice. (Interview by authors, online, July 16, 2020)

Before we finish, it is important to mention that the tensions around the disciplinary affiliation of feminist economics neither affect all feminist economists in the same way nor lead to a unique outcome. While there is a tendency toward the homogenization of economics departments worldwide, some economics departments are much more hospitable to feminist economics than others.[41] As Deere told us,

> UMass has always been so unique. I feel really fortunate that as an economist I didn't end up in a traditional economics department. My poor students, they had to go out into the real world and face economics departments. I was in Nirvana, that's what made me so productive, able to really develop as I wanted but always as an economist. I always worked in an interdisciplinary fashion but thought of myself as an economist. (Interview by authors, San Diego [2020 ASSA meeting], January 3, 2020)

Some of our interviewees who were in traditional economics departments either opted out or were pushed out. While most of them continue

40. The Twenty-Fifth IAFFE Conference held in Galway, Ireland, in 2016, was recalled by many of our interviewees as a particularly critical moment.

41. Certainly, the type of department is the main predictor of the hospitality toward feminism in economics. Nevertheless, not all fields of economics are equal. Labor feminist economists and feminists interested in intrahousehold bargaining can benefit from the convergence of interest between their research and questions raised within the mainstream before a feminist approach was articulated. Likewise, development economics, compared with other fields of economics, is a subfield where pluralism and interdisciplinarity are more established.

to think of themselves as economists, after "feeling pushed out" or having the "feeling of not fitting enough," they moved to other departments (and in one case temporarily outside academe). Most of the time these new departments host interdisciplinary programs (gender studies, women's studies, urbanization, education). Our interviewees recalled finding more flexibility and freedom, both in teaching and in research, feeling more comfortable and respected, and finding colleagues with whom to have fruitful intellectual exchanges.

7. Conclusion

We have examined the institutionalization of feminist economics through three tensions: the tension between feminist work in economics and mainstream economics at the moment of the creation of IAFFE; the tension between the different methodologies used by feminist economists; and the tension surrounding the place of feminist economics in the discipline. We identified some elements to understand how feminist economics has persisted as an approach and a community despite the differences and tensions that characterize the field.

First, interest in feminism and economics was increasing at the moment when IAFFE and the journal *Feminist Economics* were created, as is shown through the panels at the ASSA conferences and a number of publications. The group of feminist economists received the support of other well-established institutions such as women's studies departments, but especially from URPE's Women's Caucus and CSWEP.[42] As we have shown, many of the founders of IAFFE came from URPE's Women's Caucus and CSWEP. They benefited from the battles already won by these societies. This is certainly due to the moment when IAFFE and the journal were created: both arrived after some years of reflection, at a moment of relative maturity and with the intention to fill a clear need of institutions explicitly devoted to promoting feminist economics research and policies.

IAFFE was conceptualized from the start as an *international* organization. Although initially its meetings were held in the United States and its initial membership was mainly based in North America, substantial research, and networks by feminist economists outside the United States, long preceded the founding of IAFFE.

---

42. In 2018, the URPE Women's Caucus was reborn and had bylaws approved to reinstate a seat on the Steering Committee for a Caucus representative in URPE.

Second, while feminist economics is frequently considered a heterodox approach, some feminist economists use standard mainstream tools. We suggested a spectrum to capture the methodological heterogeneity within feminist economics.

Third, the institutionalization of feminist economics allowed economists working from a feminist perspective to stay in the discipline. The journal *Feminist Economics* was particularly important for feminist economics *to make a home in economics*. Likewise, certain economics departments are more hospitable to feminist economics, allowing some feminist economists to stay in economics. Some feminist economists in more standard departments were pushed out or decided to opt out of economics.

IAFFE and *Feminist Economics* are essential institutions for defending research in feminist economics. Many scholars helped build and maintain these institutions, renewing and reinventing them for three decades. They made important advances, laying the ground for younger feminist economists, and provided a supportive home for the development of a community. All that was sometimes accomplished, however, at the expense of approaches that differ from the mainstream.

What we have called, using their own words, the "big umbrella" of feminist economics is this intention of being inclusive: embracing different approaches, and accepting great diversity in educational backgrounds as well as theoretical and methodological perspectives. From the beginning, a tension between two strategies guided the institutionalization of feminist economics. One was to create an inclusive association, encouraging more and diverse people to join IAFFE and participate in the conferences. The other was to maintain the status of the journal, giving priority to "being heard by the mainstream." The relevance of discussion for current debates, the number of IAFFE members, the journal's rankings, the impact of articles, the number of positions and financed projects, the active participation in public debates and consulting—all of this augurs well for the future of feminist economics.

References

Aerni, April, and J. Nelson. 1995. "A Brief History of the International Association for Feminist Economics." *International Association for Feminist Economics Newsletter* 5, no. 1: 1–5.

Agarwal, Bina. 1994. *A Field of One's Own*. Cambridge: Cambridge University Press.

Agarwal, Bina. 2016. "Challenging Mainstream Economics: Some Reflections." In *Gender Challenges*. Vol. 3, *Environmental Change and Collective Action*. Oxford: Oxford University Press.

Albelda, Randy P. 1997. *Economics and Feminism: Disturbances in the Field*. New York: Twayne.

Barker, Drucilla, and Edith Kuiper. 2003. *Toward a Feminist Philosophy of Economics*. London: Routledge.

Bartlett, Robin L. 1998. "CSWEP: Twenty-Five Years at a Time." *Journal of Economic Perspectives* 12, no. 4: 177–83.

Becchio, Giandomenica. 2020. *A History of Feminist and Gender Economics*. London: Routledge.

Benería, Lourdes, ed. 1982. *Women and Development: The Sexual Division of Labor in Rural Societies; A Study*. New York: Praeger.

Benería, Lourdes, Günseli Berik, and Maria S. Floro. 2015. *Gender, Development, and Globalization: Economics as If All People Mattered*. New York: Routledge.

Bergmann, Barbara. 1986. *The Economic Emergence of Women*. New York: Basic Books.

Boserup, Ester. 1970. *Woman's Role in Economic Development*. London: George Allen and Unwin.

Bourdieu, Pierre. 1980. "L'identité et la représentation (éléments pour une réflexion critique sur l'idée de région)." *Actes de la recherche en sciences sociales* 35: 63–72.

Boxer, Marilyn Jacoby. 1998. *When Women Ask the Questions: Creating Women's Studies in America*. Baltimore: Johns Hopkins University Press.

Buker, Eloise. 2003. "Is Women's Studies a Disciplinary or an Interdisciplinary Field of Inquiry?" *NWSA Journal* 15, no. 1: 73–93.

Chassonnery-Zaïgouche, Cléo, Béatrice Cherrier, and John Singleton. 2020. "'Economics Is Not a Man's Field': CSWEP and the First Gender Reckoning in Economics (1971–1991)." https://papers.ssrn.com/sol3/papers.cfm?abstract_id=3510857.

Cherrier, Béatrice, and Aurélien Saïdi. 2021. "Back to Front: The Role of Seminars, Conferences, and Workshops in the History of Economics." *Revue d'économie politique* 131, no. 4: 609–35.

Cohen, Jennifer. 2018. "What's 'Radical' about [Feminist] Radical Political Economy?" *Review of Radical Political Economics* 50, no. 4: 716–26.

Cohen, Jennifer. 2019. "The Radical Roots of Feminism in Economics." *Research in the History of Economic Thought and Methodology* 37A:85–100.

Conrad, Cecilia. 2018. "Feminist Economics: Second Wave, Tidal Wave, or Barely a Ripple?" In *The Legacy of Second-Wave Feminism in American Politics*, edited by Angie Maxwell and Todd Shields, 99–136. Cham: Palgrave Macmillan.

Deere, Carmen Diana, and Magdalena León. 2001. *Empowering Women: Land and Property Rights in Latin America*. Pittsburgh: University of Pittsburgh Press.

Dimand, Robert W., Mary Ann Dimand, and Evelyn L. Forget, eds. 2000. *A Biographical Dictionary of Women Economists*. Northampton: Edward Elgar.

Doss, Cheryl. 2020. "Diffusion and Dilution: The Power and Perils of Integrating Feminist Perspectives into the Household Economics." IAFFE Presidential Address at ASSA 2020. San Diego. https://www.youtube.com/watch?v=a3uQNSy7vYA&t=1381s.

Edwards, Rosalind. 2000. "Numbers Are Not Enough: On Women in Higher Education and Being a Feminist Academic." In *Academic Work and Life*, edited by M. Tight, 1:307–33. International Perspectives on Higher Education Research. Bingley: JAI.

Emami, Zohreh, and Paulette Olson. 2002. *Engendering Economics: Conversations with Women Economists in the United States.* London: Routledge.

Ferber, Marianne A. 1987. *Women and Work, Paid and Unpaid: A Selected, Annotated Bibliography.* New York: Garland.

Ferber, Marianne A., and Julie A. Nelson, eds. 1993. *Beyond Economic Man: Feminist Theory and Economics.* Chicago: University of Chicago Press.

Ferber, Marianne, and Julie A. Nelson, eds. 2003. *Feminist Economics Today: Beyond Economic Man.* Chicago: University of Chicago Press.

Folbre, Nancy. 1994. *Who Pays for the Kids? Gender and the Structures of Constraint.* London: Routledge.

Forget, Evelyn. 2002. "A Hunger for Narrative: Writing Lives in the History of Economic Thought." In *The Future of the History of Economics*, edited by E. Roy Weintraub. *History of Political Economy* 34 (supplement): 226–44.

Forget, Evelyn. 2011. "American Women and the Economics Profession in the Twentieth Century." *Œconomia* 1, no. 1: 19–31.

Fourcade, Marion, Étienne Ollion, and Yann Algan. 2015. "The Superiority of Economists." *Journal of Economic Perspectives* 29, no. 1: 89–114.

Harding, Sandra. 1986. *The Science Question in Feminism.* Ithaca, N.Y.: Cornell University Press.

Hartmann, Heidi. 1979. "The Unhappy Marriage of Marxism and Feminism: Towards a More Progressive Union." *Capital and Class* 3, no. 2: 1–33.

Hopkins, Barbara E. 2012. "The Institutional Barriers to Heterodox Pluralism." *Review of Radical Political Economics* 24, no. 3: 489–501.

Jacobsen, Joyce P. 2020. *Advanced Introduction to Feminist Economics.* Cheltenham: Edward Elgar.

Jaggar, Alison M., and Paula S. Rothenberg, eds. 1978. *Feminist Frameworks: Alternative Theoretical Accounts of the Relations between Women and Men.* New York: McGraw-Hill.

Jenkins, K. 2014. "'That's Not Philosophy': Feminism, Academia, and the Double Bind." *Journal of Gender Studies* 23: 262–74.

Jullien, Dorian. 2019. "Interviews and the Historiographical Issues of Oral Sources." In *The Historiography of Contemporary Economics*, edited by Till Düppe and E. Roy Weintraub. London: Routledge.

Kandiyoti, Deniz. 1988. "Bargaining with Patriarchy." *Gender and Society* 2, no. 3: 274–90.

Keller, Evelyn Fox. 1985. *Reflections on Gender and Science.* New Haven, Conn.: Yale University Press.

Kim, Marlene. 2018. "URPE at Fifty: Reflections on a Half Century of Activism, Community, Debate (and a Few Crazy Moments)." *Review of Radical Political Economics* 50, no. 3: 468–86.

Kuiper, Edith, and Drucilla K. Barker, eds. 2006. *Feminist Economics and the World Bank: History, Theory, and Policy.* New York: Routledge.

Lenger, Alexander. 2019. "The Rejection of Qualitative Research Methods in Economics." *Journal of Economic Issues* 53, no. 4: 946–65.

Livingstone, David N. 2003. *Putting Science in Its Place: Geographies of Scientific Knowledge.* Chicago: University of Chicago Press.

Luxton, Meg, and Kate Bezanson. 2006. *Social Reproduction: Feminist Political Economy Challenges Neo-liberalism.* Montreal: McGill-Queen's University Press.

MacDonald, Martha. 1995. "Feminist Economics: From Theory to Research." *Women and the Economy: A Reader* 28, no. 1: 25–34.

Madden, Kirsten. 2002. "Female Contributions to Economic Thought, 1900–1940." *History of Political Economy* 34, no. 1: 1–30.

Madden, Kirsten, and Robert W. Dimand, eds, 2018. *Routledge Handbook of the History of Women's Economic Thought.* London: Routledge.

Mata, Tiago, and Frederic S. Lee. 2007. "The Role of Oral History in the Historiography of Heterodox Economics." In *Economists' Lives: Biography and Autobiography in the History of Economics,* edited by E. Roy Weintraub and Evelyn L. Forget. *History of Political Economy* 39 (supplement): 154–71.

Matthaei, Julie. 1996. "Why Feminist, Marxist, and Anti-Racist Economists Should Be Feminist-Marxist-Anti-Racist Economists." *Feminist Economics* 2, no. 1: 22–42.

Meagher, Gabrielle, and Julie A. Nelson. 2004. "Survey Article: Feminism in the Dismal Science." *Journal of Political Philosophy* 12, no. 1: 102–26.

Meulders, Daniele. 2001. "Feminist Economics." In *International Encyclopedia of the Social and Behavioral Sciences,* edited by Neil J. Smelser and Paul. B. Baltes. Oxford: Pergamon.

Mutari, E., H. Boushey, and W. Fraher IV. 1997. *Gender and Political Economy: Incorporating Diversity into Theory and Policy.* New York: Routledge.

Nelson, Julie A. 1993. "Value Free or Valueless? Notes on the Pursuit of Detachment in Economics." *History of Political Economy* 25, no. 1: 121–45.

Nelson, Julie A. 2008. "Feminist Economics." In *The New Palgrave Dictionary of Economics,* edited by S. N. Durlauf and L. E. Blume. London: Palgrave Macmillan.

Nelson, Julie A. 2009. "My Tenure War." *Committee on the Status of Women in the Economics Profession Newsletter,* Spring, 9–10.

Nelson, Julie A. 2020. "Economics, Considered." In *Gender, Considered: Feminist Reflections across the US Social Sciences,* edited by Sarah Fenstermaker and Abigail J. Stewart, 219–38. Cham: Palgrave Macmillan.

Peterson, J., and M. Lewis, eds. 1999. *The Elgar Companion to Feminist Economics.* London: Edward Elgar.

Phillips, Anne, and Barbara Taylor. 1980. "Sex and Skill: Notes towards a Feminist Economics." *Feminist Review* 6, no. 1: 79–88.

Pietrykowski, Bruce. 2000. "Book Review Essay: The History and Practice of Feminist Economics." *Review of Radical Political Economics* 32, no. 2: 331–39.

Pujol, Michèle A. 1992. *Feminism and Anti-feminism in Early Economic Thought.* Aldershot: Edward Elgar.

Rao, Smriti, and A. Haroon Akram-Lodhi. 2021. "Feminist Political Economy: A Review Essay." In *The Routledge Handbook of Feminist Economics*, edited by Günseli Berik and Ebru Kongar, 34–42. London: Routledge.

Shackelford, Jean. 1999. "The International Association for Feminist Economics." In *The Elgar Companion to Feminist Economics*, edited by Janice Peterson and Margaret Lewis. London: Edward Elgar.

Strassmann, Diana. 1993. "Not a Free Market: The Rhetoric of Disciplinary Authority in Economics." In *Beyond Economic Man: Feminist Theory and Economics*, edited by Marianne A. Ferber and Julie A. Nelson, 54–68. Chicago: University of Chicago Press.

Strober, Myra. 1994. "Rethinking Economics through a Feminist Lens." *American Economic Review* 84, no. 2: 143–47.

Strober, Myra. 2016. *Sharing the Work: What My Family and Career Taught Me about Breaking Through (and Holding the Door Open for Others).* Cambridge, Mass.: MIT Press.

Tejani, Sheba. 2019. "What's Feminist about Feminist Economics?" *Journal of Economic Methodology* 26, no. 2: 99–117.

Tong, Rosemarie. 1989. *Feminist Thought: A Comprehensive Introduction.* Boulder, Colo.: Westview.

Waring, Marilyn. 1988. *If Women Counted: A New Feminist Economics.* San Francisco: Harper and Row.

Weintraub, Roy E. 2005. "2004 HES Presidential Address: Autobiographical Memory and the Historiography of Economics." *Journal of the History of Economic Thought* 27, no. 1: 1–11.

Woolley, Frances R. 1993. "The Feminist Challenge to Neoclassical Economics." *Cambridge Journal of Economics* 17:485–500.

Wu, Alice H. 2017. "Forum, Gender Stereotyping in Academia: Evidence from Economics Job Market Rumors." Undergraduate thesis, UC Berkeley.

Tracing Barbara Bergmann's Occupational Crowding Hypothesis: A Recent History

Sarah F. Small

Civil rights and feminist movements in the United States in the 1960s and 1970s brought issues of race- and gender-based discrimination to the forefront of social consciousness, and economists responded. They responded with increased attention to issues of representation within the discipline and with a burgeoning body of research on discrimination: from detailed empirical analyses to new theories and criticisms of old theories.[1] Barbara Bergmann, a lifelong feminist and Harvard-trained economist, emerged as a key contributor to debates on the economics of discrimination with her occupational crowding hypothesis.

When Bergmann died in 2015, she was known as a leading feminist economist who spent most of her career tackling issues of discrimination

Correspondence may be addressed to Sarah F. Small, Department of Economics, 260 Central Campus Drive, University of Utah, Salt Lake City, Utah 84112. I would like to thank the anonymous reviewers, Elissa Braunstein, Steven Medema, and the faculty and fellows at the Center for the History of Political Economy during the 2020–21 academic year for their comments on earlier drafts of this article. I would also like to thank participants and conference organizers in the HOPE 2021 conference for their helpful feedback.

1. The Caucus of Black Economists, now the National Economic Association, was founded in 1969, and the *Review of Black Political Economy* was established in 1970 (Simms 2020). The Committee on the Status of Minority Groups in the Economics Profession (CSMGEP) and the Committee on the Status of Women in the Economics Profession (CSWEP) both became standing committees of the American Economic Association in the early 1970s.

History of Political Economy 54 (annual suppl.) DOI 10.1215/00182702-10085696

in the economy (Olson 2007). However, her career did not start in the realm of discrimination: her early career covered several different topics, and her occupational crowding hypothesis was her first work to directly tackle the issue of discrimination. Bergmann introduced the crowding hypothesis in her 1971 publication, "The Effect on White Incomes of Discrimination in Employment." Bergmann's theory suggested that because Black men were "crowded into a comparatively small number of occupations," their marginal productivities and their wages were driven down while White wages were simultaneously inflated by the suppression of Black labor supply.

Published in the *Journal of Political Economy*, Bergmann's model of racial discrimination in employment temporarily stood alongside other neoclassical theories of discrimination (like those of Gary Becker, Kenneth Arrow, Anne Krueger, and Lester Thurow), but was largely relegated to the margins of economics by the 1980s. Today, most economists continue to rely predominantly on the canonical Becker models of discrimination, but some heterodox economists, namely, stratification and feminist economists, often still turn to Bergmann's crowding hypothesis, as I discuss in subsequent sections of this article.

In the following sections, I consider how Bergmann's personal and professional experiences brought her to the crowding hypothesis and what informed her understanding of the economy and discrimination. I then situate Bergmann's hypothesis in the debates on the economics of discrimination taking place during the 1950s, 1960s, and 1970s. I consider how it was initially received and then pushed outside the mainstream of a renewed labor economics. This historical examination of the occupational crowding hypothesis serves as an examination of a famous feminist economist's first step into a lifetime of research on discrimination.

Though traditionally in the periphery, recent historians of economic thought have increasingly focused on feminist economic thought. Michèle Pujol (1992) famously examined feminism in early economic thought, including Adam Smith, John Stuart Mill, Alfred Marshall, and A. C. Pigou. More recently, several have studied feminist economic thought as it developed during the 1990s, when the International Association for Feminist Economics (IAFFE) was founded and the subfield thus institutionalized. For instance, Camila Orozco Espinel and Rebeca Gomez Betancourt (this volume) research the development of the IAFFE. Others have researched the work of IAFFE's founders, including Bergmann. For example, Giandomenica Becchio (2021) studies Bergmann's economic theory of marriage.[2] Ultimately, this increasing focus on historicizing feminist economic thought is important to the mission of feminist economics as a whole. Feminist economists' goals have historically been able to overcome androcentric bias in the field (Ferber and Nelson 2009). Because the history of economic thought plays a role in deciding the importance of economic ideas for future generations, documenting and historicizing the work and lives of feminist economists helps meet this goal by pulling feminist perspectives from the periphery and pushing them closer to the center stage of the economics discipline.

1. Who Was Barbara Bergmann? And What Brought Her to the Crowding Hypothesis?

Barbara Bergmann was known for many contributions in academic and policy spaces. She was a Harvard-trained economist who spent most of her career as a professor at the University of Maryland and American University. But many know Bergmann from her congressional testimonies on poverty and discrimination, or from her role as a staff economist for President John F. Kennedy's Council of Economic Advisers. Others know of her as a president and founding member of the International Association for Feminist Economics, or as the first president of the Eastern Economic Association. Many others might know of her outspoken opposition to the Nobel Prize for economics, her appearance on late-night American television shows in defense of affirmative action, and her cartoon book on social security. Yet, among a great deal of notable and often controversial work, Bergmann is perhaps most widely known in academic circles for her occupational crowding hypothesis. As noted above, she presented the hypothesis formally in her 1971 *Journal of Political Economy* article, "The Effect on White Incomes of Discrimination in Employment."

Who was Bergmann before the crowding hypothesis? And what led her, as a young economist, to write about labor market discrimination? Understanding a researcher's background and overlapping social locations is important from the perspective of feminist standpoint theory (Harding 2004) and scholars in the history of economic thought (Howson 2013; Forget 2002). For instance, Forget (2002: 240) argues that historians

---

2. Becchio's 2020 book also delves into several case studies on the development of gender and feminist economics.

of economic thought should take advantage of life writing to guide narratives on economic works and to enhance our understanding how economists' lives inform their research. Similarly, standpoint theory is often used by feminist researchers to understand and reflect on how knowledge production is embedded in social, political, and historical contexts. In general, a standpoint epistemology argues "that knowledge is constructed from specific positions and that what a knower can see is shaped by the location from which the knower's inquiry begins" (Sprague 2016: 47). More simply, "ideas cannot be divorced from the individuals who create and share them" (Collins 2015: 252).

Bergmann's background provides an understanding of her perspectives within economics and within debates on the economics of discrimination. Namely, Bergmann's understanding about occupational segregation grew out of lived experiences: she faced a great deal of labor market discrimination as a Jewish woman born in New York City in 1927. In her later years, she reflected that she had faced discrimination in her career every step of the way. Her early-career experiences and frustrations with occupational segregation may have indeed been part of the spark for her development of the crowding hypothesis. Further, it is part of what made her analysis and perspective unique from that of other prominent economists working on competing theories in labor market discrimination. For instance, Becker, Thurow, and Arrow were certainly not experiencing gender- or race-based discrimination, nor did they face the occupational barriers Bergmann faced as a Jewish woman.

Bergmann grew up in the Bronx with an immigrant mother and an absent father. Although neither of her parents had graduated from high school and she did not receive much support from her own high school, Bergmann applied to Cornell University and the Massachusetts Institute of Technology (MIT). The admissions committee at MIT "thought she was crazy" for expressing interest in civil engineering as a young woman (Olsen and Emami 2002: 56). She was rejected by MIT but accepted at Cornell. After Bergmann graduated with a degree in mathematics from Cornell in 1948, she experienced firsthand the occupational segregation about which she would later theorize: upon graduating in the midst of a recession, Bergmann looked for a job in the "male categories" for months. She eventually gave up and took a job as a typist "in the female category," but "couldn't endure the boredom" and quit after two days (Bergmann 2005: 12). She eventually found a low-ranking job at the Bureau of Labor

Statistics (BLS) office in New York City in 1950. Though she had read Gunner Myrdal's 1944 book, *An America Dilemma*, as an undergraduate and was a member of her university's NAACP branch, it was during her time at the BLS that she realized the discrimination she read about in Myrdal's book was not just confined to the South. Bergmann was frustrated with the way in which the BLS office's sole Black employee was not permitted to advance in his career. Bergmann was deeply affected by this experience and even returned to a BLS office more than a decade later to see if similar types of discrimination were still in practice. She was disappointed to find that they were.

Ultimately, her interactions with economists at the BLS inspired Bergmann to pursue a doctorate in the field. In 1953 she was accepted at Harvard. Her time at Harvard was not free from the discriminatory behavior she had hoped to escape at the BLS. Harvard was still segregated by gender (then Radcliffe for women), and the economics department had been rife with anti-Semitism.[3] Bergmann wrote her dissertation on regional consumer expenditures in New York City, and her work had nothing to do with labor market discrimination, race, or gender directly. After graduating with her PhD in economics, she again faced discrimination. As she explained in an American Association of University Professors newsletter, "I was second in my class at Harvard in 1959, but couldn't get an academic job . . . and I attribute it to sex discrimination" (Bergmann Papers, box 7, folder 2).

She lingered at Harvard for several years until she secured a job on Kennedy's Council of Economic Advisers (CEA) in 1962. This was a particularly notable CEA, as it included Arrow, James Tobin, Rashi Fein, Arthur Okun, Robert Solow, and Walter Heller, many of whom would remain Bergmann's lifelong friends.[4] Most of the CEA reports during her years there did not have to do with discrimination, aside from one issued in September 1962. The report was titled "A Study on the Costs of Racial Discrimination." This study included empirical modeling of wage losses occurring as a result of racially minoritized workers being excluded from certain jobs (Papers of John F. Kennedy, White House Staff Files of Walter W. Heller). The report did not indicate which members had

---

3. For discussion of anti-Semitism in the Harvard economics department during the 1930s and 1940s (largely from the perspective of former economics graduate student Paul Samuelson), see Backhouse 2014 and Weintraub 2014.

4. For discussion on the Kennedy administration's CEA, see Romani 2018.

authored it; however, the CEA in 1962 had only nineteen full-time staffers, so Bergmann likely knew about the study if she was not immediately involved. Bergmann was at least motivated to write about discrimination during this time: in a 2006 letter to Kenneth Arrow, Bergmann bemoaned, "I remember that many of us on the CEA staff at the time were unhappy with Kennedy—slowness to move in civil rights and taking economic advice from Bobby and his dad instead of from Walter Heller" (Arrow Papers, box 2, folder 13). Bergmann's curiosity in the economics of discrimination was certainly simmering while at the CEA. This curiosity received a significant boost after her move to the Brookings Institution as a senior staff member in 1963. While her early years at Brookings were spent traveling to Peru and Bolivia to research the impacts of highway investment on development, she acknowledged that her work on the crowding hypothesis began during this Brookings period (Bergmann 1971: 294) and may have had to do with the numerous labor movements taking place on the continent during the 1960s (Bergquist 1986).

Bergmann slowly began to dip her toes into issues of race and discrimination in 1967. The first Bergmann-authored publication that considered the role of race in the economy was a 1967 report to the US Department of Commerce on structural unemployment. Bergmann and David Kaun, who had both been affiliated with Brookings, coauthored the report. In the section titled "Negro Unemployment and Structural Unemployment," Bergmann and Kaun attempted to explain why Black unemployment rates were higher than White unemployment rates and estimated how this may change during periods of high output. They wrote primarily about the role of migration patterns and only briefly engaged with theories of discrimination. For instance, they referred to the "last-hired, first-fired" hypothesis but indicated that they did not find conclusive evidence in support of it. They also referred to Harry G. Gilman's (1965) work, which showed, using 1960 Census data, that a great deal of non-White unemployment had to do with the distribution of Black workers by occupation and industry. Gilman (1965: 1079) argued that Black workers were "concentrated in low-skilled occupations which have a high incidence of unemployment." Gilman did not explicitly explain the ways in which this influenced worker's wages, but Bergmann was hooked: she eventually used this same data set and trends to motivate her 1971 paper to explain how this occupational segregation affected marginal productivity and wages.

Bergmann later published "Investment in the Human Resources of Negroes" in 1968, in which she discussed gaps in Black and White workers' human capital and estimated the ultimate toll this took on the nation's economy. She continued to largely avoid explicit discussion of the consequences of racism and only wrote that "dollars which should have been invested in enhancing Negroes' ability to be economically productive . . . were not invested, in part because of discrimination, and in part because of the poverty and ignorance of the Negroes themselves." In this piece, she takes no clear stance: she waffles between blaming the plight of Black Americans on themselves and on discrimination. Similarly, Bergmann's 1969 publication "The Urban Economy and the 'Urban Crisis'" briefly discussed the well-being of Black individuals, but again did not directly engage with theories of discrimination.

All her publications related to race prior to her 1971 crowding hypothesis were purely empirical and did not directly engage with racism or discrimination, often relegating the words to footnotes or brief sentences, if they were included at all. The 1971 crowding hypothesis, as described in the next section of this article, dealt with the issue of discrimination head-on and examined the benefits accruing to White workers as a result of labor market discrimination. In this sense, the crowding hypothesis dealt with issues of power and group conflict more than any of Bergmann's preceding work, and these became central topics for her as she continued her career. For example, she was among the founders of the International Association of Feminist Economics, which was organized in the 1990s to challenge patriarchal power both in the economy and in the economics discipline. Bergmann also continued to work on issues of race-based discrimination after her 1971 publication: for example, she wrote a book about affirmative action and collaborated on work with the founder of stratification economics.[5] Stratification economics is a subfield that focuses on intergroup inequality and identifies material benefits that accrue to dominant (and often discriminatory) groups as a result of economic discrimination. I discuss the crowding hypothesis's role in modern feminist and stratification economics in section 4.

Ultimately, the bold shift reflected in Bergmann's 1971 paper, where she directly faced issues of discrimination, may be related to her career becoming less precarious: Bergmann had been an assistant professor at

---

5. Namely, in work with William Darity Jr., who is known as the founder of stratification economics (Darity 2005; Darity, Hamilton, and Stewart 2015).

the University of Maryland for six years but by 1971 had received tenure.[6] That same year, she received a grant from the Office of Economic Opportunity to initiate and direct a project on the economics of discrimination. She used the grant funding to develop research, including her occupational crowding hypothesis, as well as a course on poverty and discrimination, one of the first of its kind in the country (Olson 2007).

Bergmann's own exclusion from certain occupations, her experiences witnessing race-based occupational segregation firsthand, and her activity in public policy circles during pivotal civil rights events in the United States and Latin America situated her perfectly to revive the occupational crowding hypothesis. Her tenure status and funding from the Office of Economic Opportunity likely bolstered her bravery to not just write empirical papers observing differences in economics outcomes by race but actually theorize about discrimination.

2. What Is the Occupational Crowding Hypothesis? Bergmann's Contributions to the Theory

Bergmann's 1971 article, "The Effect on White Incomes of Discrimination in Employment," introduced the occupational crowding hypothesis and would become Bergmann's first publication in a long line of work on issues of racism and sexism in economic life. She began the paper with some empirical motivation: she provided US Census data indicating that Black men were excluded from many high-earning occupations and crowded into a comparatively small number of occupations. She then presented a theoretical model that indicated the consequences of crowding were lower marginal productivities and wages for Black men, enforced by abundance of labor supply, and higher White marginal productivities and wages as a result of the reduced labor supply and competition.

Though Bergmann included a mathematical model, she explained her hypothesis most simply with an example.

> If Negroes were allowed only to be janitors and the number of Negroes in the labor force (plus the number of whites completely specialized to janitorial jobs) were larger than the number of janitors demanded in a

6. Archival data indicate that Bergmann felt she was being underpaid as a result of gender discrimination while at the University of Maryland. She drafted letters documenting her pay and accomplishments compared with those of her male colleagues, and eventually investigated similar gender pay gaps that existed in other departments across campus.

colorblind economy, then restricting Negroes to this occupation alone would surely have the effect of driving the wage of janitors down below what it would be in a colorblind economy. In order to clear the market for janitorial labor, into which Negroes would be forcibly crowded, the marginal productivity of janitorial labor would have to be pushed to an abnormally low level. Even if the employers who restricted Negro labor to janitorial jobs paid Negro janitors a wage equal to their marginal productivity, such a wage would be below that paid to whites for jobs requiring similar talents. (Bergmann 1971: 298)

Bergmann went on to explain that the opposite dynamic would hold for White workers: in jobs reserved for White workers, she argues their marginal productivity would be higher because of the exclusion from competition with Black workers.

Through her mathematical model, Bergmann demonstrated that the more rigorous the racial restriction, the bigger the difference in marginal productivities of Black and White workers. But in a world where occupations were opened to both races, she showed that labor would move until the marginal productivities were equal in both types of work. This would result in increased marginal productivities of Black workers and decreased marginal productivities of White workers, and therefore, increased and decreased wages, respectively. However, she was sure to point out that this would also lead to an increase in national income, which would offset the decrease in White wages (300). In fact, after introducing the theoretical model, she went through an entire empirical exercise to demonstrate that the wage losses to White workers would be limited to those less educated, and these wage losses would be minimal. She summarized by writing that the marginal productivity of Black workers "is lowered in comparison with that of whites of equivalent education" (310) because of crowding, and that "very considerable gains could be made by Negroes in rate of remuneration at the expense of trivial losses for most white males and moderate losses for virtually all other white males" (303).

The crowding hypothesis was unlike contemporary theories on race-based discrimination, which I discuss in section 3. But the theory was not entirely new to those studying gender discrimination, a fact that Bergmann made clear in her 1971 article. The crowding hypothesis stemmed largely from Francis Y. Edgeworth's (1922) work on *gender* differences in wages. "He argued that the main factor responsible for women's lower pay was the circumstance that they were crowded into a comparatively small number of occupations" (Bergmann 1971: 295). Bergmann acknowledged that

Edgeworth's work inspired her own, but did not recognize the woman who had inspired Edgeworth's conceptualization: Millicent Fawcett. This came to Bergmann's attention later in her life. In 1994 Kenneth Arrow was rereading Edgeworth 1922 for an essay on Edgeworth's ethics, became aware of Edgeworth's citations of Fawcett's work, and wrote to Bergmann to alert her of this omission. Bergmann replied to Arrow, "I was pleased with your revival of the contribution of Millicent Fawcett, but mortified that I had neglected it" (Arrow Papers, box 2, folder 13).

The application to race was surely inspired by the civil rights movements taking place while Bergmann was writing the 1971 piece, as well as the burgeoning of economic literature on discrimination, which I discuss in the next section. But it certainly stemmed from her own interests in race-based discrimination, which were planted by Myrdal's *American Dilemma*. She recollected that "Myrdal's book sparked a lasting interest in race discrimination, which was later extended to an interest in sex discrimination" (Bergmann 2005). Bergmann read the book while in college at Cornell, and the book includes discussions that connect to the crowding hypothesis.

The main theoretical contribution of *An American Dilemma* was Myrdal's assertion that "discrimination breeds discrimination" (381), otherwise described as a "vicious circle of cumulative causation." This is ultimately at the core of Bergmann's hypothesis: Bergmann showed that crowding Black workers into a limited selection of occupations maintained higher wages for White workers, which incentivized them to maintain discrimination. A section from *An American Dilemma* made connections to an occupational crowding idea: "By excluding Negroes from the competition for jobs, the white workers can decrease the supply of labor in the market, hold up wages and secure employment for themselves" (Myrdal 1944: 391). Myrdal further explained that "to give white workers a monopoly on all promotions is, of course, to give them a vested interest in job segregation." Though Bergmann did not cite Myrdal in her 1971 paper, her life-changing experience reading *An American Dilemma* as an undergraduate certainly resurfaced indirectly in the paper.[7]

---

7. It is also possible that Bergmann 1971 did not cite Myrdal because the book "was not regarded as an economic work, which may explain why its impact was more significant on the other social sciences" (Fleury 2012: 5). Indeed, though the book was groundbreaking on many fronts, only a few sections had distinctly to do with the economics of discrimination, and those sections were primarily empirical analyses of the economic conditions of Black families.

Bergmann's other main addition to Fawcett's (1892, 1916) and Edgeworth's occupational crowding hypotheses is of course the formalization of the theory. The understanding of marginal productivity theory in monopolistic settings and the mathematical tools at Bergmann's disposal were products of the time in which she was writing: Edgeworth and Fawcett would not have presented their theories in such a way. The tools she developed as a PhD student at Harvard brought these skills, and her perspectives on their use were influenced by her work under Edward Chamberlin. Bergmann classified Chamberlin's *Theory of Monopolistic Competition* as "an attempt to get away from the never-never land of perfect competition, and to describe the messier and more complex real-world phenomenon." Bergmann's occupational crowding hypothesis took tools like production functions and marginal productivity theories and combined them with her tutelage under Chamberlin on imperfect competition. The crowding hypothesis is, in essence, an examination of labor markets as an imperfectly competitive market, as stratified by gender and race discrimination.

Working under Chamberlin at Harvard inspired Bergmann to critique economists like Gary Becker, whose theories of labor market discrimination operated in the world of perfectly competitive markets. In her autobiographic notes, Bergmann (2005: 14) reflected as follows:

> [Chamberlin's] lesson of skepticism I was able to apply to Gary Becker's theory that race and sex discrimination in employment, if ever they appeared, could not long persist. He claimed that any employer who discriminated would be driven out of business by competitors who didn't discriminate, who would be able to hire a labor cheaper, and produce the product at a lower price, drawing away all the customers of the discriminating employer. Becker's theory, neat but totally negated by the facts, gained wide acceptance among economists, and continues to be quoted with approval today.

These criticisms of Becker's work were harsher than the brief criticisms she presented in her 1971 work. This perhaps stemmed from decades of being pushed to the periphery while Becker's theories took center stage. In the 1960s and 1970s, Becker's work was the most prominent of theories on labor market discrimination, and in many circles, remains so. Even by the 1980s, Bergmann had changed her tune and had begun criticizing Becker's work more harshly. In the subsequent sections, I discuss Bergmann's crowding hypothesis in the context of the 1960s and 1970s debates on labor market discrimination theories, and examine why Becker's theories stuck in mainstream circles while Bergmann's was eventually relegated to heterodox circles.

3. Situating the Crowding Hypothesis: Familiar Methods, Unconventional Conclusions

During the 1960s and 1970s, many economists were writing about labor market discrimination, most empirically and some theoretically. Many of Bergmann's colleagues contributed to the empirical literature. For instance, Rashi Fein (1965), with whom Bergmann worked at the CEA, wrote empirical pieces on the social profile of Black Americans. Similarly, Heller (1970), who ran the CEA while Bergmann worked there and cited her (1968) in his work, also wrote about the status of Black families in the country. Both Fein and Heller compared incomes, unemployment, and education rates between Black and White workers and, like Bergmann (1968), emphasized the toll that racial-economic disparities took on the nation's economy.

While there was a great deal of empirical literature during this period comparing the incomes of Black and White workers, only a few prominent works focused on connections between occupational segregation and income differences.[8] For example, Norval D. Glenn (1963), whom Bergmann cited in her 1971 piece, showed that the occupational status of White workers was higher in localities where the size of the Black population was larger. Previously, Herbert R. Northrup (1943, 1946) had examined how Black workers were excluded from unions, and thus many occupations, and Donald Dewey (1952) demonstrated the heavy concentration of Black workers in relatively few occupations. Thus, while Bergmann's empirical analyses were not especially novel, her theoretical contribution surfaced during a period when prominent economists were reexamining theories of labor market discrimination.

Much of the preexisting theoretical literature, for instance, that of Krueger and Arrow, built on Becker's work and focused on individual preferences and applied the same tools used to understand all forms of

8. Some focused on the intersections between housing segregation and consumption. For example, Hazel Kyrk (1950) described how urban Black families suffered housing discrimination, which led them to be charged higher prices than White families, which limited Black families' ability to express character in consumption.

market behavior to their models. Theories outside the dominant perspective often pointed to power and group distributional incentives as explanations of labor market discrimination. Bergmann's crowding hypothesis fell into both categories. At the time of its publication, Bergmann's hypothesis stood among other mainstream theories (like those of Becker, Arrow, Krueger, Thurow) but was later relegated to largely heterodox approaches.

Most theories on the economics of discrimination were built on Becker's seminal book *The Economics of Discrimination* (1971; first edition 1957). Though not immediately popular, Becker's theories had risen to prominence by the time of Bergmann's publication. In addition to the reasons described in Jean-Baptiste Fleury's (2012) research, Becker's book may have had a difficult time penetrating the contemporary dominance of theories on competitive markets, especially general equilibrium theory. Traditionally, models of perfect competition left little room for analyses of discrimination: in competitive markets, discrimination should not exist. But Becker successfully fit his model into this world of competitive markets by modeling discrimination as a good with a positive price. Becker (1957: 15) explained that if an individual has a "taste for discrimination," then they would act as if they were "willing to pay something, either directly or in the form of a reduced income," to avoid being associated with certain groups of people. This logic was also applied to employers: employers act as though the employment of Black workers imposed an extra monetary cost on them.

In Becker's models, employers were faced with the money wage rate plus an additional cost, the discrimination coefficient, that varied based on the intensity of the employer's taste for discrimination. Becker wrote that Black and White workers would be hired in the same firm only if the wages owed to the White workers were the same as those of the Black workers plus the additional cost of a "taste for discrimination." In other words, an employer hires laborers up to the point at which marginal product is equal to the marginal cost. For White workers, their wage is therefore equal to their marginal product. For Black workers, their wage is less than their marginal product, because the marginal cost of hiring a Black worker includes the discrimination coefficient (Becker 1957: 51). Bergmann's occupational crowding hypothesis was even more "neoclassical" than Becker's theory in that Bergmann brought marginal productivity theory back into the fold. In Bergmann's hypothesis, crowding reduces the marginal productivity of Black labor and therefore their wages.

She assumed wages equal to marginal product. In Becker's model, Black workers' wages are less than their marginal product. Bergmann's training under Chamberlin was perhaps what brought Bergmann to this understanding. Chamberlin brought marginal productivity theory into imperfectly competitive contexts in his 1949 *Theory of Monopolistic Competition*. Bergmann used similar techniques in her 1971 crowding hypothesis, which is, in essence, a description of an imperfectly competitive market.

Bergmann's hypothesis was also well situated within other prominent literature on discrimination, most of which built directly from Becker's theories. For instance, Bergmann frequently relied on and cited the work of her friend Arrow. The majority of Arrow's work on theories of discrimination were simply extensions of Becker: Arrow (1973: 5) declared that his goal was to "develop further Becker's models and to relate them more closely to the theory of general competitive equilibrium." Arrow was very clear in his intention to continue the use of neoclassical tools in his theories, and he relaxed many of the assumptions made by Becker to provide them with more mathematical rigor.[9] Arrow and Bergmann seemed to be working in tandem on the economics of discrimination in the late 1960s. In her 1971 publication, Bergmann made it clear that correspondence with Arrow was formative in many aspects of the paper: Bergmann wrote that she had "profited from reading a draft of a paper by Arrow [forthcoming] who has been working independently along parallel lines." She specifically pointed to "The Treatment of Returns to Capital" section in her paper, writing that she owed "a great deal to an extended comment by Professor Arrow" (Bergmann 1971: 304). Her work alongside Arrow seemed to help Bergmann more closely fit her model into a Beckerian, general equilibrium framework.[10]

Bergmann aligned her 1971 work with Becker's and did not offer scathing criticisms of his work, though they would have heated disagreements later in her life. She went a step further in siding with Becker when she disparaged a contemporary work that sparred with his: Thurow's 1969 *Poverty and Discrimination*. Thurow was a fellow Harvard PhD and another Brookings staffer. Bergmann and Thurow had agreed on several

9. Specifically, he relaxed the "convexity of indifferent surfaces, costless adjustment, perfect information, and perfect capital markets" (Arrow 1973: 4) assumptions and provided theoretical support for relaxing them.

10. For a more detailed discussion of Arrow's theories on the economics of discrimination, see Chassonnery-Zaïgouche and Larrouy 2017.

key aspects of the debates on the economics of discrimination. For instance, their criticisms of Krueger's (1963) model of discrimination were nearly identical.[11] However, in her 1971 paper Bergmann was highly critical of the key mechanisms underlying Thurow's theory.

At the core of *Poverty and Discrimination*, Thurow had rejected Becker's assumption that people had a taste for discrimination and postulated that discriminators did not necessarily seek *physical* distance from Black individuals, as Becker claimed, but instead sought "social distance." Thurow (1969: 117) described this "social distance" as "specifying the relationships under which the two parties will meet and how the Negro will respond." In other words, Thurow emphasized the role of relative power and status that White individuals sought over Black individuals. Many of Thurow's theories were focused on explaining how discriminators would arrange the economy to maximize their gains from discrimination. In his discussion on wages, Thurow explained that a discriminating employer would allocate White and Black labor efficiently but would seek to maximize the distance between Black workers' wages and their marginal productivity. This would result in Black workers being paid below their marginal product at a subsistence wage, and the discriminators would "appropriate part of the marginal product of Negro labor" and then there would "have been no losses coming from any inefficient distribution of economic resources" (Thurow 1969: 120).

Both Bergmann and Thurow postulated that discriminators continue to discriminate because of the material gains they accrue from being in power. In this way, their models' conclusions align. However, the discriminating agents behave differently in Bergmann's world compared with Thurow's: Bergmann pointed out that the "villain" in Thurow's model was "the man who hires Negroes and pays them low wages" and then appropriates their marginal product. However, "under the crowdedness hypothesis (and both Becker models) the villain is the entrepreneur who will not hire Negroes, perhaps on behalf of or under pressure from his white worker" (Bergmann 1971: 310). She did not directly spell out the goals of the entrepreneur or their workers, a weakness for which she was

11. Krueger's (1963) model built from one of Becker's (1957), where both economists modeled White and Black communities as separate economies, much like international trade models. Bergmann disliked this model, writing that in the real world, Black and White workers do cooperate in production and labor is not restricted to separate economies.

later criticized.[12] Bergmann pointed out that "under Thurow's hypothesis white workers would lose nothing at all if wage discrimination ceased." So while the White employer benefited from discrimination in Thurow's model, in Bergmann's model, White workers had a vested interest in maintaining discrimination.[13]

The conclusions one can draw from Thurow's model were more closely aligned with some of the "radical" theories on the economics of discrimination at the time. These works were defined as such because they largely trivialized issues of race-based discrimination due to the dominance of class conflict, and therefore missed the ways in which White workers gain economic advantages from racism. In other words, they focused more on capitalist-labor conflict and less on intra-labor conflict. For example, Victor Perlo (1975: 166) briefly expressed intra-labor conflict, but sloughed off the issue, writing that "whatever the advantage whites may gain from their more complete racial monopoly on better jobs in the South, they lose much more because of the existence of a deeply oppressed Black population used by employers to lower the income of all workers in all kinds of jobs." In this sense, Thurow's theory is similar: discrimination exists to benefit White capitalists because they can appropriate portions of Black workers' marginal product.

The conclusions of Bergmann's crowding hypothesis were not "radical" in this sense: her work did not fall back on class analyses. Instead, the hypothesis indicated that discrimination benefits White workers of similar income and education groups as Black workers. She also relied heavily on marginal productivity theory and other neoclassical tools to make her arguments.

However, her work was not entirely distant from those in the radical tradition. For example, Marshall (1974: 858) identified Raymond S.

12. Donald Harris, the chair of a search committee to find a new economics faculty member researching in "feminist studies" at Stanford University in 1984, pointed out this key weakness of Bergmann's work. In a letter to Nathan Rosenberg, the chair of the economics department at Stanford, Harris listed Bergmann as one of the candidates for the position, and regarding her crowding hypothesis, wrote that "the actual implementation and working out of her ideas has met with mixed reception. Some find the crowding model to be not sharply specified as to which agents do the excluding and what are their goals" (Arrow Papers, box 5, folder 7).

13. In her 1974 paper, Bergmann clarifies how employers benefit from occupational crowding. This was perhaps in response to some of the criticism mentioned in the previous footnote. Bergmann contrasted her model to Beckerian models which argued that a discriminating employer is one who was "missing out on the cheapness of a group of laborers." In contrast, Bergmann (1974: 108) emphasized that many employers *do* take advantage of the cheapness of Black men's labor and maintain that cheapness by limiting their occupational choices.

Franklin and Solomon Resnick (1973) as "two writers in the radical tradition" and argued that their work reduced "to the crowding of blacks in
particular industries and occupations, or in social spheres that limit the
opportunities or experiences of blacks in relation to whites." And like
Franklin and Resnick, Bergmann was focused on group conflict, but the
group was not class: it was race. Bergmann's conclusions ask readers to
consider group conflict and power imbalances, as opposed to individual
rational agents in perfectly competitive markets. As nicely put by Francine
D. Blau (1984: 121), Bergmann's hypothesis suggested, "in contrast to
Becker's (1957) analysis, segregation may play a *causal* role in producing
discriminatory pay differentials." So her conclusions were aligned with
more radical theories in that they focused on group distribution and power,
but her methods and tools (namely, marginal productivity and general
equilibrium theories) belonged to neoclassical economists. She largely
worked to align herself with Becker in her 1971 paper but introduced conclusions that were not aligned with his Chicago-style world of perfect
competition.

Ultimately, Bergmann's crowding hypothesis was published during a time
where a distinct heterodox and mainstream labor economics were being
established. Frederic S. Lee (2004) discusses how, starting in the 1950s,
efforts were made to marginalize contributions to labor economics from institutional and imperfect, nonmarket-clearing perspectives. He argues that, by
1970, labor economics became a branch of applied neoclassical microeconomics through a hegemonic perfect competition, market-clearing approach.
In this sense, Bergmann's hypothesis sat in between two increasingly diver-
gent worlds: the heterodoxy and the mainstream. However, among neoclassical theories of discrimination, hers was not the most "radical." Thurow in
many ways had a more Marxist approach to discrimination. So if Bergmann
did not directly align herself with heterodox theories on class-based discrimination, and still approached the problem using a neoclassical mindset, why
has Becker's theory prevailed over Bergmann's since the 1970s? And in which
schools of thought did the crowding hypothesis thrive?

4. Bergmann Brushed Aside: The Crowding Hypothesis after the 1970s

As any perusal of modern economics textbooks will show, Beckerian
models of labor market discrimination are now dominant, and Bergmann's
crowding hypothesis only occasionally merits a passing mention. For
instance, a widely used graduate-level labor economics textbook by Pierre

Cahuc, Stéphane Carcillo, and André Zylberberg (2014) does not include any discussion of Bergmann's model and continues to rely solely on Becker's. Some undergraduate texts (e.g., Borjas 2017; McConnell, Brue, and Macpherson 2017) briefly mention occupational crowding, often in an exclusively gendered context, and only sometimes citing Bergmann. In this section, we trace how and why occupational crowding receded from the mainstream.

The legacy of Bergmann's occupational crowding hypothesis, and her opposition to Becker's theories, becomes even more clear when tracking Bergmann's changing tone as time passed. Between 1971 and 2005, Bergmann's writing about Becker's work became increasingly oppositional. In her 1971 and 1974 pieces, she contrasted her work with Becker but often aligned parts of her crowding hypothesis with parts of his theories. She presented several criticisms of his work but provided no sweeping statements on the quality of the theory on the whole. Her 1973 work with Irma Adelman subtly suggested the "tastes for discrimination" approach failed to address the core of the socioeconomic issues at play. By 1989, Bergmann blamed Becker for widespread disbelief among economists in even the very existence of labor market discrimination. In the *Journal of Economic Perspectives,* Bergmann (1989: 50) wrote, "For many economists, disbelief in the existence of substantial discrimination is based, not on empirical evidence, but on a theory due to Becker (1957), that if a firm discriminated it would fail." She went on to suggest that Becker's theory needed "a confrontation with reality" (51). By 1995, she was calling Becker's work on family economics "preposterous," and by 2005 she wrote that Becker's theory on labor market discrimination was "neat but totally negated by the facts" and lamented that it had "gained wide acceptance among economists, and continues to be quoted with approval today."[14] She went on to write that most economists were "not capable" of seeing that "employment practices were and are affected by societal systems of status difference. . . . They are trained to explain all business behavior on the basis of simple profit maximization" (Bergmann 2005: 14). As time passed, Bergmann became harsher in her views on Becker's work, but also, as evidenced by the passages above, became increasingly frustrated with the profession at large and what she saw as

14. In the first issue of *Feminist Economics,* Bergmann also published a piece titled "Becker's Theory of the Family: Preposterous Conclusions" in which she mercilessly critiqued Becker's New Home Economics.

an inability or unwillingness to see labor market discrimination the way she did.

The lasting influence of Becker's model has largely to do with the shift in economics in the 1970s. The "never-never land of perfect competition" that Bergmann described was prevalent in the 1970s, and Chicago school ideals were penetrating several corners of the economics discipline. Chicago-style models of perfect competition were incompatible with Bergmann's hypothesis: occupational crowding does not fit into a world of perfect competitive labor markets, where different groups of similarly qualified workers are easy substitutes for one another. For these economists, perfect competition should eventually prevail. By contrast, Bergmann highlighted a world in which imperfect competition was maintained because it benefited White workers and thereby maintained their group privilege. And though Bergmann's model was not class-focused in the same way that other heterodox theories were, Bergmann's conclusions highlighted issues of collective power that were inconsistent with how perfectly competitive labor markets work.

It is also possible that Bergmann's hypothesis was pushed aside by mainstream researchers as the motives for her work became clearer: Bergmann was concerned with social justice, and her work became thus more normative in nature. For instance, her 1986 book *The Economic Emergence of Women* shows the extent of her willingness to speak about norms and standards of justice that societies should uphold. Bergmann (1986: 218) openly claimed the goal of the book was to guide building new family and workplace arrangements with "justice, common sense, and humanity." In the book, she revisits the occupational crowding hypothesis, this time describing the occupational crowding of women instead of Black workers, and focusing on injustices rather than pure economic efficiency.

In her 1971 work, Bergmann's occupational crowding hypothesis was largely couched in a discussion on how reducing occupational segregation would raise national output. In her 1986 reexamination, Bergmann couched the crowding hypothesis in issues of women's liberation, discussing how crowding limited women's potential and forced them to "spend their lives doing things they hate" (83). She wrote that "part of the problem is misogyny—the desire on the part of some men to keep women in an inferior status, and therefore out of jobs that would make them equal or superior of male employees" (89). Bergmann's newfound feminist frankness applied to the crowding hypothesis may have scared away citations from economic researchers who aimed to discuss the economics of discrimination in a positive, rather than normative, manner, and who preferred to focus on economics "laws of nature" rather than power, racism, and patriarchy.

Still, in the 1970s and 1980s, the crowding hypothesis was used in a number of empirical papers.[15] Many of these papers extended the application of the crowding hypothesis to gender segregation, perhaps encouraged by the description in *The Economic Emergence of Women* or by Bergmann's 1974 publication in the *Eastern Economic Journal*, in which she briefly mentioned her hypothesis could be extended to sex discrimination. For example, Ferber and Lowry (1976) referenced Bergmann's work when demonstrating that a large part of the gender wage gap was attributable to occupational distributions, that earnings were lower in occupations dominated by women, and that discrimination was the most prominent explanation for these trends. They, along with Paula England (1982), June E. O'Neill (1983), Mark Aldrich and Robert B. Buchele (1986), and Elaine Sorensen (1990) found women earned less if they worked in a job that hired women exclusively as opposed to a gender-mixed occupation.

In addition to empirical applications of the hypothesis in gender-based labor market discrimination, many works pitted Bergmann's and Becker's theories against each other. Isabel V. Sawhill (1973) used Current Population Survey data to demonstrate that employment discrimination was more relevant than pure wage discrimination for women. She tied this result to Bergmann's crowding hypothesis and suggested the results could serve as ammunition in a Becker versus Bergmann battle comparing theories of taste-based discrimination to occupational crowding. Blau reviewed the hypothesis in a 1979 work with Wallace D. Hendricks and in a 1984 edited volume for the National Academy of Sciences on sex segregation in the workplace. In these works, she updates previous studies on occupational segregation and, in her 1984 work, suggests that data on occupational segregation induce her to view Bergmann's theory as more persuasive than Becker's (Blau 1984: 130).

This post-1970s shift from a racial application of the crowding hypothesis to a gendered one may have simply been a reflection of changing interests at the time. In the United States, the civil rights movement and issues of race-based discrimination were prominent in

---

15. Many continued to focus on race, including Bergmann and Lyle 1971; Bergsman 1982; Bergmann and Darity 1981.

the 1950s and 1960s, but second-wave feminist movements began a bit later in the 1960s and 1970s. Given this chronology, it makes sense that many economists focused on race-based labor market discrimination in the mid-twentieth century, then turned to gender-based shortly after. Further, Bergmann's broader career began to shift to issues of gender-based discrimination. She published her first works on gender issues in the economy in 1973, just after her first work on the crowding hypothesis. Her first work on gender was a coauthored piece with Irma Adelman (1973: 509), where they argued that "a proper analysis of discrimination is yet to come" and that economists needed to move beyond unexplained tastes for discrimination to understand the true social forces at play, which was a direct and critical reference to Becker. Her second 1973 piece was focused on the "economics of women's liberation," where within the first few pages she briefly revisited her crowding hypothesis in gender applications. Thus Bergmann herself seemed interested in shifting the crowding hypothesis back to its gender-oriented origins. Additionally, her heavy involvement in the newly formed International Association for Feminist Economics in the 1990s may simply have meant that her work, including the 1971 and 1974 articulations of the crowding hypothesis, had been publicized among feminist economists more than those in other fields.

Feminist economics was in fact the perfect subdiscipline to carve out a home for the crowding hypothesis. Feminist economics and IAFFE were largely founded to combat androcentric bias in economics research. Marilyn Power (2004: 3) has proposed that feminist economics, among other things, be made up of "analysis of economic, political, and social processes and power relations; inclusion of ethical goals and values as an intrinsic part of the analysis; and interrogation of differences by class, race-ethnicity, and other factors." Bergmann's crowding hypothesis, unlike Becker's theories of taste-based discrimination, offered an analysis of power relations by race and eventually by gender. Even today the crowding hypothesis is regularly referenced by feminist economists as an important determinant of gender differences in labor market outcomes (for instance, Seguino and Braunstein 2019; Aidis 2016; Grybaite 2006).

Similar to feminist economics, stratification economists also regularly draw on occupational crowding as an explanation of labor market dynamics. Stratification economics focuses on "the structural and intentional processes generating hierarchy and, correspondingly, income and wealth inequality between ascriptively distinguished groups" (Darity 2005). It is a subfield that acknowledges that "there are *material benefits* that redound to dominant groups that motivate their efforts to maintain privilege" (Darity 2005). In many ways, this description fits the crowding hypothesis perfectly, as it explains how White workers accrue material (wage) gains when Black workers are shunted into a small group of occupations. Indeed, the term *stratification economics* was coined by William Darity Jr., who had previously coauthored work with Bergmann in 1981 on explanations for occupational segregation by race and gender. Recent stratification economists à la Darity still use the crowding hypothesis in research on racial disparities in labor markets (for instance, Holder 2017, 2018; Hamilton and Darity 2012; Willow 2011; Gibson, Darity, and Myers 1998).

Ultimately, while Bergmann's crowding hypothesis has had a lasting impact in several disciplines, these have primarily been in the heterodoxy.[16] Feminist economists and stratification economists are rarely considered part of the mainstream, and many recent papers that make use of the crowding hypothesis have been published in *Feminist Economics*, which hails from the IAFFE organization that Bergmann helped found, and the *Review of Black Political Economy*, which was established in 1970 during the burgeoning of interest and concern about issues of racism in the economy and in the economics discipline. Ultimately, Bergmann's hypothesis successfully expanded from merely a model on race-based discrimination to one that could be applied to both race- and gender-based discrimination, and it seems that Bergmann's hypothesis was accepted by these heterodox scholars because of its insights about power and group privilege. It was perhaps pushed out of the mainstream because it was based on an imperfectly competitive labor market, but also because the ties Bergmann made to Becker's theories in 1971 dissipated rapidly soon after. As Bergmann's disdain for Beckerian discrimination models (and for his models of the family) got progressively less subtle, one has to wonder if her increasing assertiveness in critiquing Becker distanced her work on crowding from those who favored Becker. Bergmann indeed had a reputation for being straightforward, undiplomatic, and staunch in her convictions, which could perturb some, probably partly because these characteristics were associated with a woman. Yet, as her colleague Susan Himmelweit in IAFFE's commemoration of Bergmann upon her death in

16. In addition to providing foundations for feminist and stratification economics, the crowding hypothesis has also penetrated literature on immigrant labor (e.g., Lindley and Elliott 2008; Meng 1998; Stevans 1998, 1996).

2005 noted, "She was straightforward, fearless, and ruthlessly honest—just what feminist economics needed to get started" (Bergmann Papers, box 8, folder 1).

5. Conclusion

Bergmann had a personal and professional reputation far beyond her famous crowding hypothesis.[17] However, this article serves to investigate Bergmann's first contribution to the literature on the economics of discrimination: her occupational crowding hypothesis. As standpoint theorists might hypothesize, Bergmann's own experiences with discrimination as a Jewish woman working to become an economist in the 1950s were related to her development of the hypothesis. Her experiences with discrimination as a woman in economics pushed her to examine workplace inequality throughout her life.

Bergmann's hypothesis was initially compared to work done by other prominent economists like Becker, Arrow, Thurow, and Krueger. Hers was not the most "radical" in the group, but was still eventually pushed out of the mainstream. This may be because of the shift in the mainstream to perfectly competitive worldviews, because of Bergmann's increasingly normative stances in economics, or because the conclusions of Bergmann's model ultimately suggest that discrimination is used to maintain *group* privilege and thus moves away from mainstream theories on individual rationality.

One could do similar historical examinations on the development and trajectory of Bergmann's other key contributions. For instance, her work on affirmative action, or her activity in policy spaces, or her involvement with founding IAFFE and the Eastern Economic Association. Yet because the occupational crowding hypothesis was Bergmann's first in a long line of work that dealt with group inequality and discrimination, studying its history is, in many ways, a study of the intellectual origins of a pioneering feminist economist.

As the economics of race and gender continue to become more mainstream, it is important that historians of economic thought help the discipline revisit works that were pushed out of the mainstream because of their focus on the power dynamics of racism and patriarchy. Further, if the goal of feminist economics is to overcome androcentric bias in the field,

---

17. Partially described in work by Paulette Olson (2007).

historians of feminist economics must point out the androcentric biases experienced by feminist economists in their careers and in the reception of their works. This study on Bergmann's occupational crowding hypothesis, and indeed many other works in this volume, are certainly efforts in these directions.

References

Aidis, Ruta. 2016. "Business and Occupational Crowding: Implications for Female Entrepreneurship Development and Success." In *Women's Entrepreneurship in Global and Local Contexts*. Cheltenham: Edward Elgar.

Aldrich, Mark, and Robert B. Buchele. 1986. *The Economics of Comparable Worth*. Cambridge, Mass.: Ballinger.

Arrow, Kenneth J. Papers. David M. Rubenstein Rare Book & Manuscript Library, Duke University.

Arrow, Kenneth J. 1973. "The Theory of Discrimination." In *Discrimination in Labor Markets*, edited by Orley Ashenfelter and Albert Rees, 3–33. Princeton, N.J.: Princeton University Press.

Backhouse, Roger E. 2014. "Paul A. Samuelson's Move to MIT." In *MIT and the Transformation of American Economics*, edited by E. Roy Weintraub. *History of Political Economy* 46 (supplement): 60–77.

Becchio, G. 2020. *A History of Feminist and Gender Economics*. London: Routledge.

Becchio, G. 2021. "Bergmann versus Becker on Marriage Theory: The Emergence of Feminist Economics as a Challenge to New Home Economics." Unpublished manuscript.

Becker, Gary S. 1957. *The Economics of Discrimination: An Economic View of Racial Discrimination*. Chicago: University of Chicago Press.

Becker, Gary S. 1971. *The Economics of Discrimination: An Economic View of Racial Discrimination*. 2nd ed. Chicago: University of Chicago Press.

Bergmann, Barbara. Papers. David M. Rubenstein Rare Book & Manuscript Library, Duke University.

Bergmann, Barbara R. 1968. "Investment in the Human Resources of Negroes." Joint Economic Committee of the US Congress, Federal Programs for the Development of Human Resources, vol. 1, pt. 2.

Bergmann, Barbara R. 1969. "The Urban Economy and the 'Urban Crisis.'" *American Economic Review* 59, no. 4: 639–45.

Bergmann, Barbara R. 1971. "The Effect on White Incomes of Discrimination in Employment." *Journal of Political Economy* 79, no. 2: 294–313.

Bergmann, Barbara R. 1973. "Successful Women in the Sciences: An Analysis of Determinants; The Economics of Women's Liberation." *Annals of the New York Academy of Sciences* 208:154–60.

Bergmann, Barbara R. 1974. "Occupational Segregation, Wages and Profits When Employers Discriminate by Race or Sex." *Eastern Economic Journal* 1, no. 2: 103–10.

Bergmann, Barbara R. 1986. *The Economic Emergence of Women.* New York: Basic Books.

Bergmann, Barbara R. 1989. "Does the Market for Women's Labor Need Fixing?" *Journal of Economic Perspectives* 3, no. 1: 43–60.

Bergmann, Barbara. 1995. "Becker's Theory of the Family: Preposterous Conclusions." *Feminist Economics* 1, no. 1: 141–50.

Bergmann, Barbara R. 2005. "Pushing for a More Humane Society." *American Economist* 49, no. 2: 11–15.

Bergmann, Barbara R., and Irma Adelman. 1973. "The 1973 Report of the President's Council of Economic Advisers: The Economic Role of Women." *American Economic Review* 63, no. 4: 509–14.

Bergmann, Barbara R., and William Darity. 1981. "Social Relations, Productivity, and Employer Discrimination." *Monthly Labor Review* 104, no. 4: 47–49.

Bergmann, Barbara R., and David Evan Kaun. 1967. *Structural Unemployment in the United States.* Vol. 46. Washington, D.C.: US Department of Commerce, Economic Development Administration.

Bergmann, Barbara R., and Jerolyn R. Lyle. 1971. "The Occupational Standing of Negroes by Areas and Industries." *Journal of Human Resources* 6, no. 4: 411–33.

Bergquist, Charles. 1986. "Labor in Latin America." In *Labor in Latin America: Comparative Essays on Chile, Argentina, Venezuela, and Colombia.* Stanford, Calif.: Stanford University Press.

Bergsman, Joel. 1982. "Apartheid, Wages, and Production Costs in South Africa: An Application of the Crowding Hypothesis." *Journal of Human Resources* 17, no. 4: 633–45.

Blau, Francine D. 1984. "Occupational Segregation and Labor Market Discrimination." In *Sex Segregation in the Workplace: Trends, Explanations, Remedies,* edited by Barbara F. Reskin, 117–43. Washington, D.C.: National Academy Press.

Blau, Francine D., and Wallace E. Hendricks. 1979. "Occupational Segregation by Sex: Trends and Prospects." *Journal of Human Resources* 14, no. 2: 197–210.

Borjas, George. 2017. *Labor Economics.* 7th ed. New York: McGraw Hill.

Cahuc, Pierre, Stéphane Carcillo, and André Zylberberg. 2014. *Labor Economics.* Cambridge, Mass.: MIT Press.

Chamberlin, Edward. H. 1949. *Theory of Monopolistic Competition: A Reorientation of the Theory of Value.* London: Oxford University Press.

Chassonnery-Zaïgouche, Cléo, and Lauren Larrouy. 2017. "'From Warfare to Welfare': Contextualising Arrow and Schelling's Models of Racial Inequalities (1968–1972)." *European Journal of the History of Economic Thought* 24, no. 6: 1355–87.

Cohen, Malcolm S. 1971. "Sex Differences in Compensation." *Journal of Human Resources* 6, no. 4: 434–47.

Collins, Patricia Hill. 2015. "Black Feminist Epistemology." In *Just Methods: An Interdisciplinary Feminist Reader*, edited by Alison M. Jaggar, 252–56. New York: Routledge.

Darity, William. 2005. "Stratification Economics: The Role of Intergroup Inequality." *Journal of Economics and Finance* 29, no. 2: 144.

Darity, William A., Jr., Darrick Hamilton, and James B. Stewart. 2015. "A Tour de Force in Understanding Intergroup Inequality: An Introduction to Stratification Economics." *Review of Black Political Economy* 42, nos. 1–2: 1–6.

Dewey, Donald. 1952. "Negro Employment in Southern Industry." *Journal of Political Economy* 60: 279–94.

Edgeworth, Francis Y. 1922. "Equal Pay to Men and Women for Equal Work." *Economic Journal* 32, no. 128: 431–57.

England, Paula. 1982. "Skill Demands and Earnings in Female and Male Occupations." *Sociology and Social Research* 66, no. 2: 147–68.

Fawcett, Millicent G. 1892. "Mr. Sidney Webb's Article on Women's Wages." *Economic Journal II*, March, 173–76.

Fawcett, Millicent G. 1916. "The Position of Women in Economic Life." In *After War Problems*, edited by W. H. Dawson, 404–6. London: Allen & Unwin.

Fein, Rashi. 1965. "An Economic and Social Profile of the Negro American." *Daedalus* 94, no. 4: 815–46.

Ferber, Marianne A., and Helen M. Lowry. 1976. "The Sex Differential in Earnings: A Reappraisal." *ILR Review* 29, no. 3: 377–87.

Ferber, Marianne A., and Julie A. Nelson, eds. 2009. *Beyond Economic Man: Feminist Theory and Economics*. Chicago: University of Chicago Press.

Fleury, Jean-Baptiste. 2012. "Wandering through the Borderlands of the Social Sciences: Gary Becker's Economics of Discrimination." *History of Political Economy* 44, no. 1: 1–40.

Forget, Evelyn L. 2002. "A Hunger for Narrative: Writing Lives in the History of Economic Thought." In *The Future of the History of Economics*, edited by E. Roy Weintraub. *History of Political Economy* 34 (supplement): 226–44.

Franklin, Raymond S., and Solomon Resnik. 1973. *The Political Economy of Racism*. New York: Holt, Rinehart, and Winston.

Gibson, Karen J., William A. Darity Jr., and Samuel L. Myers Jr. 1998. "Revisiting Occupational Crowding in the United States: A Preliminary Study." *Feminist Economics* 4, no. 3: 73–95.

Gilman, Harry. 1965. "Economic Discrimination and Unemployment." *American Economic Review* 55, no. 5: 1077–96.

Glenn, Norval D. 1963. "Occupational Benefits to Whites from the Subordination of Negroes." *American Sociological Review* 28, no. 3: 443–48.

Grybaite, Virginija. 2006. "Analysis of Theoretical Approaches to Gender Pay Gap." *Journal of Business Economics and Management* 7, no. 2: 85–91.

Hamilton, Darrick, and William A. Darity Jr. 2012. "Crowded Out? The Racial Composition of American Occupations." *Researching Black Communities: A Methodological Guide*, edited by James S. Jackson, Cleopatra Howard Caldwell, and Sherrill L. Sellers, 60–78. Ann Arbor: University of Michigan Press.

Harding, Sandra G. 2004. *The Feminist Standpoint Theory Reader: Intellectual and Political Controversies.* New York: Psychology Press.

Heller, Walter W. 1970. "Economics of the Race Problem." *Social Research* 37, no. 4: 495–510.

Holder, Michelle. 2017. "African American Men's Decline in Labor Market Status during the Great Recession." In *African American Men and the Labor Market during the Great Recession*, 35–62. New York: Palgrave Macmillan.

Holder, Michelle. 2018. "Revisiting Bergmann's Occupational Crowding Model." *Review of Radical Political Economics* 50, no. 4: 683–90.

Howson, Susan. 2013. "The Uses of Biography and the History of Economics." *History of Economics Review* 57, no. 1: 1–15.

Krueger, Anne. 1963. "The Economics of Discrimination." *Journal of Political Economy* 71, no. 5: 481–86.

Kyrk, Hazel. 1950. "The Income Distribution as a Measure of Economic Welfare." *American Economic Review* 40, no. 2: 342–55.

Lee, Frederic S. 2004. "To Be a Heterodox Economist: The Contested Landscape of American Economics, 1960s and 1970s." *Journal of Economic Issues* 38, no. 3: 747–63.

Lindley, J. K., and R. J. R. Elliott. 2008. "UK Immigrant Earnings and Occupational Crowding." *Journal of the Royal Statistical Society Series A* 171, no. 3: 645–71.

Marshall, Ray. 1974. "The Economics of Racial Discrimination: A Survey." *Journal of Economic Literature* 12, no. 3: 839–71.

McConnell, Campbell, Stanley Brue, and David Macpherson. 2017. *Contemporary Labor Economics.* 11th ed. New York: McGraw Hill.

Meng, Xin. 1998. "Gender Occupational Segregation and Its Impact on the Gender Wage Differential among Rural-Urban Migrants: A Chinese Case Study." *Applied Economics* 30, no. 6: 741–52.

Myrdal, Gunner. 1944. *An American Dilemma: The Negro Problem and Modern Democracy.* New York: Harper & Brothers.

Northrup, Herbert R. 1943. "Organized Labor and Negro Workers." *Journal of Political Economy* 51, no. 3: 206–21.

Northrup, Herbert R. 1946. "Unions and Negro Employment." *Annals of the American Academy of Political and Social Science* 244, no. 1: 42–47.

Olson, Paulette I. 2007. "On the Contributions of Barbara Bergmann to Economics." *Review of Political Economy* 19, no. 4: 475–96.

Olson, Paulette I., and Zohreh Emami. 2002. *Engendering Economics: Conversations with Women Economists in the US.* New York: Routledge.

O'Neill, June E. 1983. *The Determinants and Wage Effects of Occupational Segregation: Final Report.* Washington, D.C.: Urban Institute.

Papers of John F. Kennedy. Presidential Papers. White House Staff Files of Walter W. Heller. Subject Files, 1953–1964. Discrimination report, 1962. JFKWHSFWWH-MF31–011. John F. Kennedy Presidential Library and Museum.

Perlo, Victor. 1975. *Economics of Racism USA: Roots of Black Inequality.* New York: International Publishers.

Power, Marilyn. 2004. "Social Provisioning as a Starting Point for Feminist Economics." *Feminist Economics* 10, no. 3: 3–19.

Pujol, Michèle A. 1992. *Feminism and Anti-feminism in Early Economic Thought.* Cheltenham: Edward Elgar.

Romani, Roberto. 2018. "On Science and Reform: The Parable of the New Economics, 1960s–1970s." *European Journal of the History of Economic Thought* 25, no. 2: 295–326.

Sawhill, Isabel V. 1973. "The Economics of Discrimination against Women: Some New Findings." *Journal of Human Resources* 8, no. 3: 383–96.

Seguino, Stephanie, and Elissa Braunstein. 2019. "The Costs of Exclusion: Gender Job Segregation, Structural Change, and the Labour Share of Income." *Development and Change* 50, no. 4: 976–1008.

Simms, Margaret C. 2020. "The National Economic Association at Fifty: Where Have We Come From and Where Are We Going?" *Review of Black Political Economy* 47, no. 2: 118–24.

Sorensen, Elaine. 1990. "The Crowding Hypothesis and Comparable Worth." *Journal of Human Resources* 25, no. 1: 55–89.

Sprague, Joey. 2016. *Feminist Methodologies for Critical Researchers: Bridging Differences.* Lanham, Md.: Rowman & Littlefield.

Stevans, Lonnie K. 1996. "Immigration and Occupational Crowding in the United States." *Labour* 10, no. 2: 357–74.

Stevans, Lonnie K. 1998. "Assessing the Effect of the Occupational Crowding of Immigrants on the Real Wages of African American Workers." *Review of Black Political Economy* 26, no. 2: 37–46.

Thurow, Lester. 1969. *Poverty and Discrimination.* Washington, D.C.: Brookings Institution.

Weintraub, E. Roy. 2014. "MIT's Openness to Jewish Economists." In *MIT and the Transformation of American Economics*, edited by E. Roy Weintraub. *History of Political Economy* 46 (supplement): 45–59.

Willow, Moriah. 2011. "Occupational Crowding by Race in the Pacific Northwest: A Comparative Study of Portland, Oregon and Seattle, Washington." *PSU McNair Scholars Online Journal* 5, no. 1: 24.

Controlling for What? Movements, Measures, and Meanings in the US Gender Wage Gap Debate

Daniel Hirschman

Each year, the National Committee on Pay Equity (NCPE) announces a new "Equal Pay Day." In 2021, NCPE tells us that Wednesday, March 24, represents "how far into the year women must work to earn what men earned in the previous year." The NCPE bases its moving calendar on measurements of the "gender wage gap" (also called the gender pay gap), typically defined as the ratio of women's average earnings to men's, among those working full-time. In 2021, the pay gap sat around eighty-two cents on the dollar; put differently, the average earnings of full-time employed women are about 18 percent lower than the average incomes of full-time employed men ("Women Are Paid Less Than Men" 2022). The gender wage gap figures prominently in debates around inequality. Along with the NCPE, progressive organizations like the Economic Progress Institute and the American Association of University Women routinely publish explainers with titles like "The Simple Truth about the Gender Pay Gap," foregrounding the apparent obviousness of the gap and its stubborn refusal to close (AAUW 2020). These publications summon ritualized counterperformances, as each year the conservative American

Correspondence may be addressed to Daniel Hirschman, Department of Sociology, Cornell University (dan.hirschman@cornell.edu). I thank Laura Adler, Cléo Chassonnery-Zaïgouche, Kira Lussier; members of the Work, Organizations, and the Economy workshop; participants at the 2021 HOPE conference on women and economics; and two anonymous reviewers for comments on prior versions of this article.

History of Political Economy 54 (annual suppl.) DOI 10.1215/00182702-10085710

Enterprise Institute and its fellow travelers offer rebuttals with titles like "The Gender Wage Gap Myth" (Hoff Sommers 2014).

This article explores how debates around economic inequality between men and women came to focus on this particular *stylized fact*, and how that fact circulates within academic, policy, and public debates. How did the gender wage gap come to be the sort of thing that can have a "simple truth" or a status as "myth"? What sorts of politics does the gender wage gap enable or frustrate? What can our shifting interpretations of the gap tell us about our understandings of men and women's places in economic life, and about ideologies of agency and structure?

This article is part of a larger project attempting to understand the role of stylized facts in the production and circulation of economic knowledge (see Hirschman 2016). Attempting to formalize the folk concept used by economists since the 1960s, I define stylized facts as *empirical regularities in need of an explanation*. Stylized facts include trends, correlations, and rates of incidence. The most famous stylized fact, one of the first to be explicitly called out as such, was the observed stability in labor's share of national income (Kaldor 1957). For Kaldor, treating labor's share as a stylized fact was useful because it drew attention to the relative stability of the figure over long periods of time rather than the small amount of year-to-year variation. More generally, stylized fact claims are attempts to identify a pattern in economic life stable enough to be worth explaining, even as scholars acknowledge that economic relationships change over time such that no correlation is stable forever and no trend continues indefinitely. Put differently, these quantitative descriptions act in economics (and other social sciences) the way that phenomena function in some natural sciences (Hacking 1983). That is, stylized facts are what (some) economic models are built to explain.

Stylized facts do not stay confined to the pages of economics journals. The trends, correlations, and rates identified by academics are capable of traveling out into political discourse (on how facts travel, see Howlett and Morgan 2010). When they travel, stylized facts may serve as a "hinge" (Abbott 2005) bringing researchers and their theories into public discourse and policy conversations. Or stylized facts may travel disconnected from larger bodies of scholarship, instead meeting up with "folk economics" (Swedberg 2018), nonexpert understandings that offer alternative explanations of the workings of the economy. In turn, these folk economic understandings may be shaped especially strongly by "legal consciousness" (Ewick and Silbey 1998). As sociolegal scholars have shown, the law has an outsized role in shaping how people believe society *ought* to work and how it *actually* works. Social movements may vie to foreground particular stylized facts or particular academic or folk interpretations of those facts that they believe will help sway public opinion. This article explores these dynamics in the contexts of debates over the extent and causes of the gender wage gap in the United States.

The history of the gender wage gap in the United States begins with debates over women's increasing presence in the paid labor force. I briefly review debates in the late nineteenth to mid-twentieth century, and especially the demands of labor feminists for what later came to be called equal pay for *comparable* work. In this period, occupational gender segregation was both extreme and widely acknowledged, and feminist activists thus recognized that demands for equal pay for the *same* work would have relatively little impact on overall economic gender inequalities. Academic debates on gender inequality focused on comparisons *within* occupations. Data on overall wages broken down by gender were scarce; instead, studies focused on particular industries, occupations, or employers.

In the 1960s, both the politics and study of pay disparities shifted. In 1963, Congress passed the Equal Pay Act, which enacted a narrow version of labor feminists' demands: only differential pay for the *same* work would be considered illegal. With the rise of human capital theory and high-quality household survey data, economists and sociologists began to study pay disparities at an aggregate level *and* to attempt to tease apart the sources of that gap, usually focusing on the relative weights of education, experience, occupation or industry, and discrimination. This research, along with the publications of the Women's Bureau of the Department of Labor, settled on the modern formulation of the gender wage gap, which compared the wages of full-time employed men and women, not controlling for anything else.

This choice was not entirely obvious—why control for full-time work when women are much more likely to work part-time? Why not control for hours, given that men employed full-time work, on average, more hours? But it stuck. And spread. Discussions of discrimination were framed around the Equal Pay Act, and many studies attempted to rebut the simplistic interpretation of the wage gap as entirely or even largely reflecting unlawful discrimination. Instead, scholars argued that pay differentials came from women's relatively lower levels of education and experience, and from working in lower-paid occupations.

The limits of the Equal Pay Act, and Title VII of the Civil Rights Act of 1964, which banned sex discrimination more generally, became rapidly apparent to a new generation of feminist activists. Throughout the 1960s and 1970s, the gap stayed stubbornly flat, around 60 cents on the dollar. In the late 1970s, feminist activists, frustrated with this apparent stagnation, mobilized around the banner of "comparable worth." Returning to the demands of labor feminists from the first half of the twentieth century, organizations like the NCPE, NOW, labor unions, and allies in the federal government fought to reinterpret Title VII as prohibiting employers from paying lower wages to heavily feminized occupations that otherwise required similar levels of education, skill, and effort. Drawing on employers' own job evaluation systems, scholars and activists tried to prove that women's work was devalued, whether or not the particular occupant of a job was a man or a woman.

The fight for comparable worth yielded some initial successes in the early 1980s before coming to a halt after a series of setbacks. I draw on a hand-coded corpus of newspaper articles to document trends in the invocation and interpretation of the gender wage gap from 1970 through 2014. Absent pressure from the feminist movement, the stylized fact of the gender wage gap became largely delinked from questions of occupational segregation. Rapid improvements in the gender pay gap during the 1980s flattened out near their current levels. This trend, alongside other transformations, has led scholars to characterize this era as one of an "uneven and stalled" gender revolution (England 2010). While extensive occupational segregation persists, motherhood came to occupy the most prominent space in the debate over the enduring gender wage gap. The folk economics of the gender pay gap came to contrast illegal pay discrimination with freely chosen family obligations as the dominant back-and-forth explanatory debate.

At the same time, the gender wage gap continues to be widely misunderstood, as many actors assume it refers to the kind of same-work, different-pay discrimination outlawed by the Equal Pay Act. This misunderstanding is reinforced when the gender wage gap is mobilized in support of policies designed to improve enforcement of the Equal Pay Act (policies that likely cannot address most of the remaining gap). And this misunderstanding is exacerbated by the limits of the household survey-based knowledge infrastructure of labor economics and sociology (Hirschman 2021). Without employer-employee matched data, researchers are not able to definitively answer the question of how much less women are paid than men working in the same jobs.

In the following history, I try to attend simultaneously to the interactions of academics, activists (feminist, labor movement, and conservative), politicians, data, method, and theories. The history of the gender pay gap is at once the history of the development of modern economics and sociology, the shifting fortunes of the American feminist and labor movements, the outsized importance of the law in shaping debates over (in)equality, and dramatic transformations—and nontransformations—in the "arrangement between the sexes" (Goffman 1977). To tell this crisscrossing story, I rely heavily on existing histories of these various movements and dynamics, alongside my own reading of newspapers, academic journals, and political debates, as well as a handful of oral history interviews with key scholars. In this effort, I am especially indebted to Laura Garbes and Clare Wan for their research assistance.

Before the Gender Wage Gap

Before the 1960s, the "gender wage gap" was not yet a thing. Neither government statisticians nor academic social scientists calculated the average earnings of a representative sample of all full-timed employed women and compared it with that of men. They did not do so in part because the tools needed to do so were simply unavailable. Before the 1940s, household survey data were scarce. The Current Population Survey (CPS) would not launch until 1948 (although it was based on a survey of unemployment that began in 1940), and the influential Panel Study on Income Dynamics (PSID) did not begin until 1968. Processing those data that existed was difficult and expensive. And theoretical debates did not yet focus on the earnings of individuals, as they would after the rise of human capital theory in economics and stratification research in sociology.

Although the gender wage gap was not yet a recognizable object, let alone a stylized fact, economic gender inequality was well recognized in the late nineteenth to mid-twentieth century. Debates focused on the question of fair wages for women and what that implied about women's and men's roles in the family and the workplace (Kessler-Harris 2014).[1] Feminist labor groups mobilized for equality in the workplace (Cobble 2004), and feminist bureaucrats published reports and

---

1. For parallel discussions in Britain, see Chassonnery-Zaïgouche 2018.

investigations in support of that mobilization (Laughlin 2000). These debates mobilized statistics in support of women's claims for equality, but the statistics available tended to be much narrower, emphasizing specific employers, specific professions, or specific locations. From the 1870s to the 1930s, the debate focused largely on whether women should work at all, and whether they deserved equal pay to men when they did so. Informed by the doctrine of "separate spheres" of family and public life, these debates centered White women and their family obligations while ignoring the experiences of Black women who were more likely to work outside the home (often as servants for those same White women). Starting in the 1940s, labor feminists expanded the debate to focus both on occupational segregation and on comparable worth, with the experiences of World War II making a strong case for women's ability to do traditionally male jobs and thus laying the groundwork for the argument that traditionally feminine occupations were undervalued compared with those dominated by men.

In this period, some forms of gender pay inequality were stark. For example, a 1906 *New York Times* story reports on the launch of a campaign for equal pay among schoolteachers in New York City ("Women Teachers Open Equal Pay Campaign" 1906). While women teachers started at a salary of six hundred dollars per year, men teachers started at nine hundred dollars. This kind of explicit pay disparity was legal and typically justified by pointing to men's family obligations, or sometimes their productivity or competitiveness on the labor market.

Although these stark disparities between men and women working in the same jobs for the same employer were perhaps the easiest to document and mobilize against, feminist activists recognized that tackling gender disparities in the workforce would require addressing occupational segregation as well. Most jobs were highly segregated, with women concentrated in a handful of occupations like secretary and nurse, and men dominating the rest of the labor market.

The labor needs of the wartime economy in World War I put a few dents into the segregated occupational structure. Given the opportunity, women moved into jobs previously occupied by men in large numbers (Kessler-Harris 2014: 28), increasing the salience of the question of equal pay. Feminist labor activists and their allies in the government, including the Women's Industry Service (which would become the Women's Bureau of the Department of Labor in 1920), pressured for policy changes to force employers to pay women and men equally, a "rate for the job"

(Kessler-Harris 2014: 35).[2] This pressure continued through the 1920s and 1930s, uniting the efforts of different factions of the feminist movement around the principle of equal pay for equal work with some successes (Kessler-Harris 2014). This pressure ramped up in World War II, which followed the same pattern as World War I but to an even greater extent. Somewhat ironically, the push for equal pay in this period also drew in decidedly antifeminist actors, including some in the labor movement concerned with *maintaining* occupational segregation by preventing employers from undercutting men's labor with lower-paid women (Kessler-Harris 2014: 77).

Although gender segregation fell during World War II, it remained a stark feature of the American occupational structure. This fact was recognized by feminist activists and academics alike. During and immediately after the war, feminist labor activists began to coalesce around a stronger demand: equal pay for *comparable* work. That is, they began to demand that women's work be compensated comparably to men's work that required similar effort, skill, risk, experience, and so on. In 1943, Z. Clark Dickinson, an economist at the University of Michigan, put the argument starkly: "The slogans 'equal pay for equal work' and 'the rate for the job' both express too narrowly the real objective of equality of economic opportunity between the sexes, for they concentrate attention too exclusively on the rather few occupations which are common to both sexes in peacetime, or in which women replace men during wartime" (Dickinson 1943: 711; also cited in Kessler-Harris 2014).

Dickinson's article drew on available data to try to assess the level of inequality between men's and women's wages. Like most research in this period, Z. Clark Dickinson was limited by the lack of representative national data. Instead, Dickinson focused his account on twenty-five specific manufacturing industries where data were available. As he noted, "If we seem unduly preoccupied with factory workers, that is only because the data concerning them are most nearly adequate for our analysis" (Dickinson 1943: 703). Reports in this period from the Women's Bureau (e.g., Pidgeon 1937) relied similarly on data about particular industries,

2. The Women's Bureau of the Department of Labor has an interesting and complicated history (see Laughlin 2000). The bureau served as a foothold for the feminist movement inside the executive branch of the federal government. Its main outputs were research reports and conferences on women's economic position. Although the bureau's position on other issues (notably the Equal Rights Amendment) shifted over the period discussed here, the bureau was a consistent proponent of the Equal Pay Act throughout the post–World War II era.

most of it focused on particular states. Dickinson's analysis showed that women were typically paid less, even within the same industry. The overall gender wage gap figure in its modern form was not present, although his article does provide related statistics in a footnote (Dickinson 1943: 708). These statistics were not given any special significance. In contrast, Dickinson lamented the lack of data from within individual establishments: "Let me here express the hope that compilers of wage statistics will publish more data on intra-plant averages of earnings by sex, within same-named occupations" (714). As I show, this hope remains largely unfulfilled to this day.

After World War II, feminist activists from varying backgrounds united to apply pressure to achieve wage justice for women. This campaign involved calls for equal pay for comparable work, including introducing legislation at both the national and the state level. At the federal level, the first Equal Pay Bill was submitted in 1945 and would have prohibited wage differentials for "work of a comparable character" (Cobble 2004). Writing in a 1947 special issue of the *Annals of the American Academy of Political and Social Science* titled "Women's Opportunities and Responsibilities," Dorothy Brady (an economist in the Department of Labor) made the case for the proposed bill. Like Dickinson, Brady (1947) pointed to the absence of data about specific workplaces, which made it difficult to substantiate claims of within-job discrimination. She drew on a small study of manufacturing plants in East Liverpool, Ohio, to illustrate both the extent of within-job discrimination but also the larger problem of occupational segregation and the devaluation of women's work.[3] The Women's Bureau held a prominent conference on equal pay in 1952 (Laughlin 2000). This conference gave birth to the National Committee for Equal Pay, with the American Association of University Women (AAUW) and the National Federation of Business and Professional Women's Clubs (BPW) taking leading roles. At the same time, labor unions were increasingly successful in negotiating equal pay provisions into union contracts, and unions continued to support legislative efforts (albeit sometimes motivated by the desire to prevent employers from undercutting men's labor rather than

3. Interestingly, Brady (1947: 59–60) does cite figures on the aggregate gap in median full-time earnings (the modern gender wage gap) at the end of her article—but largely to make the point that many men and women did not make a sufficient income to support a family. Nonetheless, this remains one of the earliest examples of this statistic's use in the equal pay debate.

the push for wage justice). These efforts yielded success at the state level: just two states had equal pay laws on the books as of 1940, but twelve had them by 1952, and twenty-two by 1963 (Laughlin 2000: 40).

Throughout this period, the Women's Bureau continued to publish reports on gender differences in pay, but also continued to note problematic absences in data. For example, in the early 1950s, Women's Bureau statistician Mildred Barber circulated an extensive memo within the Bureau of Labor Statistics (BLS) calling the BLS out for failing to provide data on women workers by industry (Laughlin 2000: 54). Women's Bureau publications began to include more data on earnings in the mid-1950s, including figures like the contemporary gender wage gap; for example, Beyer (1957: 34) reports a comparison of the annual earnings of men and women who work full-time. This comparison is presented alongside many others, is given no special significance, and follows extensive discussions of women being less likely to work full-time, more likely to work in lower-paid occupations, and also likely to be paid less even working in the same jobs (which was still legal in most states). These figures were also given little attention in media debates around gender inequality, which tended to focus on statistics about women's increased participation in the paid labor force rather than differences in earnings, even when the topic was equal pay legislation ("Congress Urged to Equalize Pay" 1955: 26; "Bill for Equal Pay" 1962).

By the early 1960s, then, data on gender wage inequality were beginning to circulate more widely, linked partly to pressure from the feminist movement to pass a national-level equal pay bill. These efforts would pay off, in part, in 1963 with the passage of the Equal Pay Act (EPA). The next section traces the passage of the EPA, and the 1964 Civil Rights Act, and the compromises in the language of those acts that would help to set up the next five decades of confusion surrounding the gender wage gap.

Equal but Incomparable

The first federal bill proposing to ban sex discrimination in wages was introduced in 1945. Legislators would continue introducing versions until the Equal Pay Act was finally passed and signed in 1963. After an initial flurry of activity in the immediate postwar period, the bill got little traction for more than a decade. Congress held one hearing on the Equal Pay Act proposal in 1950 and then no further hearings until 1962. In this section, I briefly recount the process by which the Equal Pay Act passed, with special attention to how labor union leaders, feminist activists, and business groups mobilized statistics and data to make claims about the necessity of an equal pay law. This section also shows how the debate revolved around the interpretation of the words *comparable* and *equal*, with the final language of the bill only banning pay disparities between "equal" work, in line with the requests of employers and over the objection of many union groups and feminist activists who worried that such narrow language would weaken the law to the point of complete inefficacy given the extent of gendered job segregation. Readers interested in more detailed accounts should consult the excellent history by Dorothy Sue Cobble (2004).

Academics were notably absent from these events. In the hearings held in 1950, and the four hearings held in 1962–63, not a single academic testified as an expert on gender earnings inequality. The main experts, and almost the only sources of economy-wide statistics, come from the Women's Bureau, especially Assistant Secretary of Labor Esther Peterson, who testified at each of the hearings in 1962–63 and provided extensive information and analysis. The only academic social scientists to testify were economists who presented themselves as representatives of the American Association of University Women testifying in their organizational capacity rather than as experts on labor markets or discrimination. And virtually no social scientific research was cited by any of the labor leaders, business groups, or feminists who testified. This absence contrasts markedly with the number and diversity of academic perspectives on gender wage inequality that emerged in the 1970s, and which dominated the debates over comparable worth discussed below. Through the early 1960s, before the growth of human capital theory (Blaug 1976) and the take-up of survey-based micro data (Stafford 1986), there was very little academic research on the topic, and none that made it into the political conversation.

Although the absence of academics was constant across the hearings, there was a notable change in the amount and kind of statistical information presented in the 1962–63 hearings as compared with 1950. Assistant Secretary Peterson was one of the first to testify at each of the four hearings, and her testimony included an extensive summary of research by the Women's Bureau. This research included multiple kinds of evidence about the extent of disparities, as well as details about the twenty-two state-level equal pay acts already in effect. The main forms of evidence included information on occupation-level disparities, examples of employers specifically advertising different starting pay rates for men and women, and,

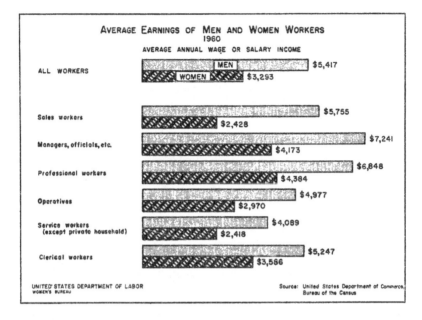

Figure 1. From Senate Hearing 1962: 62.

interestingly, statistics on what we now identify as the gender wage gap: the difference (and/or ratio) between the median annual earnings of full-time employed men and women. Figure 1, from the 1962 Senate hearings (Senate Hearing 1962: 47), showcases both the overall gap as well as the gap within particular occupations.

The accompanying testimony and documents made clear that the overall gap could not be attributed solely to the kind of discrimination that would be banned by the Equal Pay Act (whether in its weaker "equal work" or stronger "comparable work" language): "These differences are related primarily to the different types of jobs men and women hold, but they reflect also a variety of other factors, including amount of education and work experience, industry of employment, size of company, location of plant or office, and even wage differentials based on sex" (Senate Hearing 1962: 45). Despite this seemingly large caveat about its direct relevance to the narrower question of specific employers paying men and women different wages for similar work, the aggregate pay gap statistics seemed to strike a chord. They were frequently cited by proponents of the bill, including legislators like Representative Jessica McCullough (a cosponsor of one of the equal pay bills and a member of the influential

President's Commission on the Status of Women), union leaders like William Schnitzler (secretary-treasurer of the AFL-CIO), and feminist activists like Katherine Peden of the BPW. Some of these supporters were careful to note that the aggregate wage gap included many factors, while others made stronger connections to the kind of discrimination they hoped to make unlawful. For example, Senator Maurine Neuberger testified as follows: "The evidence of discrimination is overwhelming, and is rarely denied. When women work full time their levels of earnings compare unfavorably with those of men. In 1960 they amounted to about 60 percent of the men's total" (Senate Hearing 1963: 14).

In a pattern that came to define the debate over the gender wage gap, business groups were quick to point out the inadequacy of these aggregate statistics for measuring same-job (or similar-job), different-pay discrimination. While business groups like the National Association of Manufacturers (NAM) claimed to support the principle of equal pay for equal work, they repeatedly argued that federal intervention was unnecessary. To make this case, business groups contested the extent of pay discrimination, arguing that collective bargaining agreements and modern techniques for pay setting like job evaluation had largely eliminated pay disparities. Pointing to the gender wage gap, they specifically argued that "comparisons of the average weekly and hourly earnings of men and women are especially misleading" (House Hearings 1962: 165). These discrepancies, they argued, reflected differences in seniority, experience, and overtime hours worked, among other factors. The Chamber of Commerce echoed NAM, arguing that "it is practically impossible to determine statistically whether or not men and women now receive 'unequal' pay when doing 'equal' work" (Senate Hearing 1962: 101). This conclusion was far stronger than that reached by the Women's Bureau, although it rested on a similar understanding of the complexity of interpreting aggregate pay gaps, and it showcases how the gender wage gap was from the very beginning poorly matched to policy debates about pay discrimination.

The final bill was a compromise. Employers could not prevent the passage of the law, but the final bill did include one of their main requests: replacing the language of "comparable work" with the language of "equal work." In 1962, the bill reached the floor of the House, where it was debated and amended. Representative Katharine St. George, a Republican from New York, offered the amendment to replace "comparable" with "equal," and gave a stirring speech invoking Susan B. Anthony to argue that "equality is what we want: nothing less and nothing more."[4] Representative Herbert Zelenko, a Democrat from New York who was overseeing the equal pay bills, argued that this language would dramatically weaken the bill by making it trivial for employers to evade by introducing small differences between men's and women's jobs: "If you put in the word 'equal,' we will have no equal pay bill."[5] St. George's amendment passed narrowly, and the language was changed to "equal." Although both houses of Congress subsequently passed bills in 1962, the two versions could not be reconciled for procedural reasons, and the whole process was restarted in 1963 with the new Congress. Zelenko had lost his seat, and the new bills that were introduced adopted the "equal work" language that had passed in the previous year over the continued objections of some longtime supporters, like Peterson, and Representative Edith Green, a Democrat from Oregon who had been pushing for an equal pay bill since 1955. The Equal Pay Act was signed into law on June 10, 1963.

In its coverage of the law's passage, the *New York Times* included the same statistics on the aggregate gender wage gap that were referenced so frequently in the congressional hearings. The 1963 article "Equal Pay for Women" noted the limitations of the law and specifically how those limitations would prevent it from closing the wage gap: "The 1960 census indicated that the average women worker earned $3,293, as against $5,417 annual average for men. Most of that differential will vanish only when the principle of equality extends from wage rates to job advancement." In 1964, Congress did just that, passing the Civil Rights Act, which included Title VII's ban on sex discrimination in all aspects of employment. Title VII did not, however, expand on the Equal Pay Act's narrow definition of pay discrimination. Nonetheless, the aggregate disparities in the gender wage gap that were cited so frequently in the hearings over the Equal Pay Act would persist and remain remarkably stable for the next fifteen years. And they would become a routine statistical production, widely reported and cited. The recognized persistence of this pay gap in spite of formal legal prohibitions on employment and wage discrimination would help fuel a massive increase in research around wage disparities, as well as a new generation of feminist activism frustrated with the tepid rate of progress on achieving economic equality.

4. 108 Cong. Rec. H14768 (July 25, 1962).
5. 108 Cong. Rec. H14771 (July 25, 1962).

Studying the Gender Wage Gap

Before the 1960s, the gender wage gap was not a stylized fact. After the debates surrounding the passage of the Equal Pay Act in 1963, it rapidly became one. By the mid-1970s, the gender wage gap had become a standard indicator used to track progress (or the lack thereof) in achieving economic gender equality, as well as for comparing the relative levels of gender inequality across nations. This rise in public attention also coincided with a massive increase in the amount of research on gender wage inequality. This research fit neatly into the emerging research program in labor economics that brought together human capital theory, survey data, and statistical regression methods. This combination made it possible for scholars to try to put precise numbers on the importance of education, experience, industry, occupation, age, hours worked, and more, as explanatory factors that led to women making about 40 percent less than men throughout the 1960s and 1970s.

Starting in the 1960s, the Women's Bureau began to include statistics on the gender wage gap in its publications. These statistics drew on the Census Bureau's regular reports on income based on CPS data. In doing so, the Women's Bureau extended the statistics presented in the Equal Pay Act debates, making it possible to track movement (or, in this case, stagnation). For example, in 1965, the Women's Bureau reported that full-time employed women's median wages were still about 60 percent of men's. These reports drew some media attention ("Women's Pay Gap" 1964). Such attention increased in the early 1970s as the aggregate data continued to show flat or increasing gaps (Lyons 1972). By the end of the 1970s, the gap would become more central in the framing of economic inequality. For example, in 1976 the Women's Bureau published "The Earnings Gap between Men and Women," and the wage gap statistic moved from being just one of many numbers cited to being the first sentence of the report, around which was framed twelve pages of analysis. A sequel with the same title in 1979 expanded to twenty-two pages. These publications were in turn written up in the media, which highlighted both the aggregate trend and also the explanations offered by the Women's Bureau: the combination of women's continued concentration in lower-paid occupations, the large increase in women's labor force participation, which meant that women were disproportionately earlier in their careers than men, and the persistence of discrimination (Shanahan 1976; "Pay Gap Has Widened" 1976).

At the same time, the gender gap also began to be used by international organizations seeking to compare the status of women across countries. The Organisation for Economic Co-operation and Development (OECD) began publishing reports surveying the situation of women workers across countries as early as 1965 (Klein 1965).[6] Notably this initial publication included no comparative discussion of wages or wage gaps. By 1975, the updated report "The Role of Women in the Economy" included some data on earnings gaps, although it noted the paucity of statistics for most countries, rendering "full international comparisons" impossible (Darling 1975: 58). The OECD (2021) now maintains a standardized annual data series on the gender wage gap, covering the thirty-seven OECD countries and going back as far as 1970 where data are available.

This increased national and international attention to earnings gaps was matched by a rapid increase in academic research. While some academics, like Dickinson (1943) discussed above, had treated the topic of wage differences between men and women, there were relatively few accounts, and those that existed drew on smaller-scale data. Starting in the 1960s, and increasing rapidly in the early 1970s, academics began to research the determinants of the economy-wide gender wage gap with a focus on the extent to which that gap could be attributed to discrimination. In 1960, Henry Sanborn completed a dissertation at the University of Chicago titled "Income Differences between Men and Women in the United States," results from which were published a few years later (Sanborn 1964). Drawing on 1950 Census data, Sanborn attempted to statistically adjudicate how much of the gap was attributable to occupation, hours worked, education, age, race, and geography (rural vs. urban). Sanborn (1964: 548–49) concluded his analysis by arguing that pay disparities were mostly explicable by productivity-related factors, and thus "if discrimination is an important cause of male-female income differences, it is not discrimination by employers but by consumers and fellow employees that is effective." As far as I can tell, this is the first example of what became an entire research tradition devoted to decomposing the gender pay gap and attempting to determine what, if anything, was attributable to discrimination (and what sort of discrimination).

6. I thank Ruud Bruijns at the OECD for helping me find and access the OECD's earliest reports on women and work.

In the early 1970s, many more papers adopted versions of this approach, including an extremely influential paper by Ronald Oaxaca (1973) that explicitly decomposed the gender pay gap using a technique now known as the Oaxaca-Blinder-Kitagawa decomposition. Controversially, Oaxaca argued that the residual earnings disparity that existed after controlling for observable variables should be treated as an estimate of discrimination. In turn, his analysis suggested that while "unequal pay for equal work does not account for very much of the male-female wage differential," it was the case that "a substantial proportion of the male-female wage differential is attributable to the effects of discrimination" (Oaxaca 1973: 708). In this account, discrimination acted primarily by concentrating women into lower-paying occupations, thus ensuring that women earned less than men with similar personal characteristics (such as education). By 1973, Isabel Sawhill could summarize an emerging literature on explanations of the gender wage gap, citing Sanborn, Oaxaca, and four other similar works that tried to decompose the overall gap, along with her own analysis.[7] Like Oaxaca, Sawhill (1973: 391) argued against controlling for occupation because the main routes for discrimination involved placing women into lower-paying occupations rather than the sort of discrimination banned by the Equal Pay Act: "It would, of course, be quite easy to substantially reduce the remaining differential by resorting to an occupational adjustment. . . . However, this procedure would not explain why women who are well qualified with respect to education and experience continue to be relegated to relatively low-paid occupations."

Sawhill ended her analysis by noting the relative futility of equal pay laws and the promise of strongly enforced equal opportunity legislation to breakdown occupational barriers. But she also warned that "wholesale reform of sex roles and of the existing institutions of marriage and childrearing is the necessary prerequisite to equal opportunities in the labor market" (394). Employer discrimination, for Sawhill, resulted from a partially accurate, partially false, belief that women would prioritize family obligations and their husbands' careers over their own.

The debate over the interpretation of these earnings regressions and decompositions was heavily influenced by the rise of human capital

7. A handful of sociologists was involved in this conversation at the time, including Larry E. Suter and Herman P. Miller (1973), who are included in Sawhill's review. Overall, the conversation was dominated by economists, and even the sociologists tended to write in dialogue with economic theories (for an exemplary review of the literature, see Marini 1989).

theory. Since the late nineteenth century, mainstream economists had argued that wages were a function of productivity. The "marginal productivity theory of income distribution" argued that employers in a competitive economy would pay workers exactly as much as their labor was worth (Pullen 2009). In the 1950s and early 1960s, economists expanded this theory by arguing that workers would rationally invest in their own productivity, for example, by seeking out education or training, increasing their "human capital" (Teixeira 2007, 2014). This theory offered explanations for numerous stylized facts, such as the gap in earnings between more and less educated workers, and also promised to unify distinct phenomena from education to health to migration into a single framework, imagining individuals as forward-thinking investors in their own future productivity (Blaug 1976).

In the early 1970s, human capital theorists turned to the debate over discrimination and the gender wage gap. Perhaps most influentially, Jacob Mincer and Solomon Polachek (1974) analyzed sex differentials in earnings using human capital theory's model of the family as a single economic unit that shares consumption and production decisions. In this model, women specialize in nonmarket labor, including planning for career interruptions related to family obligations, and thus invest less in their careers and career-relevant training. In turn, these career interruptions lead to market-relevant skills decaying, and thus reduced productivity when women do reenter the labor force. Men, in contrast, plan for uninterrupted working careers and make investments accordingly. As a result, not only do women of the same age have fewer years of work experience, but also their work experience produces lower rates of return. Mincer and Polachek (1974: S104) were reticent to rule discrimination in or out, especially what they termed "indirect" discrimination where expectations of labor market discrimination might rationally lead women to invest less in job-relevant skills (why bother going back to school for an MBA if no corporation would ever promote you into management?). And somewhat tellingly, they noted that if the definition of discrimination is broadened to include the division of labor within the family itself (as many feminists might argue), "all of the gap is by definition a symptom of discrimination" (Mincer and Polachek 1974: S104). Rather than adopting this expansive definition, human capital theorists instead foregrounded women's occupational choices—shaped by their family priorities—as the drivers of occupational segregation (Chassonnery-Zaïgouche, Cherrier, and Singleton 2019: 28).

Mincer and Polachek's findings, and human capital theory explanations of gender inequality more generally, were and remain controversial. Alongside the human capital model, Francine D. Blau and Carol L. Jusenius (1976) identified at least four other economic explanations, including overcrowding (that discrimination forces women into a small set of occupations where supply then outstrips demand, as in Bergmann 1974) and internal labor market theory (which focuses on how men's entry-level jobs are much more likely to have clear opportunities to advance). And later researchers, including feminist sociologists, argued that the empirical predictions of human capital theory were not borne out. For example, Paula England (1982) argued that human capital theory's attempts to explain occupational sex segregation were inconsistent with evidence showing that women who left the labor force faced similar penalties whether they were employed in primarily female or primarily male occupations, undermining the argument that women were rationally opting to work in occupations that favored interrupted careers.

Stepping back from the ins and outs of the academic debates of the 1970s, what is striking is simply the amount of research that came into existence and how much the gender wage gap became a focal point for the conversation. It became a stylized fact, something to be explained. This intense academic attention meant that when public attention turned again to debating the causes of gender wage inequalities, academics were ready to play a central role in a way they had not been in the 1950s and 1960s. At the same time, academic research in labor economics (and sociology) was relatively unable to assess the dynamic governed by the Equal Pay Act: different pay for the same work by the same employer. The studies in this period—and almost all the research done through to the present—rely on either data from the Census or from large-scale household surveys. None of these data sets matched employers and employees.[8] Academics largely agreed that this now-illegal form of discrimination was a relatively small part of the remaining gender wage gap, and focused their attention elsewhere: on issues of the division of labor within families, occupational segregation, the role of on-the-job training, and career tracking through internal labor markets.

At the same time, attention to the stagnation in the aggregate gender wage gap helped fuel a new generation of feminist activists who blamed

---

8. For a rare exception from a government statistician, see Buckley 1971, which reported within-establishment differentials for ten narrow occupations.

the lack of progress on the failures of the government to adequately enforce civil rights law. In turn, these activists would revive debates about equal and comparable work, eventually arguing that women's work was devalued *because* women did it, and that this form of discrimination was amenable to legal remedy under the Civil Rights Act, if not the Equal Pay Act. These issues would take center stage as the feminist movement initiated a new campaign in the late 1970s to address the stubbornly persistent gender wage gap.

Fighting the Stalled Wage Gap

When the Equal Pay Act passed in 1963, the reported gender wage gap was around sixty cents on the dollar. Over the next two decades, that number moved very little. As early as the mid-1960s, feminist activists noted the apparent stagnation and mobilized around it. By the late 1970s, the stalled pay gap would become a motivating frame for a new movement around pay equity and comparable worth. This movement won several major legal and economic victories, but fizzled out after a string of hostile regulatory and court decisions undermined its core strategy in the mid-1980s. These legal and regulatory debates, unlike those of the 1960s, would be deeply informed by the new economics of gender inequality that emerged in the 1970s.

Title VII of the Civil Rights Act of 1964 banned sex discrimination in employment. The political compromises that led to the inclusion of sex discrimination were complicated—a strange alliance of feminist legislators and southern Democrats trying to sink the entire bill—but in the end, the sex discrimination provisions were passed into law. The Equal Employment Opportunity Commission (EEOC) was then set up to enforce the act. In its first years of operation, the EEOC faced a flood of complaints, including many alleging sex discrimination in pay, benefits, hiring, promotions, and more (Kessler-Harris 2001). While these complaints clearly fell under the heading of the EEOC's legal mandate, the EEOC instead prioritized racial discrimination claims. Many public discussions of sex discrimination went so far as to ridicule the very idea that sex discrimination in employment ought to be unlawful (Kessler-Harris 2001: 249).

In 1966, in response to these dismissals, feminist leaders associated with the President's Commission on the Status of Women (most notably Betty Friedan and Pauli Murray) and the EEOC (including Aileen Hernandez, Sonia Pressman Fuentes, and Richard Graham) founded the

National Organization for Women (NOW) (Kessler-Harris 2001; Turk 2016). NOW's founding statement of purpose, adopted in October 1966, explicitly drew attention to the apparent *increase* in the wage gap:

> Despite all the talk about the status of American women in recent years, the actual position of women in the United States has declined, and is declining, to an alarming degree throughout the 1950's and 60's. Although 46.4% of all American women between the ages of 18 and 65 now work outside the home, the overwhelming majority—75%—are in routine clerical, sales, or factory jobs, or they are household workers, cleaning women, hospital attendants. . . . Working women are becoming increasingly—not less—concentrated on the bottom of the job ladder. As a consequence full-time women workers today earn on the average only 60% of what men earn.[9]

These statistics offered a focal point for diagnosing gender economic inequality. For the next two decades, the feminist movement, including NOW, would emphasize the connections between occupational segregation, the devaluation of women's work, discrimination in promotions, and the overall gender wage gap. For example, in the late 1960s, NOW successfully lobbied and protested the EEOC, pressuring it to take sex discrimination more seriously (Kessler-Harris 2001: 250).

Although the EEOC began to adopt clearer and more uniform standards, debates over racial and sex discrimination moved in somewhat different directions. While the absence of Black employees was taken as evidence for discrimination and as cause for government intervention (such as mandated affirmative action hiring), the same did not hold for the absence of women. Employers argued, and many agreed, that occupational sex segregation reflected not discrimination but "women's own preferences for raising families, their willingness to place their own careers second to their husbands', and their ambivalent attitudes toward wage work" (Kessler-Harris 2001: 277). This choice versus discrimination framing launched what Kessler-Harris aptly calls "an endless debate" (277), one that persists into the present.

By the end of the 1970s, the feminist movement had achieved many concrete goals. Sex discrimination was banned, the EEOC had implemented new enforcement mechanisms, and corporations had begun to at

---

9. See National Organization of Women, "Statement of Purpose," https://now.org/about /history/statement-of-purpose (accessed February 25, 2021).

least nominally increase the hiring of women into managerial and professional roles (Kelly and Dobbin 1998). And yet, the overall wage gap had not budged. News stories around gender inequality noted this stagnation, dating it back as far as the 1930s, and feminists circulated the statistic widely, stamping it into buttons and printing it on leaflets (McCann 1994: 23; Cobble, Gordon, and Henry 2014: 141; Rosenbaum 1980). Feminists argued that the flat gender wage gap had a clear underlying explanation: the persistence of occupational sex segregation coupled with the devaluation of women's work. Frances Hutner, an economist who later authored a book on comparable worth (Hutner 1986), put the issue starkly to the *New York Times*: "The main problem . . . is that women are trapped in female occupational ghettos" (quoted in Bennetts 1979).

Although some economists offered competing explanations—such as human capital theorists' emphasis on women's family-related obligations and the burdens of motherhood—this occupational segregation–focused story helped galvanize a new coalition of labor leaders and feminist activists who mobilized around revitalizing and expanding an old strategy: comparable worth. In 1979, the National Committee on Pay Equity was launched as a collaboration eventually containing more than one hundred organizations, including labor unions and NOW, among many others (Turk 2016; Hower 2020). The movement to revalue women's jobs had two major prongs: a legal strategy centered on Title VII (McCann 1994; Nelson and Bridges 1999) and a workplace activism strategy taken up by public-sector unions (Hower 2020).

Both approaches identified employers' own job evaluation practices as strategically useful for establishing that women's jobs were systematically undervalued. Formal job evaluations involve scoring jobs based on various features (such as skill, effort, responsibility, and working conditions) and then assigning a pay rate to each job based on its score (National Research Council 1981; see Adler 2020 for a comprehensive overview and history). Job evaluations had existed for decades, and employers even cited their extensive use as one reason why the Equal Pay Act was unnecessary: because job evaluations assigned a "rate for the job" rather than for the particular employee who occupied it, sex discrimination was (in their telling) impossible. Comparable worth advocates argued that while job evaluation practices might have eliminated the sort of same-job, different-pay disparities that the Equal Pay Act targeted, they also showcased the pervasive underpayment of jobs occupied primarily by women. For example, a study made at the request of employees from the State of

Washington in 1974 showed that "for jobs rated equally by the job evaluation system, those held mainly by men were paid 20 percent more on the average than those held mainly by women" (National Research Council 1981: 3). In the case of Washington state, this study became the focal point for a decades-long campaign for pay equity, and government employees across the country followed suit, from municipal workers in San Jose, California, to state employees in Connecticut and Florida (Hower 2020).

These local and state-level labor actions were matched by a national-level effort that centered on the EEOC and the legal interpretation of Title VII. In 1980, EEOC chair Eleanor Holmes Norton held extensive hearings on the relationship between job segregation and wage discrimination with a focus on the comparable worth question.

In stark contrast to the 1962–63 debates over the Equal Pay Act, the 1980 EEOC hearing would include a wealth of social scientific expertise from different perspectives. Alexis Herman, director of the Women's Bureau, testified to the stability of the gender wage gap and offered two main explanations: that women remained concentrated in lower-paying, traditionally female occupations, and that a recent large increase in women's participation in the paid labor force led to "an even larger concentration of women who are at the bottom of the economic ladder" (EEOC 1980: 346). Notably this explanation implied that the wage gap might soon improve absent any notable policy changes as this cohort of women gained more work experience.[10] Mary Corcoran, a political science professor from the University of Michigan, testified about her research that drew on PSID data to show how white men had much better access to job training and that this training explained some of the persistent wage gap. Barbara Bergmann, an economics professor at the University of Maryland, reinforced the centrality of sex segregation to explaining the wage gap, and also argued that women were more often required to pay for their own training—a finding consistent with Corcoran's research but incompatible with human capital theory. Bergmann put the point clearly:

10. Goldin (1990) provides evidence for precisely this argument in her book-length treatment of the gender wage gap. This narrative offers an explanation for why the wage gap appeared to stagnate in the 1970s, when EEOC enforcement and affirmative action programs were at their height, and then appeared to improve rapidly in the 1980s, when these programs were in decline. In this argument, the gender wage gap was a lagging indicator of changes in gender equality in the labor market.

"[Women] have already at their own expense provided themselves with nurse's training. They have already at their own expense given themselves master's degrees in social work, and these social scientists are alleging that these women, the problem, the reason women have lower pay is that these poor women don't feel like accumulating human capital, but that is trash" (EEOC 1980: 316).

In contrast, Andrea Beller, an economics professor from the University of Illinois, drew on CPS data to argue that much of the wage gap could be explained by human capital theory and that labor market discrimination seemed to be on the decline precisely due to the enforcement of the Civil Rights Act. An exchange between Beller and EEOC commissioner Ethel Bent Walsh is revealing for how it showcased competing understandings of choice and discrimination. Beller agreed that discrimination could manifest in terms of lower pay to women's occupations, but argued that economists must first rule out nondiscriminatory explanations rooted in women's preferences for flexibility or safety (for example), and that to the extent wage discrepancies were rooted in those preferences, it would be wrong for policymakers to intervene.

> *Professor Beller:* "In order to determine by how much wages in women's occupations are discriminatorily depressed, we must first establish to what extent women's occupational distribution reflects choice and to what extent discrimination."
> *Commissioner Walsh:* "I am trying to get on that theory what came first, the chicken or the egg, because when you talk in terms of reflecting choice, if that choice is very limited, does that not, in effect, extend to discrimination?" . . .
> *Professor Beller:* "What I am trying to say is that it is not true that the entire wage difference between women's jobs and other jobs is the result of discrimination, . . . preferences have some role in which occupations people go into, and to the extent that that is operating and wage differences reflect those preferences, we would not want to intervene. There would be no justification for doing anything about that because it is what people want." (EEOC 1980: 300–301)

Here we see another example of the "endless debate" that Kessler-Harris identified between explanations of gender disparities in terms of choices versus discrimination. What changes are the details and who is authorized to speak. In contrast to earlier periods, social scientists were increasingly tasked with interpreting the quite technical details. In so doing, particular disciplinary understandings of concepts like discrimination and preferences came to the fore. For Beller, and for orthodox economists more generally, if a difference was rooted in women's and men's different preferences, then there was nothing to be done about it. Preferences were sacred. In contrast, feminist economists like Bergmann rejected both the empirical analysis provided by human capital theorists *and* their interpretations of gendered preferences as exogenous and outside the political sphere.

The EEOC hearings included testimony from more traditional labor and business sources as well. Testimonies from the Business Roundtable and Chamber of Commerce are particularly revealing because both specifically engaged with the gender wage gap to argue that it should not be interpreted as a measure of discrimination. William Knapp, a lawyer testifying on behalf of the Chamber of Commerce, cited the Women's Bureau (1979) publication showing the wage gap at fifty-nine cents on the dollar but then went on to say, "The statistic alone is meaningless and can be very misleading" (EEOC 1980: 716). Similarly, Virgil Day from the Business Roundtable argued that "this unrefined statistic, however, is not proven sex discrimination, let alone a pay difference prohibited by federal law" (EEOC 1980: 671). Instead, Day continued, the wage gap should be seen as a reflection of women moving into entry-level jobs, along with other nondiscriminatory factors like differences in education and industry.

The growing centrality of social scientific expertise was not limited to the EEOC hearings. Increasingly, social scientists testified in employment discrimination cases (Chassonnery-Zaïgouche 2020). The EEOC also sought more conclusive expert guidance in the form of an expert report from the National Research Council of the National Academy of Sciences (Turk 2016: 119). Published in 1981, *Women, Work, and Wages: Equal Pay for Jobs of Equal Value* (Treiman and Hartmann 1981) largely endorsed arguments in favor of comparable worth, and specifically in favor of using employers' own job evaluation practices to judge whether women's occupations were systematically underpaid.

The combined efforts of labor unions, NCPE, and the EEOC seemed initially to bear fruit. In the early 1980s, public-sector unions won various disputes that led to significant increases in the pay for some women (Hower 2020). And the 1981 US Supreme Court decision in

Gunther seemed to open the door to a legal theory that held that comparable worth claims could be brought under the Civil Rights Act (Nelson and Bridges 1999; Turk 2016). But these initial victories were fleeting. By 1985, the EEOC, now under the leadership of Clarence Thomas, soundly rejected comparable worth (Turk 2016: 121–22). And, as Robert L. Nelson and William P. Bridges (1999: 37–38) document, federal courts rejected comparable worth-based arguments so consistently that by the late 1980s plaintiffs simply stopped making them.

Interestingly, the comparable worth movement did have one lasting implication: employers abandoned job evaluation systems en masse (Adler 2020). The threat of litigation in the early 1980s turned job evaluation's standardized pay-setting process into a liability that seemingly exposed inequalities between men's and women's occupations. In court, employers were able to successfully argue that their practices were, in fact, dictated by market pressures, and these arguments were routinely upheld by the courts as sufficient justification no matter how flimsy the evidence provided (Nelson and Bridges 1999). Nonetheless, human resources professionals began to advise employers to make their practices match their rhetoric, and employers rapidly switched away from formal job evaluation systems in favor of market surveys (determining the market rate for specific jobs) and individual negotiations (often based on a candidate's salary history) that still dominate pay-setting practices today (Adler 2020).

By the end of the 1980s, then, the gender wage gap had become institutionalized as one of the key indicators of gender inequality, various groups of experts (largely economists) competed to provide explanations for the gap, and the comparable worth movement had largely faded. While the NCPE continues on, and organizations like the AAUW continue to promote "Equal Pay Day" and other efforts to draw attention to the gender wage gap, no similar effort has emerged to replace the comparable worth movement in the fight against gender wage inequality. As a result, as I show in the next section, the conversation around the gender wage gap has turned away from explanations rooted in occupational segregation (despite its relative persistence) and toward explanations rooted in family life and women's choices. At the same time, misunderstandings of the gender wage gap rooted in its historical connection to the narrow legal definition of discrimination inscribed in the Equal Pay Act continue to characterize the debate.

Opting Out, Leaning In, and Persistent Misunderstandings

To understand the trajectory of conversations about economic gender inequality before and after the comparable worth movement, the following section draws on a data set of newspaper articles about the gender wage gap. The sample includes all articles from the *New York Times*, *Washington Post*, and *Wall Street Journal* from 1970 to 2014 that include either of the terms *wage gap* or *pay gap* and at least one of *women, female*, or *sex*. This search yielded 912 articles. These articles were hand-coded for their discussions of issues related to gender inequality and their use of quantitative measures of gender inequality; 520 articles were deemed relevant (about the gender wage gap, and focused on the United States). The full codebook is available upon request.

These data show how the end of the comparable worth movement, and other forces like the decline of labor unions and the rise of an antifeminist backlash (Faludi 2006), led to a change in the conversation around gender wage inequality. After the 1980s, the gender wage gap persisted as a key hinge connecting policy debates, academic research, and public understandings, but the narratives around the gender wage gap shifted. Absent pressure from the feminist labor movement forcing attention to occupational segregation and the devaluation of women's work, we see an increasing emphasis on women's choices such as the "opt-out revolution" made prominent by a 2003 *New York Times Magazine* article. As Joan C. Williams, Jessica Manvell, and Stephanie Bornstein (2006) show, media narratives about women leaving the workplace emphasized women's choices without addressing the structural constraints (such as the absence of maternity leave or affordable childcare) under which women were forced to choose. Similarly, we see the rise of both academic research on motherhood pay gaps and media narratives that foreground that explanation.

At the same time, occupational segregation persists, and social scientists agree that it remains one of the most important explanations for the gender wage gaps. For example, figure 2, reproduced from Hegewisch and Hartmann 2014, makes this link explicit, graphing trends in the two aggregate statistics. Notably, both occupational segregation and the wage gap barely budged between 1990 and 2010 (see also England, Levine, and Mishel 2020; Goldin 2014).

Figures 3 and 4 show results from the hand-coded analysis of newspaper coverage of the gender wage gap. Figure 3 shows the centrality of the

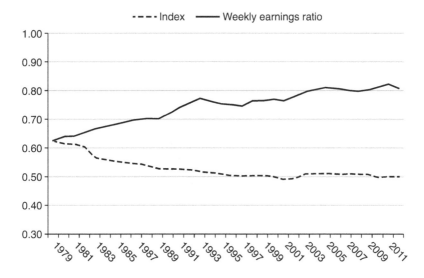

Figure 2. Change in the Index of Occupational Segregation and the Gender Earnings Ratio, 1979 to 2012. Originally figure 5 in Hegewisch and Hartmann 2014.

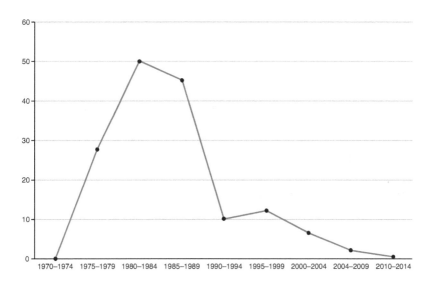

Figure 3. Percentage of articles about the gender wage gap that mention comparable worth.

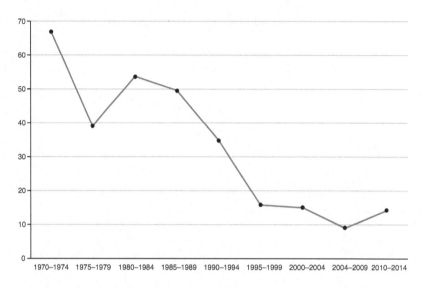

Figure 4. Percentage of articles about the gender wage gap that mention occupational segregation as an explanation for that gap.

comparable worth movement to the conversation in the 1980s. At the movement's peak, about half of all coverage of the gender wage gap discussed comparable worth or pay equity. This period also saw a significant uptick in the amount of coverage, from about one article per year in the first half of the 1970s to thirty-one articles in 1985. The movement both put the gender wage gap on the public agenda and also provided a narrative to understand it. Figure 4 shows how discussions of occupational segregation as an explanation for the gender wage gap fell with the decline of the comparable worth movement. Between 2000 and 2014, only 10–15 percent of articles about the gender wage gap discuss occupational segregation as a potential explanation. In contrast, explanations foregrounding women's choices steadily appear in about 30 percent of articles. Together, these data show how the gender wage gap has become relatively delinked in public conversations from occupational segregation but has remained linked to discussions of women's choices around balancing work and family. This trend was epitomized by the publication in 2013 of Sheryl Sandberg's controversial *Lean In: Women, Work, and the Will to Lead*.

Work-family conflicts are not the only persistent explanations for the gender wage gap. Explanations emphasizing discrimination also

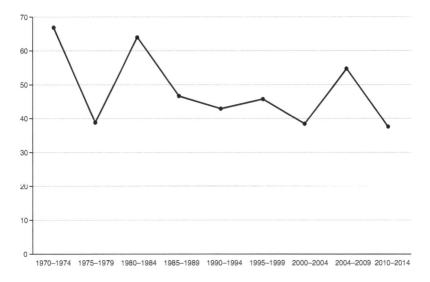

Figure 5. Percentage of articles about the gender wage gap that mention discrimination as an explanation for that gap.

occur at a steady clip. Figure 5 shows that throughout this period, discrimination is a prominent explanation, from around 40 percent of articles to over 60 percent in some periods. Discrimination here includes both same-job, different-pay discrimination (made illegal by the Equal Pay Act); hiring, firing, and promotion discrimination (made illegal by the Civil Rights Act); and discrimination against women's occupations (i.e., the kind of discrimination identified by comparable worth advocates, which remains legal in most states). These forms of discrimination were difficult to disentangle, as many articles referred to discrimination in a broad sense without specifying particular sites or mechanisms. Nonetheless, the persistence of discrimination messaging is important because it furthers one of the central dynamics in public discourse around the gender wage gap: the misunderstanding of the gap as one that captures solely same job, different pay.

For example, as early as 1974, when *Time* magazine reported on the first-ever Equal Pay Act Supreme Court case, they misreported the gender wage gap: "According to a recent Labor Department study of jobs, women who do work similar to men's earn 60c for every 1$ earned by their male equals" ("Wages and Women" 1974: 90).[11] This sort of misunderstanding is pervasive to present. A recent example comes from a 2016 video produced by *Huffington Post* for a series called "Celebs Have Issues," where the actress Kristin Bell humorously argues that employers should engage in "pinksourcing" rather than outsourcing, replacing men with women working the same jobs and paying them just seventy-seven cents on the dollar.[12] In turn, this kind of misunderstanding from advocates of gender equality occasions a constant stream of debunking narratives. In this case, Karin Agness Lips (2016) wrote a rebuttal in *Forbes*, arguing that Bell's use of the gender wage gap—as well as many others, including those by then presidential candidate Hillary Clinton—was misleading because it failed to account for "choices such as education level, years of experience, type of job, and hours worked." Here, Agness Lips seizes on the inaccuracy of Bell's claims to assert that the wage gap can be accounted for by women's choices, categorizing education, hours, and type of job under that heading.

The centrality of illegal forms of discrimination to the folk interpretation of the gender wage gap constrains the ability of researchers to inform the public conversation (and perhaps results from past failures to do so). In an oral history interview with the present author in December 2018, the sociologist Paula England put it like this:

> In my experience as a public speaker, and I'll include in this teaching it to undergraduates, explaining it to people at family dinners, talking to professionals, [EEOC], whatever, the hardest thing is that everybody thinks of sex discrimination as either hiring discrimination or lack of equal pay for equal work in the same job.

In turn, as seen above, conservatives call out these misunderstandings and use them to undermine the argument that remaining gender inequalities are a problem at all. Echoing arguments made in the 1960s, contemporary conservative writers assert that the wage gap is a myth and misrepresentation because it does not control for various factors, and what is left after those controls reflects women's choices.

This endless debate persists in part because researchers are surprisingly unable to answer the central question of just how pervasive

---

11. Note that the *Time* article was found separately from the systematically coded corpus.

12. See *HuffPost*, "Pinksourcing with Kristen Bell," YouTube, https://www.youtube.com/watch?v=k_m5AlsQqcs (accessed September 19, 2021).

same-job, different-pay discrimination is. Employer-employee matched data are rare in the United States, and none exist at a representative scale for the whole economy. For example, a recent paper by Smith-Doerr et al. (2019) looked specifically at pay within jobs in federal science agencies precisely because they are a unique setting in which information about individuals' jobs, gender, and salary are all available. According to Smith-Doerr et al. (2019: 542), theirs is just the fifth published paper using employer-employee matched data from multiple employers to examine gender wage gaps. This lack of representative data exacerbates popular (mis)understandings of the gender wage gap, since academics cannot definitively say how much of the remaining gender gap results from same-job, different-pay discrimination.

Conclusion: Is the Gender Wage Gap a Good Description?

The gender wage gap has become a ubiquitous indicator used to capture aggregate inequality. It is an object of academic study, an index used to rank nations, a frequent topic of public debate, and a site of partisan politics as liberals and conservatives vie to interpret the number's significance for proposed policies. Tracing the history of the gender wage gap from its emergence in postwar debates over working women, through the rise of human capital theory and neoclassical labor economics, to 1980s debates over comparable worth, up to the present conversation around work/family conflict and women's choices showcases how a single statistic can travel in multiple domains at once.

The gender wage gap as stylized fact thus acts as a hinge (Abbott 2005) and boundary object (Star and Griesemer 1989). That is, the gap serves as a tool by which researchers and their findings can become relevant in public discourse, but also a site of persistent misunderstanding. The folk economics of the gender wage gap, absent the interpretive pressures of the 1960s–1980s feminist movements, instead invokes women's choices, filtered through the lens of legal consciousness. That is, the gender wage gap is often read as either a measure of illegal discrimination (which it is not) or a benign reflection of women's unforced choices (which it is also not).

The gender wage gap is a particular and peculiar calculation. It is not obvious why this particular formulation won out as the stand-in for economic gender inequality. That it did so—that academics and commentators have spent so much energy on this number as opposed to others—showcases the importance of the specific choices made in deciding how to *describe* economic life. The gender wage gap controls for full-time work, and little else. This choice—to center the conversation at this level—was highly productive for decades of social scientists who have parsed and accounted for the sources of that gap. At the same time, in a pattern familiar to scholars of technopolitics (Hecht 1998), this technical choice must simultaneously be understood as an ethical or political one.

Thus, I end this article with a new question: Is the gender wage gap a good description? What even is a good description? Textbooks, handbooks, and seminars in the social sciences obsess over the question of what counts as a good causal claim. In contrast, description gets short shrift, often derided as "mere" or "just" description (see Gerring 2012). As a result, our collective capacity for evaluating the usefulness of descriptions is limited. Here, I offer some hints of how the history of the gender wage gap might inform that conversation, and how in turn we might evaluate the limits of the gap itself.

The gender wage gap is certainly useful—it coordinates academic attention, mobilizes movements, and permits consciousness raising by creating a kind of institutionalized awareness of persistent gender inequality. But it also enables confusion and a constant debunking narrative. Beyond that, its movements may not track what advocates of equality care most about. For example, the gender wage gap stagnated in the 1970s, but that was an era of feminist gains. Those gains did not manifest in the gender wage gap until the 1980s—by which point the backlash had started (Faludi 2006) and forces were in place that stalled the gender revolution by the 1990s (England 2010). In this sense, the gender wage gap lagged what it was taken to measure. Beyond that, accounts of the gender wage gap highlight that a significant portion of its decline resulted from a relative fall in men's wages in blue-collar jobs (Goldin 2014). This decline in blue-collar incomes may mechanically yield a reduction in the gender wage gap (given the persistence of occupational segregation), but it was not the kind of equality that feminists were and are fighting for (see Brady 1947). At a minimum, we must be careful not to treat the gender wage gap as a sufficient statistic for economic gender equality. Perhaps the problem is that we have asked too much of one number, one stylized fact. Perhaps a good description must be one that views from multiple angles.

References

Abbott, Andrew. 2005. "Linked Ecologies: States and Universities as Environments for Professions." *Sociological Theory* 23, no. 3: 245–74.

Adler, Laura. 2020. "From the Job's Worth to the Person's Price: The Evolution of Pay-Setting Practices since the 1950s." Working paper.

Agness Lips, Karin. 2016. "Another Celebrity Wrong on the Wage Gap." *Forbes*, September 16. https://www.forbes.com/sites/karinagness/2016/09/16/pinksourcing -is-the-latest-misleading-equal-pay-effort/.

American Association of University Women (AAUW). 2020. "The Simple Truth about the Gender Pay Gap: 2020 Update." https://www.aauw.org/app/uploads /2020/12/SimpleTruth_2.1.pdf.

Bennetts, Leslie. 1979. "The Equal Pay Issue: Focusing on 'Comparable Worth.'" *New York Times*, October 26.

Bergmann, Barbara R. 1974. "Occupational Segregation, Wages, and Profits When Employers Discriminate by Race or Sex." *Eastern Economic Journal* 1, no. 2: 103–10.

Beyer, Sylva. 1957. *Spotlight on Women in the United States, 1956–1957.* Women's Bureau of the Department of Labor.

"Bill for Equal Pay Regardless of Sex Approved by House." 1962. *New York Times*, July 26.

Blau, Francine D., and Carol L. Jusenius. 1976. "Economists' Approaches to Sex Segregation in the Labor Market: An Appraisal." *Signs: Journal of Women in Culture and Society* 1, no. 3, pt. 2: 181–99.

Blaug, Mark. 1976. "The Empirical Status of Human Capital Theory: A Slightly Jaundiced Survey." *Journal of Economic Literature* 14, no. 3: 827–55.

Brady, Dorothy S. 1947. "Equal Pay for Women Workers." *Annals of the American Academy of Political and Social Science* 251:53–60.

Buckley, John. 1971. "Pay Differences between Men and Women in the Same Job." *Monthly Labor Review* 94, no. 11: 36–40.

Chassonnery-Zaïgouche, Cléo. 2018. "Is Equal Pay Worth It? Beatrice Potter Webb's, Millicent Garrett Fawcett's and Eleanor Rathbone's Changing Arguments." In *The Routledge Handbook of the History of Women's Economic Thought*, edited by Kirsten Madden and Robert W. Dimand, 129–49. London: Routledge.

Chassonnery-Zaïgouche, Cléo. 2020. "How Economists Entered the 'Numbers Game': Measuring Discrimination in the US Courtrooms, 1971–1989." *Journal of the History of Economic Thought* 42, no. 2: 229–59.

Chassonnery-Zaïgouche, Cléo, Béatrice Cherrier, and John D. Singleton. 2019. "'Economics Is Not a Man's Field': CSWEP and the First Gender Reckoning in Economics (1971–1991)." https://papers.ssrn.com/sol3/papers.cfm?abstract _id=3510857.

Cobble, Dorothy Sue. 2004. *The Other Women's Movement: Workplace Justice and Social Rights in Modern America*. Princeton, N.J.: Princeton University Press.

Cobble, Dorothy Sue, Linda Gordon, and Astrid Henry. 2014. *Feminism Unfinished: A Short, Surprising History of American Women's Movements*. New York: W. W. Norton.

"Congress Urged to Equalize Pay for Equal Work by Both Sexes." 1955. *New York Times*, May 27.

Darling, Martha. 1975. *The Role of Women in the Economy*. Paris: OECD.

Dickinson, Z. Clark. 1943. "Men's and Women's Wages in the United States." *International Labour Review* 47, no. 6: 693–720.

EEOC (Equal Employment Opportunity Commission). 1980. *Hearings before the United States Equal Employment Opportunity Commission on Job Segregation and Wage Discrimination*. https://babel.hathitrust.org/cgi/pt?id=mdp.39015005297109&view=1up&seq=7.

England, Paula. 1982. "The Failure of Human Capital Theory to Explain Occupational Sex Segregation." *Journal of Human Resources* 17, no. 3: 358–70.

England, Paula. 2010. "The Gender Revolution: Uneven and Stalled." *Gender & Society* 24, no. 2: 149–66.

England, Paula, Andrew Levine, and Emma Mishel. 2020. "Progress toward Gender Equality in the United States Has Slowed or Stalled." *Proceedings of the National Academy of Sciences* 117, no. 13: 6990–97.

Ewick, Patricia, and Susan S. Silbey. 1998. *The Common Place of Law: Stories from Everyday Life*. Chicago: University of Chicago Press.

Faludi, Susan. 2006. *Backlash: The Undeclared War against American Women*. 15th anniversary ed. New York: Crown.

Gerring, John. 2012. "Mere Description." *British Journal of Political Science* 42, no. 4: 721–46.

Goffman, Erving. 1977. "The Arrangement between the Sexes." *Theory and Society* 4, no. 3: 301–31.

Goldin, Claudia. 1990. *Understanding the Gender Gap*. Oxford: Oxford University Press.

Goldin, Claudia. 2014. "A Grand Gender Convergence: Its Last Chapter." *American Economic Review* 104, no. 4: 1091–119.

Hacking, Ian. 1983. *Representing and Intervening: Introductory Topics in the Philosophy of Natural Science*. Cambridge: Cambridge University Press.

Hecht, Gabrielle. 1998. *The Radiance of France*. Cambridge, Mass.: MIT Press.

Hegewisch, Ariane, and Heidi Hartmann. 2014. "Occupational Segregation and the Gender Wage Gap: A Job Half Done." Institute for Women's Policy Research. https://iwpr.org/wp-content/uploads/2020/08/C419.pdf.

Hegewisch, Ariane, and Adiam Tesfaselassie. 2020. "The Gender Wage Gap: 2019; Earnings Differences by Gender, Race, and Ethnicity." Institute for Women's Policy Research No. C495. https://iwpr.org/wp-content/uploads/2020/09/Gender-Wage-Gap-Fact-Sheet-2.pdf.

Hirschman, Daniel. 2016. "Stylized Facts in the Social Sciences." *Sociological Science* 3:604–26.

Hirschman, Daniel. 2021. "Rediscovering the 1%: Knowledge Infrastructures and the Stylized Facts of Inequality." *American Journal of Sociology* 127, no. 3: 739–86.

Hoff Sommers, Christina. 2014. "The Gender Wage Gap Myth." American Enterprise Institute. https://www.aei.org/articles/the-gender-wage-gap-myth/.

House Hearings. 1962. "Equal Pay for Equal Work." Part 1. Hearings before the Select Subcommittee on Labor of the Committee on Education and Labor. House of Representatives. 87th Cong. 2nd Sess. (March 26–28).

Hower, Joseph E. 2020. "'You've Come a Long Way—Maybe': Working Women, Comparable Worth, and the Transformation of the American Labor Movement, 1964–1989." *Journal of American History* 107, no. 3: 658–84.

Howlett, Peter, and Mary S. Morgan. 2010. *How Well Do Facts Travel? The Dissemination of Reliable Knowledge.* Cambridge: Cambridge University Press.

Hutner, Frances C. 1986. *Equal Pay for Comparable Worth. The Working Woman's Issue of the Eighties.* New York: Praeger.

Kaldor, Nicholas. 1957. "A Model of Economic Growth." *Economic Journal* 67, no. 268: 591–624.

Kelly, Erin, and Frank Dobbin. 1998. "How Affirmative Action Became Diversity Management: Employer Response to Antidiscrimination Law, 1961 to 1996." *American Behavioral Scientist* 41, no. 7: 960–84. doi:10.1177/0002764298041007008.

Kessler-Harris, Alice. 2001. *In Pursuit of Equity: Women, Men, and the Quest for Economic Citizenship in Twentieth Century America.* Oxford: Oxford University Press.

Kessler-Harris, Alice. 2014. *A Woman's Wage: Historical Meanings and Social Consequences.* Updated ed. Lexington: University Press of Kentucky.

Klein, Viola. 1965. *Women Workers: Working Hours and Services.* Paris: OECD.

Laughlin, Kathleen A. 2000. *Women's Work and Public Policy: A History of the Women's Bureau, U.S. Department of Labor, 1945–1970.* Boston: Northeastern University Press.

Lyons, Richard. 1972. "Pay Gap Widens between Sexes: Labor Department Official Describes 'Grim Picture.'" *New York Times*, December 28.

Marini, Margaret Mooney. 1989. "Sex Differences in Earnings in the United States." *Annual Review of Sociology* 15, no. 1: 343–80.

McCann, Michael W. 1994. *Rights at Work: Pay Equity Reform and the Politics of Legal Mobilization.* Chicago: University of Chicago Press.

Mincer, Jacob, and Solomon Polachek. 1974. "Family Investments in Human Capital: Earnings of Women." *Journal of Political Economy* 82, no. 2: S76–S108.

National Committee on Pay Equity (NCPE). 2021. "Equal Pay Day." https://www.pay-equity.org/day.html.

National Research Council. 1981. *Women, Work, and Wages: Equal Pay for Jobs of Equal Value.* Washington, D.C.: National Academies Press.

Nelson, Robert L., and William P. Bridges. 1999. *Legalizing Gender Inequality: Courts, Markets, and Unequal Pay for Women in America.* Cambridge: Cambridge University Press.

Oaxaca, Ronald. 1973. "Male-Female Wage Differentials in Urban Labor Markets." *International Economic Review* 14, no. 3: 693–709.

OECD. 2021. "Gender Wage Gap." https://data.oecd.org/earnwage/gender-wage-gap
.htm.

"Pay Gap Has Widened between Men, Women." 1976. *Wall Street Journal*, April 27.

Pidgeon, Mary Elizabeth. 1937. *Differences in the Earnings of Women and Men.*
Women's Bureau, Department of Labor.

Pullen, John. 2009. *The Marginal Productivity Theory of Distribution: A Critical
History.* New York: Routledge.

Rosenbaum, David. 1980. "Working Women Still Seek Man-Sized Wages: Pockets of
Success, Not a Trend." *New York Times*, July 27.

Sanborn, Henry. 1960. "Income Differences between Men and Women in the United
States." PhD diss., University of Chicago.

Sanborn, Henry. 1964. "Pay Differences between Men and Women." *Industrial and
Labor Relations Review* 17, no. 4: 534–50.

Sawhill, Isabel V. 1973. "The Economics of Discrimination against Women: Some
New Findings." *Journal of Human Resources* 8, no. 3: 383–96.

Senate Hearing. 1962. "Equal Pay Act of 1962." Subcommittee on Labor of the
Committee on Labor and Public Welfare. August 1.

Senate Hearing. 1963. "Equal Pay Act of 1963." Subcommittee on Labor of the
Committee on Labor and Public Welfare. April 2, 3, 16.

Shanahan, Eileen. 1976. "Gap in Earnings between the Sexes." *New York Times*,
December 31.

Smith-Doerr, Laurel, Sharla Alegria, Kaye Husbands Fealing, Debra Fitzpatrick, and
Donald Tomaskovic-Devey. 2019. "Gender Pay Gaps in U.S. Federal Science
Agencies: An Organizational Approach." *American Journal of Sociology* 125, no.
2: 534–76.

Stafford, Frank. 1986. "Forestalling the Demise of Empirical Economics: The Role
of Microdata in Labor Economics Research." In *Handbook of Labor Economics*,
edited by Orley C. Ashenfelter and Richard Layard, 1:387–423. Amsterdam:
Elsevier.

Star, Susan Leigh, and James R. Griesemer. 1989. "Institutional Ecology,
'Translations' and Boundary Objects: Amateurs and Professionals in Berkeley's
Museum of Vertebrate Zoology, 1907–39." *Social Studies of Science* 19, no. 3:
387–420.

Suter, Larry E., and Herman P. Miller. 1973. "Income Differences between Men and
Career Women." *American Journal of Sociology* 78, no. 4: 962–74.

Swedberg, Richard. 2018. "Folk Economics and Its Role in Trump's Presidential
Campaign: An Exploratory Study." *Theory and Society* 47, no. 1: 1–36.

Teixeira, Pedro N. 2007. *Jacob Mincer: The Founding Father of Modern Labor
Economics.* Oxford: Oxford University Press.

Teixeira, Pedro N. 2014. "Gary Becker's Early Work on Human Capital—
Collaborations and Distinctiveness." *IZA Journal of Labor Economics* 3, no. 1: 12.

Treiman, Donald J., and Heidi I. Hartmann, eds. 1981. *Women, Work, and Wages:
Equal Pay for Jobs of Equal Value.* Washington, D.C.: National Academy Press.

Turk, Katherine. 2016. *Equality on Trial: Gender and Rights in the Modern American Workplace*. Philadelphia: University of Pennsylvania Press.

"Wages and Women." 1974. *Time*, June 17.

Williams, Joan C., Jessica Manvell, and Stephanie Bornstein. 2006. "'Opt Out' or Pushed Out? How the Press Covers Work/Family Conflict." Center for WorkLife Law, UC Hastings.

"Women Are Paid Less Than Men—and That Hits Harder in an Economic Crisis." 2022. https://leanin.org/equal-pay-data-about-the-gender-pay-gap.

"Women Teachers Open Equal Pay Campaign: Interborough Association Demands Same Salary as the Men." 1906. *New York Times*, October 7.

Women's Bureau. 1965. *Background Facts on Women Workers in the United States*. Washington, D.C.: Department of Labor.

Women's Bureau. 1976. *The Earnings Gap between Women and Men*. Washington, D.C.: Department of Labor.

Women's Bureau. 1979. *The Earnings Gap between Women and Men*. Washington, D.C.: Department of Labor.

"Women's Pay Gap Is Still Widening, U.S. Official Says." 1964. *New York Times*.

The Queen of the Social Sciences: The Reproduction of a [White] *"Man's Field"*

Jennifer Cohen

1. Introduction

Economics can be imagined as a set of ideas generated through the experiences and studies of their authors, who live and work in particular social and historical contexts. In one version of this imaginary, successful theories emerge through debate in a "marketplace of ideas" and shape economic thought (see Skinner 1978). Alternatively, as Thomas Stapleford (2017: 116) has suggested, economics can be understood as a social practice: "Practices, as I'm using the term here, are comprised of three components: (1) collections of actions that are (2) linked by teleology (they can be understood as elements in a goal-oriented process) and (3) are subject

Correspondence may be addressed to Jennifer Cohen, Miami University, 501 E. High St., Oxford, OH 45056 (cohenje@miamioh.edu). I appreciate the comments from several reviewers and this volume's editorial team, especially Evelyn Forget, who helped sharpen and clarify the argument. Any remaining errors are my own. I am grateful to the original members of URPE's Women's Caucus and to the current members of what is now the Caucus of Women and Non-binary People. Heidi Hartmann, Marianne Hill, Paddy Quick, Laurie Nisinoff, Barbara Bergmann, Yana van der Meulen Rodgers, Randy Albelda, Drue Barker, Suzanne Bergeron, and Sirisha Naidu have been especially helpful. Finally, S Charusheela has been a source of unwavering support and insight about this and other work and reminds us that the road to the future is not found through platitudes or veneration for those who broke the path but through our collective projects of critical world-making. Square brackets are used to clarify meaning by adding context or missing words. In this article, square brackets make implied context explicit.

History of Political Economy 54 (annual suppl.) DOI 10.1215/00182702-10085730

to normative evaluation (they, or the overall process of which they are a part, can be done poorly or well)."

If economics is understood as a social practice, then the history of economics becomes less narrowly focused on ideas that move through time/space and the intentions of practitioners and more focused on the set of activities that characterize the discipline itself. Where theoretical dominance emerges through a meritocratic marketplace of ideas in the former imaginary, economics as social practice highlights how normative criteria are brought to bear in ways that define what is and is not valuable. Hence there is a two-way relationship between the theories that are "successful" and reflect disciplinary values, and disciplinary practices. The historical marginalization of women in the profession is reflected in the way gender has been considered by economists. Marginalization established self-sustaining practices that impede challenges to it. The relationship suggests there are high-stakes connections between demographic and epistemic diversity in economics.

The lack of demographic diversity in the economics discipline has been the subject of numerous recent studies and a topic of heated debate on social media. Meanwhile, educational institutions and professional organizations have adopted *diversity, equity,* and *inclusion* (DEI) policies to attract and retain underrepresented faculty.[1] Implementation tends to be slow and incomplete, however, partly because these efforts are met with structural resistance to diversity. Structural resistance is internal to the seemingly neutral institutions that structure academic disciplines, such as the vertical hierarchy of advancement in the profession and the evaluations that entails. Institutionalized, group-based resistance to diversity in one historical period (e.g., discrimination, hostility, misogyny) can become structural resistance to diversity in the next.[2] Therefore, even if

1. *Diversity* refers to the entry and advancement of women, Black, Hispanic, Native American, Asian, LGBTQI, and differently abled economists in the profession. *Inclusion* means nonexclusion or nonmarginalization of those economists; taking seriously the research that they do, e.g., in consideration for funding, evaluation for tenure and promotion, and, more broadly, a sense that they and their work "belong" in the discipline. For some institutions, including the American Economic Association, these efforts focus on diversity and inclusion, leaving equity aside. Ironically, this may be because of the meritocratic imaginary in which people need only to be included for their ideas to be subject to the competitive marketplace and therefore to have the opportunity to emerge as "the best." This view is ahistorical, at best, and fails to acknowledge or address power relations.

2. Collective resistance is present in the group pursuit of group interests, be they material or cultural, and may be related to perceived status or prestige. Men have historically resisted

there are no racist and sexist individuals in the following period, a discipline may remain sexist, racist, or both through structural resistance.

I have sought to trace how ongoing resistance to diversity and the construction of "work" are connected by linking "women's work" to the experiences of women economists. I find that economics remains a "man's field" through (a) structural resistance to women economists, (b) interpreting women's economic activities as marginal to the "real business" of economics, and (c) delegitimizing feminist research about those activities. The next section summarizes well-known data on the current climate in economics. Subsequently, I theorize structural resistance to diversity to make its operation more visible. I then analyze theoretical content in orthodox and feminist economics, demonstrating how concepts as basic to economics as "work" reflect gendered value systems in the discipline, with negative consequences for women. Finally, I turn to women's experiences in economics. Life-history interview data illustrate how historical resistance to diversity inside the discipline is tied up in resistance to valuing women's work and to including women who study it. In practice, the delegitimization of feminists' research on the subject *is* the devaluing of women's unpaid work in economic thought. Because economic thought is influential outside the discipline, the delegitimization of feminist economic research devalues women's unpaid work outside the discipline as well. I conclude that efforts to "fix" structural resistance to diversity without addressing the devalorization of the gendered work required to reproduce people are likely to have limited impacts.

2. The Current Climate

The unusual degree of demographic homogeneity in economics has helped define the boundaries of the field. In the United States, the discipline has historically been populated primarily by white men, especially at the top of the occupational hierarchy, whose perceptions and experiences influence knowledge production. Disciplinary norms, internalized ideologies, exposure to alternative approaches, lived experiences, and perceptions all inform scholars' decisions about what to study and

---

women's entrance into higher education and male-dominated occupations, in part out of fears of feminization. Evidence suggests that feminization has a causal relationship to reduced pay and status (Levanon, England, and Allison 2009). See also *stratification economics* (Darity et al. 2017).

their theoretical and methodological approaches. For some women and underrepresented men, experiences with sexism, racism, and other systems of oppression may influence what they study and how.[3] Demographic homogeneity and epistemic homogeneity are therefore related. The potential for greater diversity of thought in the production of economic knowledge has garnered much less attention than demographic diversity.

Resistance to demographic and epistemic diversity—and especially to both simultaneously, for example, to women who are feminist economists—is likely stronger, more unified, and more persistent in economics than in other academic disciplines (Albelda 1997). Empirically, economics has wider gender gaps in tenure and promotion, salaries, and job satisfaction than other disciplines (cf. Bayer and Rouse 2016). Resistance to diversity is part of an occupational culture that embraces one set of values while excluding or devaluing alternatives.

Occupational culture contributes to the climate of a profession. The climate may be generally "chilly" but can be downright frigid for some populations (Britton 2017). To assess the climate in the discipline, the American Economic Association's (AEA) Committee on Equity, Diversity, and Professional Conduct (CEDPC) distributed a Professional Climate Survey in 2018. The survey captured data about thousands of economists' experiences.[4] For some respondents, the concerns motivating

3. The same is true of dominant groups. Members of dominant groups have often-unrecognized experiences with systems of oppression in which they are beneficiaries, and this influences their perceptions and their choices of topics and methods too. Experiences, even when some people may not recognize their position in them, matter in knowledge production. What is considered a "nonproblem" by one group is unlikely to attract its attention, while another group may find it a significant problem that merits scholarly intervention. For example, over 80 percent of women economists felt that women were not respected in the discipline, while 70 percent of socially conservative white male economists felt that women were respected (CEDPC 2019: 14, 27). Respect for women in the discipline is therefore far more likely to be an issue taken up by women economists than by socially conservative white male economists. Intersectionality—the intersections of gender, race, class, and other forms of social difference—adds complexity to these considerations.

4. Of a pool of 45,435 current and former AEA members, 10,405 returned the forty-seven-question survey. Of respondents, 55 percent were white men, 22 percent were white women, 14 percent nonwhite men, and 7 percent nonwhite women (CEDPC 2019: 9). Overall, 30 percent of respondents were women and 21 percent were nonwhite (3). As of 2017, these data roughly align with the proportion of women in the discipline in academe (23% women vs. 30% of respondents). People of color are underrepresented, as 32 percent of the academic discipline was people of color in 2017 (vs. 21% of respondents) (Sharpe 2021: 425–26).

the survey were out of alignment with the discipline's historical disposition to begin with.

> The temperament behind [the AEA's professional climate] survey is not that of the discipline I entered almost [redacted] years ago, which had earned the title of *Queen of the Social Sciences*. Rather, the temperament behind this survey is that of the *degraded, politicized, non-disciplinary* departments and programs which have either been invented or corrupted over the last several decades. (CEDPC 2019: 14; redaction in original; emphasis added)[5]

For this person, the survey seemed to indicate that the discipline, previously focused on "determining economic truths," uninfluenced by "politics," lost the status obtained through an insistence that it is the "most scientific of the social sciences" (CEDPC 2019: 14; Fourcade, Ollion, and Algan 2015). The respondent's word choice is apt. Critical economists, especially feminists, *politicize* hierarchical relationships in their research. Politicizing a phenomenon or process means identifying and analyzing relations of power and the value systems those power relations reinforce (Peterson 2003). The demographics of the economics profession suggest the presence of value systems and relations of power that may be disadvantageous to underrepresented economists, inviting this type of analysis.

Other respondents voiced discontent too. Referring to a survey question that asked whether the AEA should expend more effort to increase diversity in economics, one wrote,[6] "Devoting any time or attention to 'diversity' and 'inclusion' and 'climate' is a ridiculous 'politically correct' waste of time in the field of economics, as in most if not all fields of academia and workplaces generally. While there are certainly cases of sexual harassment, these should not be lumped together with nonexistent problems and nonexistent issues" (CEDPC 2019: 13).[7]

---

5. Some male economists are resistant to the collection of data about women in economics. Data collection has been interpreted as a threat by some, notably a former chair of the economics department at the University of Rochester, who asserted that CSWEP was "engaged in harassment rather than in the mere gathering of information" (Chassonnery-Zaïgouche, Cherrier, and Singleton 2019: 9).

6. I was unable to confirm the genders of the respondents quoted (Bertrand, pers. comm., 2021). CEDPC 2019 identifies some quotes as being from women; where gender is not identified or is not obvious, the quotes are likely from men.

7. The respondent is correct that sexual harassment is a problem: 22 percent of women respondents reported experiencing unwanted attempts at a "dating, romantic, or sexual relation-

These anonymous survey responses are windows into resistance to diversity, particularly resistance to the presence of women.[8] It may be tempting to dismiss the comments as coming from a few disgruntled individuals, but the respondents are not mere "bad apples." Their answers reflect a widely held historical fear of feminization of the discipline and sexism in the culture of economics. They reinforce to women—and men—that economics is not a space for women, and that the exclusion and marginalization of women are not "real" problems, despite their relationships to recruitment, advancement, and retention.

Such commentary is hardly novel. Historical records from the AEA, the discipline's largest and oldest professional organization, show that groups of men resisted including women in the field fifty years ago. Male "ownership" of the economics discipline was crystallized in the language of an AEA resolution about whether economics is a "man's field." In a business meeting at the December 1971 AEA meetings in New Orleans, a group of women motioned the AEA. They accused the organization "of making economics 'a man's field' and called for greater equality in training and hiring of women economists" (Mata 2005: 83; Cohen 2019). The original language of the first resolution called on the AEA to declare that "economics is not a man's field." The resolution was changed by amendment to read, "economics is not *exclusively* a man's field" (Bartlett 1997: 11; emphasis added). In other words, by male economists' amendment, the women economists' proposed resolution was changed to effectively declare that economics *is* a man's field.

In this historical case, resistance is both to women as a demographic and to the feminist critique leveled by those who raised the issue; it is resistance to demographic and epistemic diversity. It implies that economics is a profession for men (albeit no longer "exclusively") and that economics was, and would remain, a field of thought focused primarily on [men's] economic concerns, while "women's issues" would exist on the margins.[9] In contrast to this open articulation in the early 1970s,

---

ship despite your efforts to discourage it," 10 percent experienced stalking, 7 percent reported feeling threatened with retaliation for not being romantically or sexually cooperative, and 6 percent reported experiencing attempted or actual sexual assault by others in economics (CEDPC 2019: 34). Compared with women in anthropology, women in economics were two to three times as likely to have these experiences (32).

8. Resistance to other forms of diversity is likely strong as well, but these survey responses suggest that these respondents are concerned with the feminization of the discipline.

9. Because men are the "null" category, centering men and men's concerns requires no mod-

much resistance may not be visible at all, especially if women scholars and scholars of color are discouraged from entering the discipline or from using alternative theoretical approaches that challenge orthodoxy. Like power more generally, when resistance is least visible is likely when it is at its most effective. Its embeddedness in the discipline itself means that structural resistance can be a powerful, if invisible, force.

3. [In]Visibility: Theorizing Structural Resistance to Demographic and Epistemic Diversity

Early exclusion of women limited feminist contributions to economic thought.[10] Since exclusion writ large is incomplete and illegal,[11] marginalization has been a way to insulate the profession from feminization. It also insulates orthodoxy from critique by delegitimizing feminist research as "not economics." Because feminist research challenges existing power relations, this a way to maintain gendered power relations inside and outside the discipline. Marginalization is a normative process in which ongoing investment is made to differentiate relational concepts: economics from "noneconomics," paid work from unpaid work, and that which is deemed valuable from that which is not. As a form of resistance, marginalization is not always easily observed.

Gender ideology and existing structures that reinforce disciplinary norms and values can effectively marginalize certain areas of study and unorthodox interpretations of economic concepts. Concepts that appear "neutral" can act as definitional boundaries that entrench and naturalize orthodox interpretations at the expense of alternatives (Barker and Kuiper 2003; Méthot 2013).[12] Disciplinary norms have

---

ifier; that work is considered economics and those concerns are economic issues. Women and women's concerns, on the other hand, retain the qualifier of being "women's issues." Capturing how "women's issues" are considered inferior, Nancy Folbre describes disparaging comments from other economists, "I had people tell me, you're throwing your career away . . . You're focusing on issues that are just girly issues" (quoted in Peck 2021). Other feminist economists have been told that their work is not economics at all (anonymous, pers. comm., 2021).

10. This is referred to as "epistemic exclusion" in some literatures (see Settles et al. 2020). Epistemic exclusion is "an infringement on the epistemic agency of knowers that reduces her or his ability to participate in a given epistemic community" (Dotson 2012: 24).

11. Gender discrimination in hiring, promoting, and firing was made illegal in the Civil Rights Act of 1964 (sec. 7, 42 U.S.C. sec. 2000e et seq. [1964]).

12. Pierre-Olivier Méthot (2013: 121) quotes Müller-Wille (2011: 479): "The meaning of a

been deployed (consciously or not) as women and underrepresented men enter and advance in the discipline.[13] For example, disciplinary norms direct graduate students to research questions within historically constructed boundaries that define the "proper" terrain of economics, pushing other questions into the margins (Mata 2009). Those boundaries are policed (intentionally or not) by faculty members, mentors, and others, often in what is understood as the student's (or faculty member's) interest. From the perspective of dissertation committee members, if a candidate wants to graduate, get an academic job, publish, and earn tenure, many would advise her to do what is expedient and not upset the apple cart by challenging those boundaries.

The demographics and hierarchical structure of the discipline reinforce this directive: dissertation topics and journal articles need to appeal to committee members, reviewers, and editors, who, historically, have been white men. If this demographic was perceived to have preferences for certain topics or approaches—or distaste for a set of topics or approaches—pandering to these perceived preferences is strategic. They may be more likely than other demographics to view research on race or gender as "not of general interest," for example, even though women and underrepresented men are the majority of the population of any country.[14] Disciplinary norms and dominant epistemic values therefore structure economists' careers, especially prior to tenure. It is noteworthy that preferences that are shared, or are perceived to be shared, by members of a relatively powerful, relatively homogeneous group may distort group members' own perceptions.

Another mechanism that institutionalizes bias in tenure and promotion decisions is the adoption of seemingly gender-neutral student evaluations of teaching. Colleagues need not be sexists who discriminate against

---

concept [for Canguilhem] does not exhaust itself in its discursive relationship to other words and texts only"; to the contrary, concepts "articulate dynamic power relationships of authority and resistance by advancing certain evaluations in order to contest or overcome others." See also Pohlhaus 2012.

13. For women, "re-enter the discipline" is more accurate. More women graduated with PhDs in economics in the 1920s than in the following decades up to the 1970s (Albelda 1997: 13; Forget 2011).

14. Anecdotally and from personal experience as a single-blind reviewer with other reviewers, rejecting work on gender or race as "not of general interest" is common. I have yet to encounter the reverse situation, i.e., one in which women or underrepresented men find a research topic to be oriented to men's interests or the interests of white people and therefore better placed outside general interest journals.

women for bias to be present; bias is a function of the socialization of students into a gender ideology that devalues women. The adoption of teaching evaluations is an example of how apparently neutral data collection can convert bias in one period to structural resistance to diversity in the next. Student evaluations of teaching embed resistance to women's advancement in the structure of the occupation itself. Evidence indicates that the penalty for being a woman is especially high when women teach in male-dominated disciplines like economics (Lazos 2012; Mengel, Sauermann, and Zölitz 2019).

While innovations in evaluation methods *could* give rise to sexism without sexists, about 50 percent of women report directly experiencing sex discrimination, and 33 percent of men and 44 percent of women report witnessing sex discrimination between 2008 and 2018 (CEDPC 2019: 49–50). At nearly 40 percent of the full sample, sex discrimination was the most common form of discrimination witnessed, followed by that based on race, research topics, and political views, all at 23 percent. These data suggest that gender bias remains one of the most significant challenges in the discipline.

Within academic economics, gendered expectations, norms, and values are pervasive and influence recruitment, evaluation of merit in tenure and promotion, behavior within the occupation, formation of occupational attitudes, occupational culture, and occupational stereotypes (Caplow 1954: 102). Gender ideology is internal to the discipline and its "climate": it contributes to the demographics of economics and to women's—and men's—gendered experiences in the discipline.[15] Occupations with strict vertical hierarchies tend to profound conservatism (Caplow 1954). Historically, gatekeepers have been more likely to promote those who look similar and think similarly. Homogeneity has costs. Compared with other social science disciplines, economics suffers from a lack of epistemic diversity. As Janet Seiz (1993: 187) cautions, "The lack of diversity in the scientific community and the powerful influence of ideology produce a commonality of unquestioned beliefs, limitations of vision, and conscious or unconscious wishes. False arguments may not be rooted out because those who would be inclined to challenge them—members of social groups with different experiences and interests—lack numbers and influence."

15. Men have gendered experiences, but are often understood as the "null" case, as if their experiences were generalizable, while only women's experiences involve gender. Gender is relational; it cannot affect one demographic without affecting others.

Women in economics, especially feminists, have been critical of this occupational culture from the time they entered the discipline in numbers large enough to advocate for women as a group in the early 1970s (Cohen 2019). They have argued not only that women are excluded but that research *about* women is marginalized. Hence feminists have been negatively affected by the culture while they document and combat it with their research. They experienced disciplinary closure to women and the closure of intellectual space.

The marginalization of feminist research is a function not of simple misogyny or protecting material interests alone. It is resistance to the way feminist research challenges orthodox interpretations of value and related distributions of power in the discipline, in the household, and in society. In emphasizing the value of reproductive labor and the dependence of production on reproduction, feminists challenge the centrality of paid work in economic theory and the popular perception of the paid worker as the primary contributor to the household (Himmelweit, Simonetti, and Trigg 2001). In this way feminist research challenges the centrality of men as the primary actors in economics and in life more generally.

4. Defining and [De]Valuing Work

The marginalization of women within the economics profession and the devaluation of alternative theoretical approaches coincide around "work" as a category of study. Women economists are both unpaid workers in the household[16] and economists, some of whom have questioned and redefined the category of work (Seiz 2013). Women do the vast majority of reproductive labor, so what "counts" as work, and the value it generates, have been significant concerns in feminist research (Himmelweit 1995). Feminists have created innovative theoretical and practical approaches for understanding and measuring phenomena variably referred to as reproductive labor, household production, unpaid work, and care work, all of which constitute aspects of social reproduction (Badgett and Folbre 1999; Folbre 1993; Quick 2008; Cohen 2018). Social reproduction includes the

16. Gender ideology associates women and femininity with relatively lower-status work and lower pay compared with men and masculinity. As children, people are socialized into a gender ideology that tells them that women and femininity are less valuable than men and masculinity. Gendered expectations, norms, and values are elements of social structure internalized by economists and are acted on consciously and unconsciously. Gender ideology is a source of gender bias that manifests in discrimination, exclusion, and marginalization.

activities associated with reproducing human life on a daily and intergenerational basis.

Feminists argue that a realistic understanding of the economy takes seriously the factor input labor that is produced by "the household" in orthodox thought. Yet it is not "the household" that produces labor; it is largely women's unpaid work. The lack of recognition of women's labor and their subsumption into "the household" erases women from this economic theory and these analyses. As it is understood by most economists, production fundamentally depends on women's unpaid work to reproduce human beings who are collectively recognized in economics as the labor supply. Some feminist analyses examine the relationship between masculinized, paid work in production and the feminized, unpaid work on which it depends.[17] In this way, they challenge the separability of paid and unpaid work and orthodox economists' division of the production of goods and services from the production of labor.

Feminists politicize the [inflated] status of paid work and the [degraded] status of unpaid work. They argue that status is constructed relationally in the differentiation of high-status "purely occupational lives" associated with paid work from feminized, nonoccupational lives. The division distinguishes public, productive, paid, clean (when professional), masculinized work that is popularly perceived as valuable from private, degraded, reproductive, dirty, unpaid work that is popularly perceived as low skill and "natural" to women. Here differentiation, or the creation of difference, can be read as the construction of a hierarchy of relatively higher-status work and relatively lower-status feminized work. Politicizing the relationship between paid work and unpaid work challenges the naturalness or—more accurately—the naturalization of the imaginary boundary between valued work and devalued work. The construction of unpaid work as nonwork, as that which is "natural" to women and unworthy of study, is key to understanding feminization: devaluing women's unpaid work undermines the value not simply of women's economic contributions, but of women themselves.

The relationship between feminization and value is well documented empirically. An example comes from a recent study that suggests that women entering STEM fields drives a perception of those fields as "soft

17. Activities that are monetized are included on one side of A. C. Pigou's "arbitrary line," while those "services gratuitously rendered by women" are not (Pujol 1992: 171).

science" rather than "hard science" (Light, Benson-Greenwald, and Diekman 2022). The perceived "hardness"—and value—of a given field is a function of the proportion of its practitioners who are male, not a function of the substance of the field alone. The results add to existing evidence that the perceived value of women and the work they do is lower than for men, even when the work is identical. Hence, feminization is a demographic process of increasing representation of women, a cultural process in which perceived status (i.e., of an occupation) falls, and an economic process in which lower material rewards accompany reduced status and the increasing presence of women. Historically, resistance to feminization of paid work is resistance to increased competition, reduced pay, and perceived lower status. Feminization has been theorized by economists and scholars like Mary Paley Marshall and Alfred Marshall (1890: 175–76), F. Y. Edgeworth (1922), Cléo Chassonnery-Zaïgouche and Annie L. Cot (2014), and A. C. Pigou (1920: 413), who considered women's unpaid work "leisure."[18] There are several approaches to understanding how demographic feminization reduces the remunerative and perceived value of occupations: queuing (Reskin and Roos 1990), occupational segregation and crowding (Bergmann 1974), and devaluation (England 1992). Resistance to feminization was overt in the academic economics profession and persists in less visible forms.

In spite of its critical role in the economy, reproductive labor has been defined out of popular interpretations of "work." It would be difficult to overstate the importance of the definition of "work" in economics. Definitions of such concepts are powerful ways to create social reality. The bias favoring paid work (productivism) is enshrined in the census, in which wives, like children, were considered unproductive dependents by 1900, due in part to the intervention of former AEA president (1885–92) Francis Amasa Walker (Folbre 1991; Cohen 2020b; Hewitson 1999; Barker and Kuiper 2003; Nelson 1993). Likewise, women's unpaid labor was excluded in the operationalization of the System of National Accounts, a decision made in pursuit of a universal method against the advice of women hired to research the accuracy of the GDP calculation method (Messac 2018). The value assigned by this conceptualization of work is internal to orthodox economics and to basic indicators such as economic growth. That makes the discipline of economics an active participant in

---

18. "Further leisure for [women] yields a bigger return . . . in opportunities for better care of their homes" (Pigou 1920: 413).

devalorizing "women's work." Economics has long played, and continues to play, a major role in creating a social reality in which unpaid reproductive labor is seen both as "women's work" and as unskilled. It influences the perceived value of economic activities far beyond the confines of the discipline. It contributes to the division of labor, with impacts on who does which activities and whether they are considered valuable. The historical erasure of women and their economic contributions devalues women and the work that women do with material ramifications, in addition to other costs. It would not be an exaggeration to claim that the definition and value of work impact nearly all of humanity. The devalorization of "women's work" affects the lives of women workers everywhere; women economists are no exception.

5. The Politicized Is Personal: Impacts on Women in Economics

The delegitimization of women's work in economics converges with resistance to women entering and advancing in the discipline, with dire consequences for many individual women in economics and implications for women economists more broadly. Biographical material is a way to illuminate the lived experience in economics as a social practice. I collected data about feminists' experiences in the discipline by conducting a series of semistructured life history interviews with women economists associated with the Union for Radical Political Economics and URPE's Women's Caucus. A key theme in the interview data is how resistance to women inside the discipline is tied up in resistance to devalorized work—both to those doing that work and to those studying it.

One woman's experience from the mid-1980s to the early 1990s is particularly telling. In the interview she recalled a series of "gender-related career events" such that the discipline itself, not just the men who were her colleagues, played an active role. Despite egregious sexual harassment by her adviser while a graduate student and by an economist who interviewed her for a job, Kate found a new dissertation chair, finished her PhD at Yale, and got a tenure-track job in a university.[19] She continued to encounter gender-based challenges that came to a head with her tenure case in the late 1980s. When Kate went up for tenure with the necessary publications per department and university requirements, she was told that her teaching evaluation scores from a very large economics course that she taught

19. The participant chose to remain anonymous; the name used here is a pseudonym.

to predominantly male students were not high enough. She recalls teaching being a challenge because the students conveyed that she "was not the appropriate authority" on economic issues. A few of her colleagues came to Kate's classes to "see what was wrong," but they found that her teaching seemed fine, although some of them voted against her tenure anyway. The dean of the college said tenure should have been granted, but she was denied on the grounds of the teaching evaluations. She writes, "I was furious at the time—I felt that my home was being taken away, that I was a refugee from a war" (anonymous, pers. comm., February 11, 2022).

The tenure decision is easily observed, but the underlying rationale is less transparent. Kate believes that she was denied tenure for being "too unconventional." She was one of two women in her department of about ten. She had become pregnant, broken up with her partner, and against some socially acceptable mores, she planned to raise her child as an "unwed mother." While her unconventionality may have been a factor, the context in her department merits further attention. When Kate recounted her experiences, she noted that she could not relax in the department, and this made being at ease while teaching even more difficult; the department secretary gave her a harder time about typing things for her compared with other faculty members; and as the year for the tenure decision drew closer, conversations with colleagues became uncomfortable and difficult. Effectively, the economics department was not her space, a message that was transmitted in numerous ways.

One way that four members of her department conveyed their disapproval was by publishing about unwed mothers and "youth from broken families" or "nontraditional family structures." Between 1985 and 1992, the faculty members published about the impact of family disruption on children's earnings, the labor market consequences of teenage pregnancy, and the demand for abortion by unmarried teenagers. For Kate, this was personal, and it began only after it became clear that she was an "unwed mother" who was challenging norms related to paid and unpaid work.

It is entirely possible that it is a coincidence that Kate's colleagues began writing about unwed mothers during the time she was to become an unwed mother. It is also possible that the department secretary frequently had bad days when Kate requested typing and that the discomfort with colleagues had unrelated causes. What is not possible is that these incidents are "non-problems," as described by a climate survey respondent quoted above. They aggregate into hostility, exclusion, and obstacles to advancement in the discipline. Kate summarizes the period: "It was a miserable experience."[20]

As is often the case with discrimination, one cannot be certain of the degree to which her gender, her pregnancy, her colleagues' newfound interest, or other obstacles influenced the tenure decision that pushed her out of academic economics. However, one can be sure that her gender affected the decision. Prior to 1986, the year her child was born, teaching evaluations were not part of administrative decision-making; they were used on an ad hoc basis by individual instructors for self-improvement (Stratton, Myers, and King 1994). In the 1990s, after denying her tenure, three of her colleagues published the above-cited article about a student teaching evaluation instrument implemented by the department in 1986. The teaching score became the primary measure of teaching effectiveness in the department. In their study, which uses ordinary least squares regression to examine determinants of students' grades (women's grades were 13 percent lower than men's grades), they "control for gender" (i.e., for student gender).[21] They make no mention of how gender (and race) can affect student evaluations of teaching. The article was published in 1994, when there was already an extensive literature on gendered penalties in teaching evaluations due to sexist stereotypes.[22] Again, it is not possible to concretely document a relationship between the move to weighing teaching evaluations and an intention of denying her tenure. But weighing teaching evaluation scores from evaluation methods well-known to penalize women, especially from courses in which male students question women's authority, means that Kate's gender played a demonstrable role in the decision made by her male colleagues.

It is noteworthy that her interactions with individual harassers and a group of hostile colleagues are reprehensible but are *not* reasons she left academic economics. The power that determined her future was located

20. Kate turned down a job offer with a preferred university because the university had a religious affiliation and she planned on having a child. At the time, the pregnancy seemed more likely to provoke a negative response in the other university. This was a constraint on her life, work, and location that an unmarried man with a child would be unlikely to confront.

21. For a critique of "controlling" for gender in econometric analyses, see Figart 1997.

22. A Google Scholar search turns up 4,050 hits for "gender differences in 'student evaluation' of faculty teaching" between 1970 and 1993 and 2,160 hits for the same terms for the years 1970–85.

in the institutionalization of a gender-biased evaluation method. In this instance, and across the academy, the adoption of seemingly gender-neutral teaching evaluations integrates gender bias into tenure and promotion decisions.

Superficially, Kate's experience could have happened in any academic discipline. However, for many students of economics, the marginalization of women in the discipline (e.g., being unrepresented in economics textbooks, making contributions that are unrecognized in much of economic thought, being underrepresented among Nobel prize winners, and being underrepresented in the profession) presents to them a discipline in which women barely appear, much less appear as "appropriate authorities." The objectification of women contributes to this perception.[23] Historical and structural resistance to diversity specifically in economics renders the adoption and use of student evaluations of women's teaching in the discipline especially questionable.

Other economists have described marginalization in the discipline that links their paid and unpaid work as well. Sylvia Ann Hewlett (quoted in Mui 2014), who received her PhD from the University of London in the early 1970s, said, "We were encouraged as women in the economics profession to hide our gender differences. The way to succeed was to behave like the guys, to pretend you were identical. I think we lost a big piece of ourselves that way. . . . If you are a wife and a mother and managing a household, you have a much more grounded take on everyday struggles than a lot of men of that period."

As Hewlett describes it, women economists have a better understanding of practical struggles to meet needs than men have *because* of—not in spite of—their unpaid work. "Hiding" invisibilizes something one knows will provoke a negative or patronizing response; "hiding gender" means concealing difference, not drawing attention to experience-based knowledge, and not researching gendered work or power relations. In other words, the optimal strategy for women's success in economics was for them to not be women.

The exercise of power over academic careers through the hierarchical organization of the occupation influences the questions asked in economics and the explanations deemed acceptable (Seiz 1993: 186). Because

23. Francine Blau, an economics professor at Cornell University who received her doctorate from Harvard in 1975, remembers entering a classroom as a young professor only to hear a male student refer to the course as "sex ed" (Mui 2014).

advancement is contingent on the approval of those in positions of power, academic freedom for women and underrepresented minorities was and remains restricted, especially prior to tenure. Some women's experiences with discrimination in the 1960s and 1970s were linked to those in power, as quotes from administrators demonstrate. Myra Strober describes being the first woman to go up for tenure at Stanford's business school in the late 1970s and being denied. She notes, "Several of my colleagues in the business school had advised me early on that I shouldn't work on women's issues, at least not until I got tenure" (quoted in Olson and Emami 2002: 151). She says that her male colleagues were nervous about her going up: "They knew my work was solid, but they didn't want me in their exclusive male preserve. . . . Of course, with hindsight, I now realize what these men were really worried about. . . . The problem was that my field was threatening. It was questioning men's power, and they didn't like that one bit" (150).

Strober's work examined occupational segregation among highly educated people. When she was denied tenure, a male associate dean told her, apparently unironically, that her work was not "seminal."

Strober was ultimately tenured in Stanford's School of Education in the same year she was denied tenure in the business school. Women economists with feminist research were routinely denied tenure until at least the 1990s. Some report being told that publications in journals like *Feminist Economics* (impact factor: 1.8) would not "count" for tenure (anonymous, pers. comm., 2021). In the 1980s and 1990s, discrimination was institutionalized in evaluation methods, in many cases used formally for evaluation only when academe became more diverse.[24] Bias persists in the 2000s, during which women economists are more often interrupted in seminars (Dupas et al. 2021), their papers delayed for publication (Hengel 2017), and they are personally attacked on websites like Economics Job Market Rumors (Wu 2020).

6. Conclusion

Depending on one's perspective, the present moment may constitute a threat to orthodoxy, an opportunity to diversify economic thought, or

---

24. See Price 2009; 2021 NEA listserv, which notes that many economics departments have never, and still do not, employ Black economists. See Price and Sharpe 2020 on the impacts of racism in the production of economic knowledge.

both. The proportion of white male economists fell from 71.2 percent in 2001 to 44.6 percent in 2017 (Sharpe 2021: 425–26). The proportion of women economists grew (6 percent in 1973 to 14.5 percent in 2001 to 22.8 percent in 2017), as did the proportion of Black and Hispanic economists (5.5 percent in 2001 [reported as "minority"] to 10.8 percent in 2017 (3.8 percent Black; 7 percent Hispanic).[25] Most of these groups remain under-represented and white men retain positions of power. At about 33 percent of the US population and 44.6 percent of academic economists in 2017, as of September 13, 2020, white men nonetheless held 82 percent of the editorial board positions at the top five economics journals (author's analysis, Cohen 2020a). The demographic shifts in the discipline but relatively unchanged concentration of editorial influence reflect gendered and racialized disciplinary power. The *Quarterly Journal of Economics*, established in 1886, recently celebrated adding its first woman editor to the board 134 years later, in January 2020 (Oxford University Press 2020).

Aside from some very vocal outliers, economists overwhelmingly favor diversity and diversity efforts. Nearly 100 percent of women and 90 percent of men thought that the AEA should put more effort into improving diversity (CEDPC 2019: 13). Half or more of all demographic groups agree that diversity will make economics more vibrant—with the exception of socially conservative, white, male economists, two-thirds of whom disagreed (CEDPC 2019: 27). Dissatisfaction with the existing climate is rife: the majority of white men (60 percent), underrepresented men (60 percent), women of color (76 percent), and white women (82 percent) are dissatisfied with the overall climate of the profession (CEDPC 2019: 9).

Despite all this goodwill, disciplinary resistance to diversity will persist even if individuals themselves are not discriminatory. Structural resistance appears—at minimum—in the vertical hierarchy of the discipline, in evaluation methods, and in topical areas and alternative perspectives marginalized and devalued in economic thought. Entry and advancement in the discipline is subject to gendered (and racialized) power relations institutionalized in seemingly gender-neutral practices. Gender-biased

---

25. In the 2017 data the proportions of academic economists by gender and race are white men (44.6%), Asian men (23.0%), white women (11.6%), Asian women (9.0%), Hispanic men (5.6%), Black men (3.2%), Hispanic women (1.4%), other men (0.8%), Black women (0.6%), and other women (0.3%). The 2001 data are less refined but the proportions are white men (71.2%), white women (11.5%), Asian men (9.6%), minority men (4.7%), Asian women (2.2%), and minority women (0.8%). All figures from Sharpe 2021: 425–26.

student teaching evaluations and gender-biased peer review processes affecting publishing carry over to the evaluation of work for tenure and promotion review. Dominant group preferences, real or perceived, influence what economists study and how they study it. Gender ideology conditions those preferences because economists are affected by social beliefs and values related to women, men, and gender relations.

Moreover, the construction of valuable work as paid work alone in economic thought has negative impacts on the visibility and perceived value of women and the work women do, including that of women economists. The fictional separability of paid work from unpaid work, the source of the labor supply, reinforces the degradation of unpaid work and those who do it.[26] A changed understanding of the value of unpaid work could contribute to changing the perceived value of those who do the work; it would likely be equity-enhancing. However, such a shift may be unwelcome, as it could disturb existing relationships that empower those associated with paid work relative to those associated with unpaid work. If the discipline is to become inclusive, our understanding of work must change in order to value the practical and theoretical contributions of nonwhite and nonmen people.[27]

I have sought to trace how these two points—persistent resistance to diversity and the construction of "work"—are connected by linking women and "women's work" to actually existing economists. I found that economics remains a "man's field" through structural resistance to women economists, through interpreting women's economic activities as marginal to the "real business" of economics, and by delegitimizing feminist research about those activities. In practice, the delegitimization of feminists' paid work as economists *is* the devaluing of women's unpaid work in economic thought. Because economic thought is influential outside the economics discipline, the delegitimization of feminist economic research devalues women's unpaid work outside the discipline as well. The weight of the second point about work, that feminized unpaid work is associated with women to their disadvantage, is the same weight that has kept many

26. Degradation remains a force even when those people are not women. Feminist theorists make the point that this is because *the work itself is feminized and degraded.*

27. Another form of work that I have left unmentioned is the "third shift" (or fourth shift, considering the community work done by women of color that Nina Banks [2020] describes): that work which women and underrepresented men do to merely exist in worlds designed to exclude them, worlds in which microaggressions and macroaggressions undermine well-being and make daily life and intergenerational life-making dangerous.

women economists, especially feminists, from thriving academic careers. Critically, the association alone, whether or not it reflects reality for individual women, is the foundation for bias that has kept women from getting jobs, from getting tenure, and even from the discipline itself over the past fifty years. The same weight, from the same source, has kept many more women from being hired and promoted outside economics as well.

Efforts to "fix" structural resistance to diversity without addressing the devalorization of gendered work in the economics discipline are likely to have limited impacts. They may contribute to demographic diversity, but demographic diversity may not translate into epistemic diversity in a discipline that marginalizes critical thought. In effect, such efforts may have impacts inside the discipline but do little to shift the weight that the orthodox conceptualization of work puts on women economists and women more generally. Hence, DEI efforts in economics are likely to remain uniquely challenging. As those efforts continue, "good apples" with influence should ensure that underrepresented economists have pathways to advancement with scope for genuine academic freedom. This is especially necessary when their intellectual contributions challenge the value systems and the unequal power relations that economic orthodoxy reinforces.

References

Albelda, Randy. 1997. *Economics and Feminism: Disturbances in the Field.* New York: Twayne.

Badgett, M. V. Lee, and Nancy Folbre. 1999. "Assigning Care: Gender Norms and Economic Outcomes." *International Labour Review* 138, no. 3: 311–26. https://doi.org/10.1111/j.1564–913X.1999.tb00390.x.

Banks, Nina. 2020. "Black Women in the United States and Unpaid Collective Work: Theorizing the Community as a Site of Production." *Review of Black Political Economy* 47, no. 4: 343–62. https://doi.org/10.1177/0034644620962811.

Barker, Drucilla K., and Edith Kuiper, eds. 2003. *Toward a Feminist Philosophy of Economics.* London: Routledge.

Bartlett, Robin. 1997. "CSWEP: Past, Present, Future." CSWEP Newsletter, Fall.

Bayer, Amanda, and Cecilia Elena Rouse. 2016. "Diversity in the Economics Profession: A New Attack on an Old Problem." *Journal of Economic Perspectives* 30, no. 4: 221–42. https://doi.org/10.1257/jep.30.4.221.

Bergmann, Barbara. 1974. "Occupational Segregation, Wages, and Profits When Employers Discriminate by Race or Sex." *Eastern Economic Journal,* April–July: 103–10.

Britton, Dana M. 2017. "Beyond the Chilly Climate: The Salience of Gender in Women's Academic Careers." *Gender & Society* 31, no. 1: 5–27. https://doi.org/10.1177/0891243216681494.

Caplow, T. 1954. *The Sociology of Work.* Minneapolis: University of Minnesota Press.

CEDPC (Committee on Equity, Diversity, and Professional Conduct). 2019. "AEA Professional Climate Survey: Final Report." Committee on Equity, Diversity and Professional Conduct (Sam Allgood, Lee Badgett, and Amanda Bayer, Marianne Bertrand, Sandra E. Black, Nick Bloom and Lisa D. Cook). https://www.aeaweb.org/resources/member-docs/final-climate-survey-results-sept-2019.

Chassonnery-Zaïgouche, Cléo, Béatrice Cherrier, and John D. Singleton. 2019. "'Economics Is Not a Man's Field': CSWEP and the First Gender Reckoning in Economics (1971–1991)." https://papers.ssrn.com/sol3/papers.cfm?abstract_id=3510857.

Chassonnery-Zaïgouche, Cléo, and Annie L. Cot. 2021. "Sentiment and Prejudice." *History of Political Economy* 53, no. 5: 799–832. https://doi.org/10.1215/00182702-9395055.

Cohen, Jennifer. 2018. "What's 'Radical' about [Feminist] Radical Political Economy?" *Review of Radical Political Economics* 50, no. 4: 716–26. https://doi.org/10.1177/0486613418789704.

Cohen, Jennifer. 2019. "The Radical Roots of Feminism in Economics." In "Including a Symposium on 50 Years of the Union for Radical Political Economics," edited by Tiago Mata. *Research in the History of Economic Thought and Methodology* 37A:85–100.

Cohen, Jennifer (@DrJenCohen). 2020a. "Adding 39 editors @ top 5 econ journals: AER, @Econometrica, @jpolecon, @QJEHarvard, @RevEconStud 97% white-3% BIPOC; 100% white-0% Black (B/w only); 82% men-18% women; 82% white men-18% everyone else; 15% white women-85% ev else." Twitter, September 13, 1:25 p.m. https://twitter.com/drjencohen/status/1305195942677745665.

Cohen, Jennifer. 2020b. "Feminist Political Economy and the Heterodoxy." *American Review of Political Economy* 14, no. 1. https://doi.org/10.38024/arpe.208.

Darity, W., D. Hamilton, P. Mason, G. Price, A. Dávila, M. Mora, and S. Stockly. 2017. "Stratification Economics: A General Theory of Intergroup Inequality." In *The Hidden Rules of Race: Barriers to an Inclusive Economy,* edited by A. Flynn, D. Warren, F. Wong, and S. Holmberg, 35–51. Cambridge: Cambridge University Press.

Dotson, Kristie. 2012. "A Cautionary Tale: On Limiting Epistemic Oppression." *Frontiers: A Journal of Women Studies* 33, no. 1: 24–47.

Dupas, Pascaline, Alicia Sasser Modestino, Muriel Niederle, Justin Wolfers, and the Seminar Dynamics Collective. 2021. "Gender and the Dynamics of Economics Seminars." Working paper 28494, National Bureau of Economic Research. https://doi.org/10.3386/w28494.

Edgeworth, F. Y. 1922. "Equal Pay to Men and Women for Equal Work." *Economic Journal* 32, no. 128: 431. https://doi.org/10.2307/2223426.

England, Paula. 1992. *Comparable Worth: Theories and Evidence.* New York: Routledge.

England, Paula. 2001. "Gender and Feminist Studies." In *International Encyclopedia of the Social and Behavioral Sciences*, edited by Neil J. Smelser and Paul B. Baltes, 4:5910–15. London: Elsevier.

Figart, Deborah M. 1997. "Gender as More Than a Dummy Variable: Feminist Approaches to Discrimination." *Review of Social Economy* 55, no. 1: 1–32. https://doi.org/10.1080/00346769700000022.

Folbre, Nancy. 1991. "The Unproductive Housewife: Her Evolution in Nineteenth-Century Economic Thought." *Signs: Journal of Women in Culture and Society* 16, no. 3: 463–84. https://doi.org/10.1086/494679.

Folbre, Nancy. 1993. "How Does She Know? Feminist Theories of Gender Bias in Economics." *History of Political Economy* 25, no. 1: 167–84. https://doi.org/10.1215/00182702-25-1-167.

Forget, Evelyn L. 2011. "American Women and the Economics Profession in the Twentieth Century." *Œconomia* 1, no. 1: 19–30. https://doi.org/10.4000/oeconomia.1807.

Fourcade, Marion, Etienne Ollion, and Yann Algan. 2015. "The Superiority of Economists." *Journal of Economic Perspectives* 29, no. 1: 89–114. https://doi.org/10.1257/jep.29.1.89.

Hengel, E. 2017. "Publishing While Female: Are Women Held to Higher Standards? Evidence from Peer Review." Cambridge Working Papers in Economics 1753. Faculty of Economics, University of Cambridge.

Hewitson, Gillian J. 1999. *Feminist Economics: Interrogating the Masculinity of Rational Economic Man.* Cheltenham: Edward Elgar.

Himmelweit, Susan. 1995. "The Discovery of 'Unpaid Work': The Social Consequences of the Expansion of 'Work.'" *Feminist Economics* 1, no. 2: 1–19. https://doi.org/10.1080/714042229.

Himmelweit, Susan, Roberto Simonetti, and Andrew B. Trigg. 2001. *Microeconomics: Neoclassical and Institutionalist Perspectives on Economic Behaviour.* London: South-Western, Cengage Learning.

Lazos, Sylvia. 2012. "Are Student Teaching Evaluations Holding Back Women and Minorities? The Perils of 'Doing' Gender and Race in the Classroom." In *Presumed Incompetent: The Intersections of Race and Class for Women in Academia*, edited by Gabriella Gutiérrez y Muhs, Yolanda Flores Niemann, Carmen G. González, and Angela P. Harris. Logan: Utah State University Press; Boulder: University Press of Colorado.

Levanon, A., P. England, and P. Allison. 2009. "Occupational Feminization and Pay: Assessing Causal Dynamics Using 1950–2000 U.S. Census Data." *Social Forces* 88, no. 2: 865–91. https://doi.org/10.1353/sof.0.0264.

Light, Alysson E., Tessa M. Benson-Greenwald, and Amanda B. Diekman. 2022. "Gender Representation Cues Labels of Hard and Soft Sciences." *Journal of Experimental Social Psychology* 98 (January): 104234. https://doi.org/10.1016/j.jesp.2021.104234.

Marshall, Mary Paley, and Alfred Marshall. 1890. *The Economics of Industry*. London: Macmillan.

Mata, T. 2005. "Dissent in Economics: Making Radical Political Economics and Post-Keynesian Economics, 1960–1980." PhD diss., London School of Economics and Political Science.

Mata, Tiago. 2009. "Migrations and Boundary Work: Harvard, Radical Economists, and the Committee on Political Discrimination." *Science in Context* 22, no. 1: 115–43. https://doi.org/10.1017/S0269889708002093.

Mengel, Friederike, Jan Sauermann, and Ulf Zölitz. 2019. "Gender Bias in Teaching Evaluations." *Journal of the European Economic Association* 17, no. 2: 535–66. https://doi.org/10.1093/jeea/jvx057.

Messac, Luke. 2018. "Outside the Economy: Women's Work and Feminist Economics in the Construction and Critique of National Income Accounting." *Journal of Imperial and Commonwealth History* 46, no. 3: 552–78. https://doi.org/10.1080 /03086534.2018.1431436.

Méthot, Pierre-Olivier. 2013. "On the Genealogy of Concepts and Experimental Practices: Rethinking Georges Canguilhem's Historical Epistemology." *Studies in History and Philosophy of Science* 44, no. 1: 112–23.

Mui, Ylan. 2014. "New Fed Chief Janet Yellen Lets a Long Career of Breaking Barriers Speak for Itself." *Washington Post*, February 2.

Müller-Wille, Steffan. 2011. "History of Science and Medicine." In *The Oxford Handbook of the History of Medicine*, edited by M. Jackson. Oxford: Oxford University Press.

Nelson, J. A. 1993. "Value-Free or Valueless? Notes on the Pursuit of Detachment in Economics." *History of Political Economy* 25, no. 1: 121–45. https://doi.org/10 .1215/00182702-25-1-121.

Olson, Paulette I., and Zohreh Emami. 2002. *Engendering Economics: Conversations with Women Economists in the United States*. London: Routledge.

Oxford University Press. 2020. "Meet QJE's New Editor: Stefanie Stantcheva." https://academic.oup.com/qje/pages/meet-the-editor.

Peck, Emily. 2021. "Policymakers Used to Ignore Child Care. Then Came the Pandemic." *New York Times*, May 9. https://www.nytimes.com/2021/05/09 /business/child-care-infrastructure-biden.html.

Peterson, V. Spike. 2003. *A Critical Rewriting of Global Political Economy: Integrating Reproductive, Productive, and Virtual Economies*. London: Routledge.

Pigou, Arthur Cecil. 1920. *The Economics of Welfare*. London: Macmillan.

Pohlhaus Jr., Gaile. 2012. "Relational Knowing and Epistemic Injustice: Toward a Theory of Willful Hermeneutical Ignorance." *Hypatia* 27, no. 4: 715–35.

Price, Gregory N. 2009. "The Problem of the Twenty-First Century: Economics Faculty and the Color Line." *Journal of Socio-Economics* 38, no. 2: 331–43. https:// doi.org/10.1016/j.socec.2008.10.007.

Price, Gregory N., and Rhonda V. Sharpe. 2020. "Is the Economics Knowledge Production Function Constrained by Race in the USA?" *Journal of the Knowledge Economy* 11, no. 2: 614–29. https://doi.org/10.1007/s13132-018-0563-8.

Pujol, Michèle A. 1992. *Feminism and Anti-feminism in Early Economic Thought.* Aldershot: Edward Elgar.

Quick, Paddy. 2008. "Unpaid, Reproductive, Caring Labor? The Production of Labor Power? Theoretical and Practical Implications of Terms Used for Women's Work." *Review of Radical Political Economics* 40, no. 3: 308–14. https://doi.org/10.1177/0486613408320106.

Reskin, Barbara R., and Patricia Roos. 1990. *Job Queues, Gender Queues: Explaining Women's Inroads into Male Occupations.* Philadelphia: Temple University Press.

Samuelson, Paul. 1970. *Economics.* 8th ed. New York: McGraw-Hill.

Seiz, Janet. 1993. "Feminism and the History of Economic Thought." *History of Political Economy* 25, no. 1: 185–201. https://doi.org/10.1215/00182702-25-1-185.

Settles, I. H., M. K. Jones, N. T. Buchanan, and K. Dotson. 2021. "Epistemic Exclusion: Scholar(ly) Devaluation That Marginalizes Faculty of Color." *Journal of Diversity in Higher Education* 14, no. 4: 493–507. https://doi.org/10.1037/dhe0000174.

Sharpe, Rhonda Vonshay. 2021. "The Quest for Inclusion in Economics in the US." In *The Routledge Handbook of Feminist Economics,* edited by Günseli Berik and Ebru Kongar, 420–30. Abingdon: Routledge.

Skinner, Quentin. 1978. *The Age of Reformation.* Vol. 2 of *The Foundations of Modern Political Thought.* Cambridge: Cambridge University Press.

Stapleford, Thomas A. 2017. "Historical Epistemology and the History of Economics: Views through the Lens of Practice." In "Including a Symposium on the Historical Epistemology of Economics," edited by Till Düppe and Harro Maas. Special issue, *Research in the History of Economic Thought and Methodology* 35A: 113–45.

Stratton, Richard W., Steven C. Myers, and Randall H. King. 1994. "Faculty Behavior, Grades, and Student Evaluations." *Journal of Economic Education* 25, no. 1: 5–15.

Wu, Alice H. 2020. "Gender Bias among Professionals: An Identity-Based Interpretation." *Review of Economics and Statistics* 102, no. 5: 867–80.

Contributors

Jennifer Burns is an associate professor of history at Stanford University. The leading independent expert on Ayn Rand, she is author of the acclaimed biography *Goddess of the Market: Ayn Rand and the American Right* (Oxford University Press, 2009). Currently, she is completing an intellectual biography of Milton Friedman. Burns is also a research fellow at Stanford's Hoover Institution, where she directs the annual Summer Workshop on Political Economy. Burns is a graduate of Harvard College and the University of California, Berkeley. Podcasts of her American history courses are available through iTunes and on her website, jenniferburns.org.

Cléo Chassonnery-Zaïgouche is a research associate at the Center for Research on the Arts, Social Sciences, and Humanities at the University of Cambridge and a fellow of Fitzwilliam College. She works on the history of discrimination and wages and on the relationship between economic expertise, policy, and quantification.

Jennifer Cohen is an associate professor in the Department of Global and Intercultural Studies at Miami University in Ohio and holds a joint appointment in the Faculty of Health Sciences at the University of the Witwatersrand in Johannesburg. Her mixed-methods research focuses on paid work and unpaid labor. She has conducted extensive fieldwork with nurses employed in the public healthcare system in Johannesburg and with women economists in the United States. She has published health economics research in *Preventive Medicine, AIDS, Global Public Health, Public Health Ethics, PLOS One, Feminist Economics,* and *Gender, Work, and Organization* and history of economics research in *Research in the History of Economic Thought and Methodology* and the *Review of Radical Political Economics*.

History of Political Economy 54 (annual suppl.) DOI 10.1215/00182702-10085744
Copyright 2022 by Duke University Press

Evelyn L. Forget is a professor of economics and community health sciences at the University of Manitoba in Winnipeg (Canada). Her research examines the health and social implications of poverty and inequality, and she is often called upon by governments, First Nations, and international organizations to advise on poverty, inequality, health, and social outcomes. She is a fellow of the Royal Society of Canada and an Officer of the Order of Canada.

Rebeca Gomez Betancourt is a professor of economics at the University of Lyon 2 and a researcher at Triangle, ENS-Lyon. Her work focuses on the history of monetary thought and on women and economics. She is currently working on the origins of gender and feminist economics theories, institutions, and groups. Together with Camila Orozco Espinel she is working on a research project on the history of feminist economics.

Andrés Guiot-Isaac is a PhD candidate in area atudies (Latin America) at Brasenose College, University of Oxford. He is bursary of the program Pasaporte a la Ciencia (Foco Sociedad) and holder of the Global History of Capitalism Project studentship. His research explores the transfer of decision-making power to experts in modern societies by studying the formation of an economic technocracy in Colombia during the post–World War II period. He translated Albert O. Hirschman's biography into Spanish and is the author of "The Quarrel of Policy Advisers That Became Development Experts" (2020, with A. Alvarez and J. Hurtado).

Erin Hengel received a PhD in economics from the University of Cambridge in January 2017 and is currently a research fellow at the Social Research Institute at University College London. Her main research interests are applied microeconomic theory and gender economics.

Daniel Hirschman is an assistant professor of sociology at Cornell University. He studies the political power of experts and their tools, as well as the relationship between organizational practices, knowledge production, and racial inequality. His book project, *Unequal Knowledge: The Stylized Facts of Inequality*, traces the history and politics of the gender wage gap, the racial wealth gap, and top income inequality.

Marianne Johnson is a professor of economics at the University of Wisconsin–Oshkosh. Her research focuses primarily on the history of public economics and public choice, particularly as it relates to Knut Wicksell, James Buchanan, and the Wisconsin institutionalists. Her work has been published in *History of Political Economy*, the *Journal of the History of Economic Thought*, the *Journal of Economic Literature*, and *Public Choice*.

Christina Laskaridis is an assistant professor of economics at the Open University, United Kingdom. She works on the political economy of sovereign debt, international organizations, and monetary and debt debates. Her work examines the rise and nature of economic expertise in historical perspective. She is the 2022 recipient of the Joseph Dorfman Best Dissertation Prize by the History of Economics Society and a 2022–23 visiting research fellow at the University of Oxford.

Camila Orozco Espinel is an assistant professor of economics at the University of Reims Champagne-Ardenne. Her research focuses on twentieth-century history of economics, primarily the post–World War II quest for scientific authority and the mechanism producing gender imbalance in the discipline. Together with Rebeca Gomez Betancourt she is pursuing a research project on the history of feminist economics.

Sarah Louisa Phythian-Adams is a senior lecturer at the University of Liverpool. She holds a PhD in applied economics (focusing on cultural events and institutions). Her research interests are in cultural and creative sector economics.

John D. Singleton is the Wilmot Assistant Professor of Economics at the University of Rochester. In addition to work on the recent history of economics, such as examining the rise of natural experiments (with Matthew Panhans) and a history of the Committee on the Status of Women in Economics (with Cléo Chassonery-Zaïgouche and Beatrice Cherrier), he studies school choice policies and the economics of school boards. John received his PhD in economics from Duke University in 2017.

Sarah F. Small is an assistant professor of economics at the University of Utah. She holds a PhD in economics from Colorado State University and was recently a visiting scholar at the Center for the History of Political Economy at Duke University and a postdoctoral researcher at the Center for Women and Work at Rutgers University. Her research focuses on feminist economics, specifically intrahousehold bargaining, occupational crowding, and feminist methodology and pedagogy.

Index

History of Political Economy 54 (annual suppl.) DOI 10.1215/00182702-10343088
Copyright 2022 by Duke University Press